Drawing the Line

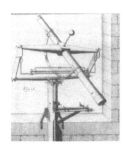

Drawing the Line

How Mason and Dixon Surveyed the Most Famous Border in America

Edwin Danson

John Wiley & Sons, Inc.

New York • Chichester • Weinheim • Brisbane • Singapore • Toronto

Copyright © 2001 by Edwin Danson. All rights reserved
Maps and drawings copyright © 2001 by Edwin Danson

Published by John Wiley & Sons, Inc.
Published simultaneously in Canada

This publication is designed to provide accurate and authoritative information in regard to the subject matter covered. It is sold with the understanding that the publisher is not engaged in rendering professional services. If professional advice or other expert assistance is required, the services of a competent professional person should be sought.

Library of Congress Cataloging-in-Publication Data:

Danson, Edwin.
    Drawing the line: how Mason and Dixon surveyed the most famous border in America.
        p. cm.
    Includes bibliographical references and index.
    ISBN 0-471-38502-6 (cloth : alk. paper)
    1. Mason-Dixon Line—History. 2. Pennsylvania—Boundaries—Maryland—
History. 3. Maryland—Boundaries—Pennsylvania—History. 4. Frontier and pioneer life—Pennsylvania. 5. Frontier and pioneer life—Maryland. 6. Mason, Charles, 1728–1786. 7. Dixon, Jeremiah. 8. Surveying—Pennsylvania—History—
18th century. 9. Surveying—Maryland—History—18th century. I. Title.

F157.B7   D36   2001
974.8'802—dc21   00-036824

For Linda
and
for Dominic and Peter

Contents

CHAPTER 21   *Legacy*   197

             Appendix   207
             Bibliography   219
             Index   223

Prologue

ON BROWN'S HILL, near the town of Mount Morris in the southwest of Pennsylvania, stands a solitary monument bearing the inscription:

MASON-DIXON LINE

Made famous as line between free and slave states before War Between the States. The survey establishing Maryland-Pennsylvania boundary began in 1763; halted by Indian wars 1767; continued to southwest corner 1782: marked 1784.

Behind these brief words lies a long and complex story with roots in an acrimonious and often violent boundary dispute between two seventeenth-century aristocratic, colonial families. For more than eighty years, the quarrel between the proprietors of Maryland and Pennsylvania was fought out in the English courts and across the border itself. The only hope for a peaceful resolution rested on a very precise survey to delineate the boundary lines, but at the time such a survey had no precedent anywhere in the world. After several valiant attempts by local surveyors to lay out the lines, the colonial proprietors were forced to conclude that the task was beyond their means. Just when it seemed that the boundary survey was "impossible for the Art of Man," two gifted English surveyors returned home, victorious, from an unusual astronomical expedition in South Africa. Their names were Charles Mason and Jeremiah Dixon.

From London, where Mason and Dixon had been found to be "persons intirely accomplished" to conduct the great survey and resolve the

1

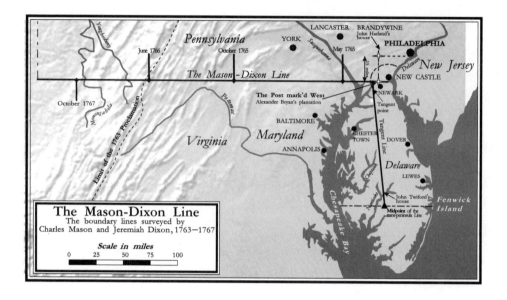

epic border dispute, these two intrepid Englishmen traveled to Philadelphia. Shortly after they landed, shocking news arrived in the bustling city. In retaliation for native uprisings along the western borders of Pennsylvania, a gang of frontiersmen known as the Paxton Boys had murdered and scalped the inhabitants of a nearby native village. Vindication for the attack on the innocent Conestoga Indians was sought in scripture and as justifiable revenge for the ravages of the great Indian war chief, Pontiac. Hatred, fueled by fear, was sweeping like wildfire through the province.

Mason and Dixon wondered what they had gotten themselves into as malice and mob violence broke out all around them. To add to their gloom, the weather was bitter cold and icy rain lashed against the windowpanes of their lodgings. A month after arriving in Philadelphia, the nights of persistent rain and snow eased sufficiently for the two surveyors to start work despite the freezing conditions. While Mason and Dixon labored in their makeshift observatory on Cedar Street, tensions in the city were rising. The provincial populace was divided; the Quakers were shocked and appalled as were most decent folk, yet a large minority supported, or at least found justification, for the actions of the Paxton Boys.

In the weeks and months ahead, as they ventured deeper and deeper into the wilderness, the two English surveyors and their Amer ican assistants ran into myriad problems. On numerous occasions the weather itself seemed to work against their mission. Heavy rains and sometimes freezing sleet or driving snow would turn the unmade roads into mires of slush and mud in which their heavy wagons sank up to their axletrees. The expedition to resolve the bitter border conflict became a woeful tale of bogged-down wagons, straining horse teams, and tired and angry men.

Indians, too, were tracking the surveying party, and Mason and Dixon had heard that there was conflict between the tribes. The Seneca were on the warpath against their traditional enemies, the Cherokee. Bands of Delaware were also about in large numbers and there was a serious chance of trouble. However, the work went forward, and finally they were into the densely forested slopes of the northern Appalachians, a strange country of steep parallel hills that stretched, ridge upon ridge, beyond Cumberland. Further west, the ridges piled upward to form the divide between the eastward and westward flowing rivers.

The last ridge before the divide was Will's Creek Mountain, where the survey crew was obliged to wade through its cold, swift stream. Mason, Dixon, and some of the men from their large survey team trekked to the peak of Savage Mountain to see what lay ahead. Mason described the magnificent view in his journal:

> Beyond the Dividing Mountain . . . is the little Yochio Geni, running into the Monaungahela, which falls into the Ohio or Allegany River at Pittsbourg . . . called by the French Fort Duquesne.
>
> The lands on the Monaungahela and Ohio are allowed to be the best of any in the known parts of North America: The Rivers abound with variety of Fish, and quantity almost incredible. At present the Allegany Mountains is the Boundary between the Natives and strangers; in these parts of his Britanic Majesties Collonies.
>
> From the solitary tops of these mountains, the Eye gazes round with pleasure; filling the mind with adoration to that prevading spirit that made them.

After almost five grueling years, Mason and Dixon completed their assignment. Their great boundary survey was the first, and for many years, the most ambitious, geodetic survey ever conducted. It set a precedent for the precise measurement and mapping of vast land distances. In addition to surveying 325 miles of boundary lines, Mason and Dixon measured the first degree of latitude and took the first scientific gravity measurements recorded in America. The professional standards and principles set by Charles Mason and Jeremiah Dixon were followed and improved upon by subsequent surveyors through the centuries. The legacy of these two great men lives on in the work of the organizations that map the cities, fields and forests, mountains and deserts of America's grand landscape.

CHAPTER I

In the Reign of George the Third

SEVENTEEN SIXTY-THREE had been one of those years. Every ship from England brought news of another irksome tax or stifling regulation to the American colonists. The long war with France was over, but the conciliatory terms of the peace treaty had brought down the British government and the cost of the war had crippled the Exchequer. The new prime minister was the unpopular Sir George Grenville, intent on rejuvenating the Treasury by taxing the colonies. He was also rumored to be planning restrictions on settlement west of the Alleghenies to appease the Indians. In the frontier lands, far to the west, there was serious trouble and reports of Indian massacres.

For the small cluster of people gathered on the quay at Philadelphia, watching a longboat pull away from the ship moored out in the river, there was at least some good news. The Falmouth packet had arrived on the afternoon tide with a group of immigrants, Pennsylvania traders returning home, and London merchants with an eye to business. Among the passengers also disembarking that gray November afternoon were two English surveyors, recently engaged by the landowners who held the royal grant, the so-called proprietors of Maryland and Pennsylvania. The appointment of the surveyors had been a secret, a last hope for settling the disputed border between the two colonies and ending eighty years of acrimony and bloodshed.

Later in history, the two men's names would become irrevocably linked with the boundary itself: the Mason-Dixon line, the border line that separates Maryland from Pennsylvania. The line's true origin has become obscured by time and is now best remembered as the symbolic divide between the North and the South during the Civil War, the partition between slave and free states.

In human terms, the Mason-Dixon line was the eighteenth century's most ambitious geodetic survey, and a project without precedent. The men who finally solved the boundary line problem were astronomers, men of science. They could measure latitude and longitude with great precision, but only on dry land. At sea, the problem was quite different and the astronomer's methods just would not work. Navigators could find the latitude by observing the stars, and followed it with reasonable certainty, but longitude was abstract. To find the longitude, seafarers needed a way of measuring the difference in time between a ship's position and some point of reference. Solving the longitude problem would save lives, safeguard valuable cargoes, and protect His Majesty's navy from shipwreck. It was the burning issue of the day and attracted a prize of £20,000 for the man who solved the riddle.

Before he accepted the American assignment, Charles Mason worked at the Greenwich Observatory, where he was a colleague of Reverend Nevil Maskelyne's, and shared with him the view that there could only be an astronomical answer to the longitude problem. However, there was a competing solution, devised by a simple clockmaker called John Harrison, a mechanical device called a chronometer. The protracted battle between Harrison and Maskelyne for the longitude prize is legendary, but in 1763 the chronometer was still a strange and uncertain thing. Maskelyne put his faith in lunar distances, rather than mechanical contraptions. *Lunars* endured a hundred years before finally succumbing to the chronometer, and their success owed much to the consummate skills of Charles Mason.

As the world took shape beneath the back staffs and quadrants of seventeenth-century roving seafarers, so knowledge of its size improved and the ghostly lines of longitude became less ethereal. Similarly, latitude was better measured and understood, and science began to take a closer interest in both of these earthly measures. Today, the intersection of a line of latitude with a line of longitude far from the nearest shore can be established with a certainty of a few meters at the touch of a button, using a piece of electronics costing a few hundred dollars. At the beginning of the eighteenth century, the same position might have been measured to a few tens of miles in latitude, but with only the vaguest idea of longitude. By the end of the century, both latitude and longitude could be found to within a few miles—if the navigator could afford the expensive technology.

While mathematicians and astronomers began to make sense of the world, so religion and politics tried to pull it apart. In the seventeenth century, the new English lords of America owed their good fortunes as much to their religious affiliations as they did to their enormous wealth. Tension between Catholic and Protestant interests waxed and waned throughout the period as monarch succeeded monarch. Toward the end of the century, the Dutch prince William of Orange became king and finally established in England the supremacy of Protestantism and Parliament, and the modern era began. British America grew apace as settlers poured into the territories and vast new trading patterns emerged. Colonial expansion outpaced the political processes, and when Mason and Dixon stepped ashore in Philadelphia on that gray November day, the America they found was substantially different from the one they expected.

At home in England, most people, and certainly most members of Parliament, regarded the American colonies as if they were distant English shires. On the long voyage to the New World, Mason and Dixon learned from homebound Americans that the colonists had neither the vote nor representation in the English Parliament. Discontent and anger was growing toward the way the British government, and especially King George III, was running American affairs. At the time, the British Empire as such did not exist and the nineteenth-century plantation regime, with its exceptional brutality, was still in its infancy. To be sure, there were slaves in America, but they were not all black.

The colonial broadsheets contained almost as many advertisements requesting the apprehension of white convicts and indentured servants as they did for black slaves. In the same month that Mason and Dixon arrived in Philadelphia, Richard Purchase, a thirty-year-old London convict, was sold into bondage to Thomas Harrison of Baltimore. Two years later he escaped and attracted a reward of £5 for "whoever will take up and secure the said Servant." Nevertheless, the overwhelming majority of slaves were kidnapped African natives, or their progeny. Dutch traders in 1619 were among the earliest to sell slaves to the settlers of Virginia. At first, these unfortunate souls were regarded akin to indentured servants brought from England, and were treated similarly. After a period of servitude, the Africans were often granted manumission, but this state of affairs proved only temporary.

In 1750, the Merchants Trading to Africa Company, the last major London company engaged in the nefarious trade, began slaving out of Bristol. In the year Mason and Dixon voyaged to America, slaving was at its height, with more than 150 ships transporting forty-five thousand Africans annually across the Atlantic to the American colonies. Thirty-five percent went to the settlements of New England, but the majority went to the middle and southern provinces; 10 percent of Maryland's population was made up of African slaves working the tobacco fields.

Although at its peak in the colonies, slavery was becoming morally unacceptable, at least in England. In 1772, Chief Justice William Murray, the earl of Mansfield, heard the case of James Somersett, a fugitive Virginian slave who had escaped to England. The judgment in Somersett's favor was not in itself a direct blow to slavery, but rather a victory for common decency; no longer could a slave be repatriated forcibly to face retributive punishment at the hand of his master. The eighteenth-century poet William Cowper was moved to write:

> Slaves cannot breathe in England; if their lungs
> Receive our air, that moment they are free;
> They touch our country, and their shackles fall.

Within ten years of Murray's judgment, the beginning of the true abolitionist movement was under way. Led by indefatigable English Quakers, the movement quickly spread abroad to be embraced by the Friends in Pennsylvania, from where it spread throughout the colonies. The abolitionists were of two camps: those for whom slavery was a moral outrage, and those who feared unrest and, with justification, outright revolt. However, all that lay in the future. During Mason and Dixon's travels in America, slaves doing sweat labor in the fields would not have been an unfamiliar sight.

The American settlers had two non-European races to contend with, neither of which was properly understood. On one hand were the imported African slave laborers, and on the other the indigenous American Indians. Ignorance and fear frequently lead to bigotry or atrocity, and, in this respect, the English settlers were not unique. To understand the America of Charles Mason and Jeremiah Dixon, one has to cast away contemporary ideas of freedom and one-man-one-vote; there was no vote for the 550,000 emigrants who flooded annually into the coastal provinces. It was a world where European men and women were carving a new land from the wilderness, a world where bravery and strength of spirit went hand in hand with the hardships of everyday life in an untamed environment. Moral yardsticks were imported from the Old World and independence was a new and cherished concept that would create a nation where freedom evolved into an article of faith. As an American friend once observed, in the United States, freedom is mandatory and requires an excessive degree of expression. In Europe, these ideas and values were to develop more slowly and with reservations.

The fragile peace that followed the end of the French and Indian War in 1763 was a time of transition that would ultimately lead to the transformation of the colonists from European vassals into American citizens. It was the era of the two Georges: George III and George Washington. To quote the 1851 edition of *A Child's History of England:* "It was in the reign of George the Third that England lost North America, by persisting in taxing her without her own consent. That immense country, made independent under WASHINGTON, and left to itself, became the United States; one of the greatest nations of the earth."

Ten years after Charles Dickens wrote those words, the slaves in the cotton and tobacco fields had helped generate enough wealth to fund the most awful of civil wars, where the Mason-Dixon line acquired a darker, more sinister meaning.

CHAPTER 2

The Fortieth
Degree

IN THE SEVENTEENTH century, granting large tracts of American wilderness to adventuresome English gentlemen was a royal prerogative. The Tudor and Stuart monarchies had failed to map accurately their new lands, and what few maps existed were unreliable. Consequently, royal land grants were mostly inaccurate and ill-informed affairs. The new colonial landowners, or proprietors, seldom, if ever, checked what they were granted before handing over large sums of gold to the grasping royals; disputes followed, inevitably leading to acrimony and bloodshed.

In 1603, a Stuart king, James VI of Scotland, had succeeded to the English throne as James I of England; although the son of a Catholic monarch, Mary, Queen of Scots, James was a Protestant. Shortly after his coronation, James reintroduced the harsh recusancy laws, which demanded penalties for those who did not attend Church of England services; this led to the Catholic plot to blow up Parliament on November 5, 1605. Although the Gunpowder Plot failed, it incensed James and reawakened anti-Catholic fervor throughout England. It was in this dangerous period of religious intolerance that the able and ambitious secretary of state, Sir George Calvert (1578–1632), a devout Catholic, had the perverse task of presenting the king's anti-Catholic policies to the House of Commons. With the king's death in 1625, anti-Catholic feelings diminished a little and Sir George felt safe enough to resign from politics. For his services to the state and Crown, he was created First Baron Baltimore in the Irish peerage and granted large estates in Ireland.

Sir George Calvert's first interest in founding an American colony was in 1621, when he employed Captain Edward Wynne to establish an expeditionary settlement in Newfoundland. To further his American interests, in 1624 Calvert secured a place in the prestigious membership of the Virginia Company of Planters. He briefly visited his settlement in Newfoundland in 1627, returning there with his wife and family the following year. However, conflict over his Catholicism, as well as the poor quality of the land and the atrocious weather, which exacted such a toll in death and illness among the settlers, prematurely ended the Newfoundland venture. Lady Baltimore moved to Jamestown, Virginia, in 1628, while her husband returned to London to petition the new king, Charles I, for a grant of Virginian land south of the James River. Without waiting for the king's decision, Calvert left England to join his wife and family in Jamestown. There he learned that his petition had been denied because of his Roman Catholic sympathies; disappointed, he returned to England.

Calvert, undaunted, tried for the area to the north of the Potomac River; this time he was more successful. The grant provided for a slice of the American wilderness from the southern bank of the Potomac River to a "point which lieth under the Fortieth degree of north latitude."

Sadly, George Calvert died on April 15, 1632, two months before the grant of the royal charter on June 20. The new territory was named Maryland in honor of Henrietta Maria, queen consort of Charles I. The new Baltimore title and the new province passed to George's son Cecilius (1605–1675), also a devout Catholic. Respecting his father's wishes, Cecilius made the province a haven of religious tolerance. While Cecilius was occupied sorting out family and business affairs, he passed to his younger brother Leonard Calvert (1606–1647) the task of colonizing Maryland. Leonard, with three hundred would-be settlers, both Catholic and Protestant, arrived at the Potomac River on May 27, 1634, aboard the ships *Dove* and *Ark*. The local Indians welcomed the new arrivals, provided them with shelter, and sold them corn and some land on which they founded their first settlement, Saint Mary's. The new colony, tolerating religious diversity, offered a sanctuary to many Englishmen of the time; three-quarters of the settlers flocking to Maryland were non-Catholic.

The new English settlers were not alone for long. In March 1638, to the northeast, a shipload of settlers from Sweden arrived. The Swedes purchased their land from the Indians and quickly laid out their first settlement, Christinahamn, and erected a defensive position, called Fort Christina, on the site of modern Wilmington. The Swedes, accustomed to the harsh Scandinavian climate, built their simple homes of hewn logs, notched and lain horizontally. With only minor changes, the Scandinavians had introduced to the continent that enduring symbol of the North American frontier, the log cabin.

During the period following Elizabeth I's death in 1603 and the start of the Long Parliament in 1640, a revolution in political thought and religious Puritanism fermented beneath the surface of English society. The full fury of the long expected war between Parliament and king broke out in 1642. With a civil war raging at home and Catholic rebels threatening stability in Ireland, England's focus became entirely introspective. Although Parliament's general, Oliver Cromwell, supported overseas settlement, the war and its aftermath effectively halted colonial activity in North America. England's colonial competitors attempted to take advantage of its disarray. In 1651, the Dutch colonists and their small army on Manhattan Island (New York) struck the Scandinavian settlements in a brief but bloody encounter. The Swedes were overwhelmed and forced to capitulate and their victors built Fort Casimar (on the site of New Castle, Delaware) to keep a wary eye on their new but dangerous subjects. Cromwell and Parliament could only react with policy, passing two Navigation Acts to protect England's monopoly of trade with its colonies. In particular, these ordinances were designed to keep the maritime Dutch out of England's North American trade, and almost immediately precipitated war with the Netherlands. The first of the Dutch Wars lasted from 1652 to 1654 and resulted in an English victory. The Swedes seized the initiative and attacked their Dutch overlords, but it was a short-lived victory; they lost everything again to the Dutch in 1656.

The Restoration of King Charles II in 1660 brought a return to English colonial expansion, which, in turn, renewed commercial rivalry with the Dutch. In 1664, the English fleet sailed into New Amsterdam and its governor, Peter Stuyvesant, surrendered the settlement without a fight. The conquerors renamed the town New York, in honor of the king's brother James, the Duke of York. The next year, aided and abetted by the French, the Dutch made the first serious challenge to England's sea power since the Armada. To compound England's agony, the Great Plague struck London with devastating effects. The following year was no better, despite a hard-fought victory over the Dutch off the French coast. On September 2, a blaze in a baker's shop started the Great Fire that destroyed 80 percent of London, including the beautiful cathedral of Saint Paul's. In June 1667, the Dutch fleet sailed boldly into London's River Thames, bombarded the royal dockyard of Chatham, and destroyed the anchored fleet. Their war successes further encouraged Dutch colonial aspirations in America.

In 1670, with the signing of the secret Anglo-French Treaty of Dover, Charles II sought an alliance with King Louis XIV of France that would remove his financial dependence on Parliament. Further, Charles wanted to declare himself a Roman Catholic and to perpetuate that faith throughout his realm. In return for French financial support and military aid, Charles bound England to support French aspirations. In May 1672, King Louis invaded the Low Countries and England provided support with its naval power, anxious to regain its damaged prestige. In British America, the conflict exploded in the territories to the east of Maryland; by 1673, the Dutch had recaptured New York and much of the surrounding area. Lord Baltimore, Cecilius Calvert, followed the events from London with alarm and urged action. King Charles had already ceded to his brother, the Duke of York, much of the territory between the Hudson and the Delaware. In turn, James had granted a part of his lands to his friends John Berkeley and George Carteret to found the province of New Jersey in 1665. There was much trade and territory at stake when James, as Lord High Admiral, in defense of his own interests and reinforcing England's dominance of the region, attacked and pacified the Dutch possessions, including New York. For England, the Third Dutch War came to an end in 1674 with the Treaty of Westminster, whereby the Dutch, impoverished by the costs of war, ceded all their territory in the New World to England.

In postwar England, times had become politically very dangerous as Catholic interests vied with Protestant aims; men of rank and consequence were examining their consciences, their loyalties, and their best interests. Charles II was a profligate sovereign, and by way of cultivating favor, Admiral Sir William Penn lent the king the vast sum of £16,000. On Sir William's death in 1670, his son, also called William, inherited the debt. The younger William Penn (1644–1718) had embraced the Quaker faith as a young man and his avowed intent was, like Calvert's before, to found a colony of religious tolerance. It was to be available to all who professed "a belief in the Holy Trinity," that is Christians, and as a refuge for the religiously oppressed.

William Penn's first experience of North American politics came in 1674 when he acted as a mediator in a conflict over ownership rights between two Quaker associates who had bought a share of the province of New Jersey from its proprietor, Sir George Carteret, after whose birthplace the colony had been named. It was an experience that should have alerted Penn to the serious difficulties owners faced in agreeing on colonial borders.

Knowing well the pecuniary difficulties of the king, and wishing to further his American objectives, Penn petitioned King Charles with an offer he could not refuse. In exchange for discharging his father's loan in full, Penn requested an American province. On January 5, 1681, he was able to write, "This day my country was confirmed to me by the name of Pennsylvania, a name the King would give it in honour of my father. I chose New Wales, being as this [is] a pretty hilly country. I proposed Sylvania (woodlands), and they added Penn to it, and though I much oppose it, and went to the King to have it struck out and altered, he said t'was past . . ." On March 4, 1681, the grant for Pennsylvania, comprising all the territory west of New York and New Jersey and to the north of Maryland, received the royal assent. The grant stipulated that the land would extend south from the forty-third parallel, as far west as five degrees longitude from the Delaware River, and "a Circle drawne at twelve miles distance from Newcastle . . . to the beginning of the fortieth degree"; that is, Maryland's northern border.

The boundary dispute between the two colonies started almost immediately when an offer to confer, agree, and mark their mutual boundary was ignored. Penn sent his cousin William Markham as deputy governor to the new province with instructions to establish the claim and its boundaries. In August 1681 Markham visited Charles Calvert, Third Lord Baltimore, at his estate on the Patuxent River, but no sooner had he arrived than he was taken ill. They agreed to postpone negotiations until October while Markham recovered. Meantime, Markham sent notices to all the settlers in northeastern Maryland to pay their taxes to Pennsylvania and not Maryland. This unfortunate, though no doubt calculated, demand further antagonized the older province and relations soured.

Some survey work around New Castle had shown that the proposed twelve-mile circle was substantially short of the critical fortieth parallel that separated the two provinces. Calvert and Markham next met at Markham's headquarters in Upland, near the modern site of Chester, Pennsylvania, to discuss the worsening situation and to try to work out an amicable solution. Lord Baltimore suggested they journey up the Delaware River and observe the location of the fortieth parallel of latitude using a back staff, a mariner's instrument for measuring latitude. Markham objected and cited the Pennsylvania charter that stipulated the boundary was to be twelve miles distant from New Castle. The difference was a matter of some thirteen miles, in Penn's favor, and potentially some four thousand square miles of territory was at stake. Markham further attested that should the two grants overlap, the matter would have to be decided by the king.

It was at about this time that Baltimore's title claim to the three lower counties, the modern state of Delaware, was challenged. Markham had already drawn his cousin's attention to the fact that without Delaware, Pennsylvania would have no seaport and, should hostilities with Maryland increase, would be denied access to the all-important sea trade.

In 1676, the province of New Jersey had been subdivided into West Jersey, under the trusteeship of Quakers, including William Penn, and East Jersey, controlled by Sir George Carteret. Following Carteret's death in 1680, the Quakers purchased the remaining eastern portion from Carteret's estate. William Penn, heedful of his cousin's worries, took advantage of the land purchase, as well as a friendly neighbor, and petitioned his old friend, the Duke of York, for the remnant of his Dutch possessions, Maryland's three lower counties or modern Delaware. With the critical conveyance in his hand, Penn set sail for the New World on his ship, the *Welcome,* arriving in New Castle on October 24, 1682. It had been a swift passage, just nine weeks to cross the Atlantic, but it had also been a tragic one. An outbreak of smallpox on the ship had carried off thirty of the company. Penn was welcomed to America by a large delegation of Dutch, Swedish, and English settlers. With these happy auspices he immediately set about consolidating the Pennsylvanian part of his claim with that assigned to him by the Duke of York. Penn then arranged to meet with his neighbor, Lord Baltimore, near Annapolis on December 13, 1682.

The two men and their advisers discussed some unlikely and impractical solutions for establishing their border. Lord Baltimore continued to press for the simple expedient of taking an instrument up the Delaware River and measuring the latitude. Penn favored more exotic and unwieldy solutions, including measuring a line northward from the known latitude of Cape Charles, and converting the distance to latitude using a value of sixty miles to the degree. In fact, at this latitude, the value would have been nearer sixty-nine miles to the degree and would have favored Penn's cause. Had Penn been advised by scientific men back home? This is likely, as the measure would have given him an additional twenty-eight miles and land for a seaport. In the event, they could not agree and the meeting ended in another stalemate, each going their separate ways, neither rejoicing.

The Catholic faith was under attack from fanatics such as the vicious conspirator Titus Oates, who invented the so-called Popish Plot. Catholic plots were seen everywhere and Lord Baltimore, as a Catholic and an influential man, was a target for Anglican intrigue. The next meeting between Penn and Lord Baltimore took place at New Castle in April 1683; again, the previous ideas were discussed without resolution. Penn tried to move forward by offering to establish the border between their provinces at his own expense, conditional on his Lordship's selling sufficient land at the head of Chesapeake Bay to provide Penn's colony with a seaport. Lord Baltimore refused and the meeting broke up in yet more acrimony.

The next curious development in the saga was a strange and unreliable survey conducted by one Colonel George Talbot. Talbot was Lord Baltimore's cousin, an able and determined individual, who had accompanied Baltimore on his return to the New World. In the summer of 1682, Colonel Talbot had conducted a survey between Octorara Creek and Naaman Creek on the Delaware River, twelve miles from New Castle. The survey line was run on an azimuth (bearing from true north) of seventy-three degrees, some nineteen miles south of the fortieth degree north parallel of latitude, greatly favoring Baltimore's claims. It was happily described by Lord Baltimore as a proper east-west line.

Clearly, something was amiss, although it is uncertain whether by error, ignorance, or design. The result made more trouble, compounded by Colonel Talbot's presenting himself to Penn and delivering a demand for the relinquishment of "all the Land upon the West Side of Delaware River and Bay, and the Seaboard side of fourtieth Degree of Northerly Latitude, and more particularly all that part thereof which lyeth to the Southward of the markt lyine aforesaid." Mr. Penn declined.

The whole issue was getting seriously out of hand; the only recourse open to the protagonists was a referral to the Crown. Penn was supportive of this move, as he commanded much influence in England and at court. The Catholic Lord Baltimore was less enamored, for his standing in the politics of state had diminished. King Charles conferred with his Privy Council, who referred the matter to the Board of Trade and Plantations. The board's commissioners carefully considered the position, with due regard for the representations of the quarreling proprietors, and finally issued its decree in 1685. The judgment of the Board of Trade was that the Delaware peninsula north of Cape Henlopen should be divided equally, the western half going to Maryland, the eastern to William Penn. The northern border was confirmed in Lord Baltimore's favor (a sign of changing times) at the fortieth degree of north latitude. That was not the end of the matter; further negotiation resulted in an amendment setting Maryland's border nineteen miles south of the fortieth parallel. The onus returned to the proprietors to set out the border marks in accordance with the decree, but this grand opportunity to end the conflict quickly slipped away.

CHAPTER 3

The Great
Chancery Suit

ON FEBRUARY 6, 1685, King Charles II died suddenly. His despotic brother James, a Catholic convert, became King James II and Catholic aspirations rose. In June, the earl of Monmouth, the illegitimate son of Charles II, and a small force of Protestant loyalists landed at Lyme Regis to launch an inauspicious rebellion in the West Country of England. The foreign seat for seditious plotting was the Protestant Netherlands, whose relationship with England had been strengthened by the marriage of Charles I's grandson, the Dutch prince William of Orange, to James II's Protestant daughter, Mary.

King James II and his wife, Mary of Modena, were ardent Roman Catholics, and it had been the intention of Monmouth to replace James with himself. James's forces proved superior in every way and hundreds of the rebels were killed or captured; Monmouth was summarily executed. In his wrath, James demanded vengeance and sent George Jeffreys, his notoriously cruel lord chief justice, on a campaign of judicial murder unprecedented in the annals of English law. In the weeks that followed, Judge Jeffreys hanged, drew, and quartered some 250 men and transported hundreds of others, including women and children, to the colonies as slaves. Word of the brutality of Jeffreys' "Bloody Assizes" spread far and wide and shocked the nation.

The king had gotten off to a bad start, and over the following two years he set in motion a series of events that were his eventual undoing. His Protestant supporters in the court and state began to find themselves eased out in favor of the king's Catholic companions. Judge Jeffreys, elevated to lord chancellor as a reward for his retribution on

Monmouth, became increasingly isolated and things turned very black indeed. The last straw for the king's unhappy reign came six months after the announcement that the queen was pregnant, raising the specter of a Catholic succession. In May 1688, James reissued his Declaration of Indulgence, suspending the laws against Catholic dissenters. The archbishop of Canterbury denounced the declaration and was immediately prosecuted for sedition. On June 10, the queen, in an event witnessed by the entire court, much to her dismay, produced for James a son and heir.

On June 30, the archbishop and seven of his bishops were acquitted of the charges against them. That same day, the earl of Danby and the bishop of London, Henry Compton, together with five other conspirators, invited the Dutch Protestant prince, William of Orange, to seize the throne of England and avert the inevitable Catholic succession. William landed in Tor Bay with an army of fifteen thousand on November 5, 1688, and his arrival in London was daily expected. The king's supporters, even his daughter the Lady Anne Stuart, deserted him. In December the king fled London for France in what became known as the bloodless Glorious Revolution. James's flight was treated as an abdication, and William and his wife Mary were crowned joint monarchs early the following year.

In an attempt to regain his crown, James landed in Ireland with a moderate force of Franco-Irish Catholic supporters. On July 1, 1690, the two contenders, James II and William III, met on the banks of the River Boyne, near Dublin. The battle of the Boyne was an indifferent affair and casualties were light; it was not the resounding defeat that William had hoped. Nevertheless, the day was William's and the Jacobite forces (those who sought to restore James II and his descendants to the English throne) withdrew to pursue the war in Ireland for another year while James returned to France. The enemies met again at the battle of Aughrim on July 12, 1691, when William's army exacted the most resounding defeat to the Jacobite cause; over seven thousand were killed. It is the battle of the Boyne that is best remembered as an event that sparked off three hundred years of Anglo-Irish tumult; it is celebrated annually by Protestant Orangemen. It also sowed the seeds of the 1715 and 1745 Jacobite rebellions, which stimulated another flood of emigrants across the Atlantic.

With a new Protestant king and queen on the throne of England, serious politics came to the fore. Monarch and Parliament enjoyed a renaissance and Catholics were purged of their Jacobite ambition. Lord Baltimore was deprived of his Maryland grant and the land reverted to a royal province, a situation that remained until 1713. William Penn also suffered a similar fate in 1691, but with friends in high places, and offering no real threat, had his lands restored in 1694, the same year Queen Mary succumbed to smallpox and died childless.

William Penn returned for his second, and last, visit to Pennsylvania in 1699. From the outset, Penn's aim was to establish a fair, by seventeenth-century standards, form of government in his colony. Penn's Quaker detractors wanted a strong legislature, but he knew the weakness of popular government, especially since the English home government was ever suspicious of Quaker motives. Instead, Penn placed power in the hands of an executive, a governor, and a council. The freemen of the colony retained a right of expression and were assured their freedom of conscience. However, this governmental framework never satisfied the provincial Friends who continued to lobby Penn. During the latter part of his stay in Philadelphia in 1701, and against his better judgment, Penn signed a Charter of Privileges that granted the colony its own elected (by freeholders) assembly.

William Penn's other concern was the twelve-mile radius around New Castle, which was still a contentious issue between the proprietors. In 1701, to start the process of demarcation, Penn engaged two surveyors, Isaac Taylor from West Chester and Thomas Pierson of New Castle, to establish and survey part of the difficult curve. The section included the provincial county boundary between Chester and New Castle and required four years work to complete. The next year, on March 8, King William died and the deposed King James's youngest daughter, the Lady Anne Stuart, was crowned queen of England.

In 1714, during the last year of Anne's reign, Parliament passed the famous act offering an enormous prize of £20,000 to anyone who solved the longitude problem. The more successful solutions to the problem would indirectly help resolve the Penn and Baltimore boundary dispute. On August 1, the queen passed away, leaving no obvious heir apparent. The next candidate in line for the throne of England was the great-grandson of James I, the German elector of Hanover, Georg Ludwig von Brunswick-Lüneburg, who was crowned George I.

An able but unpopular king, "German George" was the first of the house of Hanover. His son, George Augustus, the Prince of Wales, with his beautiful and astute wife, Lady Caroline of Ansbach, joined the new king in England. They made their home in apartments of the earl of Leicester's London mansion, a well-known Whig stronghold.

The next year both Charles Calvert, Lord Baltimore, and his eldest son and heir, Benedict, died. The family title passed to Benedict's son Charles, Fifth Lord Baltimore, who, in 1713, had successfully petitioned the king for restoration of Maryland by renouncing his own Catholicism. William Penn passed away in 1718, leaving his estates to his second wife, Hannah, to administer. At a memorial meeting for the elder Penn, his Quaker friends testified that "he was void of the strain of ambition, as free from rigid gravity as he was clear of unseemly levity." Hannah Penn transferred the lands to her sons, Thomas (1702–1775), John (d. 1746), Richard (1706–1771), and Dennis, who died young in 1723. However there was another contestant in the form of Penn's eldest son, William, by his first marriage to Gulielma Springett, and under English law, he had rights to half the estate.

The young William Penn had accompanied the family on their last visit to America, where the allures of Philadelphia had been his undoing. His heavy drinking, a social curse of the eighteenth century, and other scandalous excesses became a source of disgrace to his pious father. The old man had a chance to dwell on this, and the other woes Pennsylvania had brought him, while languishing in London's notorious Fleet debtors' prison in 1705 as his wife and friends negotiated with his creditors: "O Pennsylvania what hast thou cost me? Above thirty thousand pounds more than I ever got by it, two hazardous and mostly fatiguing voyages, and my son's soul almost."

For two years Hannah Penn struggled with the administration of her late husband's estate while William contested the will that had left him disinherited at the expense of his three half brothers. In 1720 providence came to the rescue and William Penn Jr. died in Liège, "worn out by intemperence and excesses." Pennsylvania and Penn's private estates were divided equally between Hannah's sons. John never married and died in 1746, leaving his inheritance to Thomas, who now owned two-thirds of the province. After Dennis died in 1723, Richard was the youngest of the brothers and had a reputation for being a spendthrift and a less than accomplished businessman. Thomas, on the other hand, was prudent, an accomplished merchant, and a man intent on restoring the family's fortune.

George I died at his home in Osnabrück, Germany, in 1727 and his thoroughly Anglophile son, the Prince of Wales, was crowned George II. Through all the turmoil and uncertainties of the times, the North American settlements continued to grow. In large parts of the disputed region between Pennsylvania and Maryland, settlers were still not paying their taxes and the sums involved were mounting to very large figures. Charles Calvert, Fifth Lord Baltimore, petitioned the newly crowned king to instruct the proprietors of Pennsylvania to join him in the demarcation of their mutual boundary. His Majesty referred the matter to the commissioners of the Board of Trade and Plantations, where both Thomas Penn and Lord Baltimore were present for the deliberations. The meetings were disagreeable, both sides trading insults and accusations. There was the obtuse argument by the Penn camp that because a man's fortieth year started at his thirty-ninth birthday, surely the fortieth degree of north latitude started at thirty-nine degrees. The committee concluded in 1732 that commissioners should be appointed to conduct a proper survey. Further, they stated that the decree of 1685 stood, but amended it such that the northern border of Maryland would lie fifteen miles south of Philadelphia. The Delaware peninsula would be divided equally as agreed and the northern boundary was to be "a circle twelve miles distance around Newcastle." Unfortunately, the Board did not specify the exact location for the center point.

The two proprietors duly appointed commissioners, who convened in New Castle for the first time on October 17, 1732, to discuss the decree and begin the process of practical interpretation. The first obstacle was whether the twelve-mile distance around New Castle should be a radius or a circumference. After much debate, the commissioners agreed to disagree. The governor of Maryland petitioned George II, who, by return, issued an edict that two temporary lines should be run. The first was to be 15½ miles south of Philadelphia on the east side of the Susquehanna River, the other 17½ miles south on the west side of the river. Penn appointed two surveyors from New Jersey to carry out the work in 1736, the results of which stood until 1763. However, the dispute between Pennsylvania and Maryland continued unabated. Eventually, in 1735, the whole matter was referred to the English courts in what became known as the Great Chancery Suit. The case was heard before Lord Justice Hardwicke and conducted over a laborious fifteen-year period during which the litigation costs to both sides grew to enormous proportions, and still the colonial taxes were not being collected.

Meantime, the boundary dispute was growing beyond the realms of a legal wrangle and turning into a bloody cross-border conflict. One recorded example came in 1736, when fifty Pennsylvanian raiders attacked a Maryland farmstead on the Susquehanna and one man was killed. In the same area, Lord Baltimore's surveyors fared little better when, in 1743, they tried mapping a part of the disputed territory. Some of the more belligerent Pennsylvanians of Marsh Creek, on the west bank of the river, objected to his Lordship's servants entering their land. The quarrelsome settlers, including the Agnews, the Blacks, and the Eddys, were led by a large Dutchman, Thomas Hooswick (Hooswijk) who, it is recorded, "declares yt if ye Chain be spread again he wou'd stop it, and then took ye Compass from ye Surv. Gen."

Seven years after this fracas, in 1750, Lord Hardwicke in London pronounced judgment in the Great Chancery Suit. The center of the twelve-mile circle was to be the center of New Castle, the distance would be measured as a radius, and the southern boundary of the Three Counties (Delaware) would be at the latitude of Cape Henlopen (Fenwick Island). The other provisions previously agreed upon would stand. In 1751 a new survey was commissioned and a line run from Cape Henlopen due west to Chesapeake Bay. The surveyors, led by John Watson, duly reported that the distance to Slaughter Creek, a tidal reach, was 66.00 miles and to the Chesapeake Bay waterfront, 69.93 miles. The commissioners once more met to deliberate in New Castle on November 15, where, surprisingly, they agreed that the center of New Castle should be the belfry of the courthouse. Where they could not agree was how the measurement should be made. The Penn camp was emphatic that the measurements should be made horizontally such that on a map, the curve would form a circular arc. The Maryland side disagreed and was equally emphatic that the chaining should follow the slopes of the hills and vales which would have resulted in a slightly irregular shape. The other problem was the surveyor's report and the proper way to divide the Delaware peninsula equally. The meeting was adjourned without a settlement.

Charles Calvert returned to England, where he died in 1751. His son Frederick, still a minor, inherited; Charles's brother, Cecilius Calvert, looked after young Lord Baltimore's interests. Meanwhile, the commissioners' difficulties in agreeing to definitions were referred to the court for resolution. It was ruled that the twelve miles should be a radius and measured horizontally and that the center of the circle should be the point determined by the commissioners. The important midpoint on the peninsula should lie halfway between Cape Henlopen and the Chesapeake waterfront.

Another war with France erupted in 1756; nevertheless, by 1760 the legal situation had clarified enough for surveyors, including Reverend Richard Peters, Thomas Penn's provincial secretary, and John Lukens (1720–1789), who later became surveyor general, to begin the task of setting out the first boundary lines. Their job included locating the Delaware Middle Point, setting out the twelve-mile radius around New Castle, and establishing a line from the Middle Point to a point that was at a tangent to the New Castle circle. The surveyors started work in the spring of 1761 and for a while made good progress.

The major challenge was running the boundary line from the Middle Point to its tangent with the twelve-mile radius around New Castle, a distance of some eighty miles. The surveyors first ran a trial line due north from the Middle Point towards the New Castle circle and, once they were certain they had crossed the boundary circle, set up a marker.* They next measured the radial distance from the courthouse to the marker, where they also measured the angle. It was then just a matter of trigonometry to calculate what the angle from the radial line should be to put them close to the tangent point. They also calculated that the Tangent Line should be at an angle of 3 degrees 32 minutes 5 seconds west of the meridian line. The first part of the task was completed on December 2, 1761, when the survey team stood down for the winter.

Beginning on May 25, 1762, a second trial line was run from the Middle Point towards the elusive tangent point. On September 9 they

---

*See "The Tangent Line" in the Appendix.

reached what was thought to be the tangent, but when the angle was measured with Lord Baltimore's "large Theodolite" it was found to be slightly greater than the ninety degrees demanded; that is, it was too far east of the tangent point. The theodolite, an instrument that measures both horizontal and vertical angles, although large, was not a precise instrument and its accuracy was little better than one minute of arc, maybe worse. The divisions of its reading circle were hand divided, a process requiring the greatest skill, and always prone to error. To overcome some of the error, surveying instruments were often very large, anywhere between twenty-four and thirty inches in diameter.

The commissioners and the surveyors convened on September 17 to discuss the problem. More calculations were made and a new line begun the very next day, very slightly west of the previous line. On August 18, 1763, the surveyors reached the tangent point only to find that the new line was too far west. One of the surveyors then calculated where the tangent point should lay in relationship to the twelve-mile radius markers (white painted oak posts) and the angular correction to bring their last line into correct alignment.

But it was too late; Governor Horatio Sharpe (1718–1790) of Maryland and Governor James Hamilton of Philadelphia had already decided that the geodetic problem was too complex, the surveyor's instruments inadequate for the task, and progress painfully slow, so they appealed to their respective proprietors in London to seek professional assistance. By the time the local surveyors reached the end of their last line, Charles Mason and Jeremiah Dixon had already been hired to complete the task and were preparing to leave London. Both Hamilton and Sharpe were aware of their proprietors' discussions, and Sharpe, at least, learned from Calvert in early October that Mason and Dixon were on their way.

The relationship between Thomas Penn and his governor with the legislature of Pennsylvania was at a low ebb. The Pennsylvanian commissioners for the most part were politically inclined towards the legislature's position, opposed to their province's condition as a proprietorial colony. Despite the liberality of the Charter of Privileges, the provincial Quaker movement had always opposed the governmental structure, in part because its rigidity did not represent fundamental Quaker philosophy. The Maryland commissioners, although from a less liberal colony, but rife with separatist feelings, were similarly inclined.

Beneath the surface of both colonies was a yearning for political independence from the shackles of the proprietorial system; hence the governors kept a distance from their commissioners and legislatures. This is not to say the commissioners, or their class, were "republican" or activists for devolution—that was still a few years off. That they were kept ignorant of Penn and Calvert's decision is not surprising and, for the commissioners and their American surveyors, Mason and Dixon's arrival was to come as a total surprise.

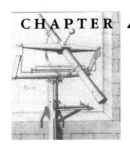 4

La Figure de la Terre

A MODERN-DAY land surveyor about to embark on a great work such as the Maryland and Pennsylvania boundary survey might start by discussing with his client certain basic specifications. He would consider which figure of Earth to use and which geodetic datum would best suit the task; in 1763, such deliberations had no meaning.

The Greek philosopher Eratosthenes of Cyrene (third century B.C.) was the first to measure scientifically Earth's circumference. He noticed that on a midsummer's day in Syene (Aswan), the Sun cast no noontide shadow, yet at Alexandria, Egypt, where he was curator of the famous library, a pillar cast a shadow of about seven degrees. Eratosthenes reasoned that the Sun was very distant and the different shadow angles were due to the curve of Earth. Official Egyptian pacers and camel drovers provided him with the distance between the two locations. His value for the circumference of Earth was 250,000 stadia, equivalent to 28,728 miles (a modern value would be about 24,755 miles), an error of only 16 percent and well within the uncertainty of the accepted value of a stadium.

More than eighteen hundred years later, in 1617, the Dutch mathematician and astronomer Willebrord Snel van Royen (Snellius) (1580–1626) improved on Eratosthenes' methods. Instead of using camel drovers' estimates, Snellius established a precise baseline between two church towers near Leiden in the Netherlands. Between 1622 and 1624, Snellius extended his baseline to cover much of the flat landscape. Observing the angles between successive church towers to form a series of triangles, a process we now call triangulation, Snellius founded modern geodetic science.

As the seventeenth century progressed, so the accuracy of maps slowly improved and the "Ghostly Lines" of latitude and longitude became more tangible. Whereas at sea longitude was proving very difficult to ascertain, on land the problem was more or less solved thanks to Galileo's astute observations of the satellites of Jupiter. The secret in measuring differences in longitude between two distant locations is actually measuring accurate differences in time. John Harrison's chronometer would eventually allow navigators and surveyors to carry a home port's time with them; however, Galileo (1564–1642) had already realized that the regular, and predictable, eclipses of far distant Jovian satellites provided the necessary clock. All one had to do was determine local time with reference to a particular eclipse. For example, if an eclipse of Jupiter's moon Io occurred at 2 A.M. London time, and the same event was observed at 4 A.M. local time at some distant location, the difference in time multiplied by 15 degrees to the hour (360 degrees/24 hours), gave a longitude of 30 degrees east of London. A decent pendulum clock and a stable telescope magnifying forty times was all that was needed on land, but such a solution was impossible on a ship's heaving deck.

Another seventeenth-century problem that required a solution was a reliable scientific estimate for the size of Earth. This was not known with an accuracy sufficient to allow angular differences in latitude or longitude to be turned into distances. In its quest to solve the longitude problem, the French Académie Royale de Sciences, under the direction of Jean-Baptiste Colbert, engaged the great Italian astronomer and mathematician Gian Domenico Cassini (1625–1712). Cassini arrived in France in 1669 to join other distinguished scientists, including Christiaan Huygens (1629–1695), inventor of the pendulum clock, and the instrument maker Adrian Auzout. The clarity of Auzout lenses, mirrors, and telescopes enabled Huygens to improve the observing accuracy of Jovian eclipses and also to discover the rings of Saturn. Even before Cassini began work on the mathematics, Colbert had realized he required more precise ground information and engaged another scientist, Jean Picard (1620–1682), to make the first precise estimate of Earth's dimensions.

Picard adopted Snellius's principles and used triangulation to cover a large distance. A baseline was chosen extending from the Pavilion at Malvoisine, near Paris, northward to the clock tower of Sourdon, near Amiens. To measure the distance, Picard observed a series of thirteen large triangles from which he was able to compute by trigonometry the length of the baseline. At each terminal point, the eclipses of Jupiter's moons provided Paris time, while other astronomical observations provided local time. The times were coordinated using two of the best pendulum clocks then in existence, and which "marked the seconds with greater accuracy than most clocks mark the half hours." After careful calculation, Picard was able to announce that the length of a degree of latitude was 57,060 *toises* (an ancient French unit equal to 2.13 yards), which equated to a spherical Earth diameter of 7,919 miles; it was an excellent start.

By the beginning of the eighteenth century, scientific men had become aware that Earth was not the perfect sphere once believed. Isaac Newton (1642–1727) predicted, by reasoned theory, that Earth was an oblate spheroid, a sphere that is flattened towards the poles. The variation from the true sphere, or flattening (also known as compression or ellipticity), was an elusive figure, and once more the enterprising French set about finding the truth. Apart from scientific curiosity, a complete understanding of the true shape of Earth would allow maps and charts to be more accurate and improve the often perilous business of navigation at sea.

In order to discover an accurate dimension for Earth and its flattening coefficient, the Académie Royale de Sciences sent two expeditions to measure meridian arcs, reasoning that by comparing the length of a degree of latitude near the equator with a similar one near the North Pole, the size of Earth and its flattening could be calculated. In 1735 the French equatorial arc expedition, led by Louis Godin, went to Mitad del Mundo, in Peru. Charles Marie de La Condamine (1701–1774) was the chief scientist of the expedition. He was accompanied by the illustrious Pierre Bouguer (1698–1758), the royal professor of hydrography, renowned for measuring the density of Earth by observing the deflection of a plumb bob caused by variations in gravity.

For various reasons, no doubt caused by the extreme heat, the humidity, and the awful food, discord grew among the scientists. Godin departed, leaving La Condamine and Bouguer to continue with their difficult meridian arc measure alone. A little later, when Bouguer detected a small error in their measurements and suggested to

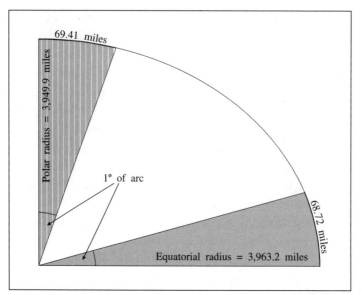

Equivalent of one degree of latitude near the North Pole and near the equator.

La Condamine that he check the results, La Condamine flew into a rage; how dare Bouguer question his work! There was an almighty row, and the two men separated. Bouguer returned immediately to France by a direct route to pursue his distinguished scientific career, most noted for his measurements of gravity using a pendulum, and for the study of light intensity and the development of Bouguer's law. La Condamine, by order of the king of France, set off from Mitad del Mundo in 1743 on a four-month botanical expedition up the Amazon, the account of which he published in 1751 as *Journal du voyage fait par ordre du roi a l'équateur*. After an uninterrupted period of ten years overseas, he arrived back in Paris in February 1745 to an enthusiastic reception. In recognition of his contributions to science, Charles Marie de La Condamine was elected to the Royal Society of London in 1748.

The Académie Royale de Sciences had sent a polar expedition, led by Pierre-Louis Moreau de Maupertuis (1698–1759), to the Tornio valley in Lapland in 1736. Assisted by Alexis-Claude Clairaut (1713–1765), Pierre-Charles Le Monnier (1715–1799), and the Académie correspondent Abbé Outhier, Maupertuis established a baseline of 7,337 *toises* (8.9 miles) across the ice-covered River Tornio. Using Snellius's pioneering methods, they extended the baseline by triangulation to cover the desired degree of latitude. Maupertuis also employed an astronomical instrument made by George Graham of London, with a movable telescope mounted on a trunnion axis, which Le Monnier described in his book *Instrument du Passages*. This instrument formed the basis of the design for John Bird's transit and equal altitude instrument, which Mason and Dixon would employ so successfully in North America.

The measured length of the triangulated arc extended from the church tower of Tornio northward to Kittisvåra; from his calculations, Maupertuis determined that in Lapland one degree of latitude was equal to 57,437.9 *toises*. Previously Picard had determined that near Paris one degree of latitude was only 57,060 *toises,* thus, a degree in the high latitudes covered a greater distance than one near Paris did. Moreau de Maupertuis published the results in his paper *La Figure de la Terre* (1738), to the delight of the scientific communities in Paris, London, and Leipzig.*

After comparing the results from the Peruvian and Lapland expeditions, and not without considerable academic acrimony, the Académie Royale de Sciences declared their results; Earth had an equatorial radius of 3,282,350 *toises* (6,996,172 yards) and a flattening ratio of $\frac{1}{216.8}$ (the ratio is simply the difference between the equatorial and polar radii divided by the equatorial radius). A hundred years would pass before the British geodesist Alexander Ross Clarke (1828–1914) developed his famous spheroid dimensions for Earth, the first to approximate modern values and which became the standard reference for surveying and geodesy in the United States. Yet another hundred would elapse before the U.S. Department of Defense defined the value as 6,378,137 meters, or 6,975,215 yards, with a flattening ratio of $\frac{1}{298.257}$.

Until Mason and Dixon made their measurements in the New World, the Académie's dimensions for Earth, with only minor corrections, were the only reliable values available. But they were not universally accepted. Mason's astronomical observations and calculations, meticulously recorded in his journal during the North American

---

*Pierre Bouguer published his results in a paper of the same name in 1749.

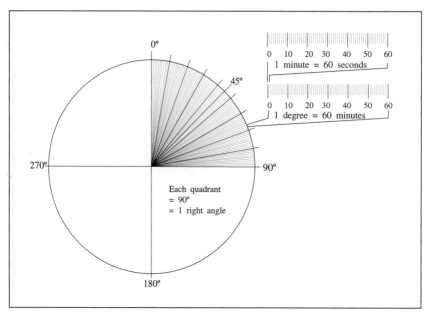

Degrees, minutes, and seconds.

campaign, include references and technical terms that may require some explanation for those unfamiliar with surveying or astronomy. Angles were measured in degrees (360 to a complete circle), each degree was divided into 60 minutes and each minute divided into 60 seconds. The conventional symbols for these units are namely, degrees (°) minutes (') seconds ("). To avoid confusion with the similar units of time, surveyors and astronomers frequently refer to minutes and seconds *of arc*. For example, the angle subtended by *1' of arc* is approximately one inch at a distance of 100 yards (useful to remember), and at one mile *1" of arc* is 0.3 inch.

The units of linear measure were English imperial and, until recently, would have been familiar to everyone; indeed, they have been better preserved in the United States than elsewhere.

The first great civilizations of Mesopotamia and Egypt, spanning some three thousand years of history, never reached a point in their long evolution where they considered Earth to be anything but an inclusive cosmic oneness. It cannot be said that they ever regarded Earth as flat—such a concept would have had little meaning—rather, they regarded Earth and everything on, above, or below it to be homo-

Measuring Units—Conversion Table

Imperial units		Metric equivalent
1 inch	=	0.025 meter
1 link = 0.66 feet or 7.92 inches	=	0.201 meter
12 inches = 1 foot	=	0.305 meter
3 feet = 1 yard	=	0.914 meter
6 feet = 1 fathom	=	1.829 meters
5½ yards = 1 rod or pole	=	5.029 meters
22 yards = 100 links = 1 chain = 4 rods	=	20.117 meters
10 chains = 1 furlong = 220 yards	=	201.168 meters
80 chains = 8 furlongs = 5,280 feet = 1 Statute Mile	=	1,609.344 meters

geneous. The firmament was either a great vault or the body of a god, depending on the dominant belief, from which were hung wonderful lamps, the stars and planets. The rise of Hellenic civilization changed that view of the world forever; the Greeks liberally absorbed the culture and science of their predecessors, adding to it reason and studied observation. Pythagoras (ca. sixth century B.C.) deduced through pure logic that Earth was a sphere. The great astronomers and mathematicians who followed him built a vast library of knowledge and theory that underpins science even to this day. Yet it was their unshakable belief in the harmony of geometry that denied them the discovery of the truth. They thought of Earth as lying at the center of creation, a theory that became epitomized in the Ptolemaic cosmic system (established by Claudius Ptolemaeus, fl. A.D. 127–145). The Greek vision was of an Earth surrounded by a nest of planetary shells working in a complex circular harmony, a vast mechanical universe, placed within a great celestial sphere on which were set the stars. This theory was to survive until the Polish astronomer Nicolaus Copernicus (1473–1543) published his Sun-centered universe concept, though Copernicus still retained the perfection of circular motion.

The Greek Earth-centered universe within its celestial sphere, while erroneous, is for convenience still used today by surveyors and astronomers. Viewed from Earth, the stars do seem to be wheeling endlessly across the sky from east to west; in reality, it is Earth turning from west to east. Centered on Earth, and of infinite radius, the celestial sphere is imagined as being a vast globe. The celestial equator is the extension of Earth's equator out into space projected onto the great celestial sphere.

• The positions of the Sun, the Moon, the planets, and the stars are described in a coordinate system synonymous with latitude and longitude. Celestial latitude is called declination and is measured from the celestial equator north or south in degrees, minutes, and seconds of arc. Celestial longitude is called right ascension (RA) and is measured around the celestial equator eastward in time units—hours, minutes, and seconds—starting from the First Point of Aries.

The First Point of Aries, denoted by the sign of the Ram (Υ), is the point on the celestial sphere where the Sun's passage among the fixed stars (the ecliptic) crosses the celestial equator from south to north on March 21 (the vernal equinox). The First Point of Aries is not a fixed direction in space; rather, it slowly precesses in a retrograde direction, in the same way a toy gyroscope moves slowly, completing a full tour of the sky every 25,800 years. Hipparchus (second century B.C.) identified this enigmatic point, together with the effect of precession, sometime around 150 B.C. In the last two millennia, the First Point of Aries has moved from the constellation of Aries, through Pisces toward Aquarius. In the 1,900 years that elapsed between Hipparchus's discovery and the time Mason and Dixon were making their calculations, Aries had precessed over 1 hour 40 minutes (an arc in the sky of some 25 degrees). Since then, it has moved east a further 13 minutes of arc.

Another strange earthly motion that affects the position of the stars is a small wobble or periodic oscillation caused by the Moon's gravitational force on Earth's rotation. This effect is called nutation (which Mason sometimes refers to as deviation) and was first explained by Dr. James Bradley, the astronomer royal, in his paper to the Royal Society in 1747. The nutation period is 18.6 years, which is the time taken for the Moon's ascending node to describe a complete revolution round the ecliptic.

The other importance of the First Point of Aries is its relevance to the measurement of time. Even in the eighteenth century, for most ordinary people, the chimes of the church clock and the shadow of the Sun were the chief means of telling the time. If it were possible to

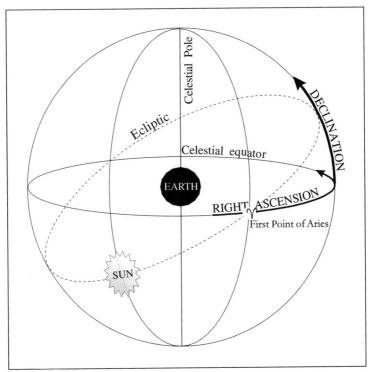

The celestial sphere, showing right ascension and declination.

see the stars during daylight, in the course of a year one would notice that the Sun would move against the fixed starry background of space. The path that it weaves among the stars is called the ecliptic. In astronomy, the Sun we see almost daily is called the apparent, or real, sun. Unfortunately, the apparent sun does not move at a constant rate along the ecliptic; it speeds up, then slows down, obedient to Johannes Kepler's laws of planetary motion (in reality it is Earth that circles the Sun). Using the apparent sun for regular and precise time measurement is impractical; instead, astronomers developed a conveniently constant but imaginary alternative called the mean sun, which is used for clock time measurement. The mean sun travels around the circular celestial equator at a constant velocity, and from this mean sun we get Greenwich mean time, in which all the hours are of an equal length and can be mechanically reproduced by a watch or clock. Had the astronomers John Harrison so despised not devised the expedience of a constant time mean sun, he would never have been able to invent the chronometer.

Local mean time—that is, mean time at any location on Earth other than on the Greenwich meridian—is measured by successive transits of the mean sun across the local meridian (north-south line). The apparent sun and the mean sun are coincident twice a year, when day and night are of equal length; these are the vernal, or spring, equinox and the autumnal equinox.

The shadow thrown by the real sun onto the face of a simple sundial shows apparent time. The difference between apparent time and mean time is the so-called equation of time, which is used to correct sundial (apparent) time to mean time. The eighteenth century was an era when all things scientific fascinated the aristocracy, and some of our finest sundials date from this period. Many examples still in existence have the equation of time scale engraved around their exquisite faces. Until 1884, mean time meant local mean time, but the advent of the forbidding railway timetable changed our concept of variable time forever. We live now in a world of time zones and digital watches. The source of all time standards was Greenwich, and to this day it remains the datum point for standard mean time as well as terrestrial longitude. To relate local mean time to Greenwich requires knowledge of the separation in longitude of the place from Greenwich, at the rate of fifteen degrees of longitude to one hour of time.

The last, and most important, time measure used by Mason and Dixon was sidereal (star) time. Sidereal time is similar to apparent time in that it is observable, but with the essential difference that its rate is constant. A sidereal day is the time taken between successive transits of the First Point of Aries (or any star) across the meridian, and is approximately 3 minutes 56 seconds shorter than a mean time day. The value of sidereal time to Mason and Dixon was that it was synonymous with a star's right ascension as it crossed the meridian. In simple terms, Mason could always find sidereal time by observing a star as it crossed the meridian, just as though the night sky was a gigantic clock face—which, of course, it is.

Until the late eighteenth century, when John Harrison's brilliant chronometer became an affordable luxury, finding longitude was a serious challenge. There had been a number of ideas put forward, all of which required either a stable and powerful telescope or advanced mathematics, or both. It was for the sole purpose of developing reliable celestial solutions for ship navigation that Charles II in 1675 founded the Royal Observatory at Greenwich under the direction of John Flamsteed. However, it was under the stern and brilliant direction of the third astronomer royal, Dr. James Bradley (1693–1762), that the observatory made its great strides towards an astronomical solution for finding longitude.

In 1714, during the reign of Queen Anne, the British government passed an "Act for Providing a Publick Reward for such Person or Persons as shall Discover the Longitude at Sea"; the prize was a queen's ransom, £20,000. Lunar distances, Bradley reasoned, might provide a means of solving the elusive problem of finding longitude. Put simply, when the moon was, say, five degrees east of an easily identified star, and one knew the time at Greenwich as well as the local time, the difference between the two times in hours, multiplied by fifteen degrees, would equal the longitude. This calculation would have taken an experienced navigator some four hours to compute.

In 1753, Johann Tobias Mayer (1723–1762), the Swiss astronomer and professor of geography at Göttingen, published a table of lunar distances he had devised based on the pioneering work of his friend Leonhard Euler. Two years later, a copy of his tables was sent to Admiral Lord Anson, the first lord of the Admiralty, who laid them before the Board of Longitude in March 1756 for its consideration in awarding Mayer the coveted longitude prize. James Bradley obtained a copy of the tables and a thorough check showed they were accurate to within one-half a degree of Bradley's own calculations. His assistant at Greenwich, Charles Mason, was given the task of compiling the observatory's version of the lunar ephemeris based on Mayer's pioneering work.

Mason's first version of Mayer's tables was sent on sea trials in 1757 with Captain (later Admiral) John Campbell aboard the *Royal George,* the same vessel that twenty-five years later suffered a spectacular but tragic capsize immortalized by the poet William Cowper. Campbell used an invention of Mayer's, called a reflecting circle, to measure the angular distances; he found the instrument next to useless and reverted to his Hadley pattern quadrant. At the end of the voyage, Campbell suggested to Dr. Bradley a refinement to the quadrant, one where the effective measuring arc was extended from 90 degrees to 120 degrees.

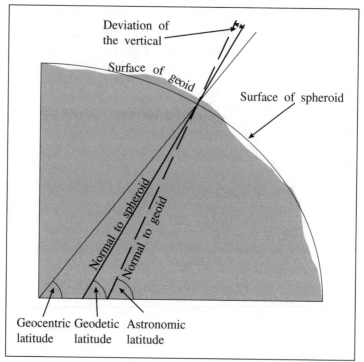

Geocentric, astronomical, and geodetic latitude.

Bradley arranged for John Bird to build the new instrument, which had a radius of eighteen inches, and thus was born the first sextant, a seafarer's instrument that remains to this day a mandatory navigation aid on all ships.

Where longitude was a challenge, latitude was reasonably straightforward. In the 1760s the true shape of Earth was, for the most part, still uncertain. It was known that Earth was slightly flattened and its shape approximated an ellipse of rotation, or spheroid. The latitude that Mason observed was the astronomic latitude shown in the figure above. The vertical, or zenith, he observed was the direction of gravity (the local vertical), as shown by a plumb bob.

In geodetic surveying, there is a small difficulty in that the vertical observed (as shown by a plumb bob) differs very slightly from the vertical to the spheroid. This effect, known as deviation of the vertical, is due to irregularities of mass within Earth's crust. These days the deviation is very well mapped and is described as an equipotential surface called the geoid, a surface that is at any point orthogonal, or at right angles, to the direction of gravity. By analogy, one might imagine a perfectly calm and tideless sea covering Earth; its imaginary, slightly undulating, surface would be the geoid.

Modern mapmakers work exclusively on a regular mathematical figure of Earth called a spheroid; throughout the world national mapping authorities have adopted specific spheroids on which to base their maps. Most of them also have a particular geodetic datum, a physical point where the theoretical Earth is connected to the real Earth. Often located at an astronomical observatory, the datum's complex parameters include the dimensions of the chosen spheroid, its mathematical relationship to the geoid, and the deviation of the vertical. In the United Kingdom, the national mapping authority is the Ordnance Survey, founded in 1791. Their datum is at the Royal Observatory's abandoned site at Herstmonceux Castle in Sussex, and the spheroid used is the one developed in 1830 by the brilliant astronomer royal George Airy. In the United States, the first official geodetic datum was the New England Datum of 1879, based upon Alexander Clarke's spheroid of 1866. As a result of successive expansion by the U.S. Coast and Geodetic Survey's (now the U.S. Geological Survey) triangulation schemes across the vast landscape, the official datum was moved to the more central location of Meades Ranch, Kansas, in 1901. The datum was renamed the North American Datum and was adopted by both Canada and Mexico.

In Mason and Dixon's time, there was neither any concept of a national datum nor any internationally accepted figure of Earth on which to base their work.

CHAPTER 5

The Transit of Venus

KING GEORGE II died in 1760 and his grandson, the twenty-two-year-old elector of Hanover, Georg Wilhelm Friedrich, was crowned George III. In London, Thomas Penn and Cecilius Calvert, representing the young Lord Baltimore, were on excellent terms and met frequently to discuss the tricky matter of surveying their boundaries. By the spring of 1762, long before they received their commissioners' appeal for help, the two proprietors were actively searching for surveying instruments. They also sought the advice of some of the foremost learned men in London just as, twenty years before in 1743, the Jersey Board of Proprietors had sought the advice of their surveyor general, James Alexander (1691–1756). The boundary then in question was that between the provinces of New Jersey and New York, where a lack of quality surveying instruments was blamed for a particularly protracted and violent dispute.

Even before the division of New Jersey in 1682, the forty-seven-mile-long borderline, extending from the Hudson River, a few miles north of Yonkers, west-northwest to the Delaware, had been the cause of a number of clashes. Following the reunification of New Jersey as a royal province in 1702, tension increased despite the will of both New York and New Jersey's assemblies to resolve their differences. In 1719, James Alexander wrote to his proprietors, exasperated by the absence of an exact instrument to survey the border accurately, even doubting that one could ever be constructed, declaring "it is impossible for the Art of Man to make an Instrument true and correct . . ." The act to survey the boundary was not passed by the Assembly of the

Jerseys until 1743, when it was agreed that the line would commence from the west bank of the Hudson exactly at the forty-first parallel, and there lay the problem; how to measure an accurate latitude. The Board of Proprietors turned to Alexander for practical advice. Alexander consulted his counterpart Dr. Cadwallader Colden (1688–1776), the lieutenant governor and surveyor general of New York, who was in correspondence with Peter Collinson (1694–1768) of the Royal Society in London, concerning the construction of a suitable instrument to settle their contentious boundary.

Collinson discussed the designing of a proper instrument with the London watch and instrument maker George Graham (1673–1751) at his workshop at the sign of the Dial and One Crown in Fleet Street. The elderly Graham recommended a large quadrant for measuring the latitude, but, as he was busy with other commissions, recommended that his former apprentice Jonathan Sisson (1694–1749) should construct the instrument. On the understanding that Graham would certify the work, Sisson was awarded the commission to construct a quadrant of thirty inches radius; his price was thirty guineas.

In any event, George Graham gallantly forewent his fee when it was found the instrument exceeded all expectations. Even before it was complete, George Parker, the second earl of Macclesfield (1697–1764), and other "very curious knowing people" visited the quadrant in its workshop and testified to its excellence. When completed, the quadrant, engraved "Property of Council of Proprietors of the Eastern Division of New Jersey," was taken to Greenwich, where it was compared with Sisson's iron-framed eight-foot radius mural (wall-mounted) quadrant in the Royal Observatory. James Short (1710–1768), another noted instrument maker and mathematician, and the renowned scientist Dr. John Bevis (1693–1771) also examined the instrument and testified to its accuracy as being better than ½ minute of arc ($\frac{1}{120}$ of a degree). With his invoice to the Jersey Board of Proprietors for £47-17s-3d, Sisson enclosed a copy of de Maupertuis's book *Degree of the Meridian*, in which was described an even more exotic instrument called a zenith sector.

The wondrous quadrant, with seven pages of user instructions, was dispatched to New Jersey in the late summer of 1745 and remained in its packing cases until almost a year later, when James Alexander and Dr. Colden finally got round to opening it. It took them three months,

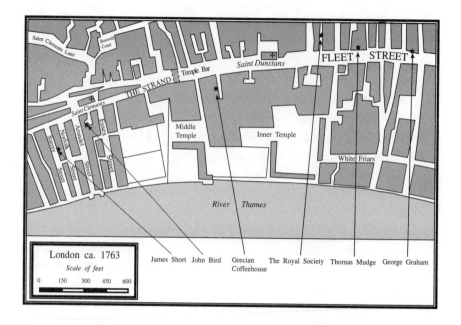

each day after work, to assemble the instrument's many parts. Known as the Jersey Quadrant, Sisson's instrument was first used by Alexander to establish the location of the forty-first parallel of latitude, opposite modern Hastings-on-Hudson. The western end of the boundary was located at the major bend of the Delaware River, opposite modern Matamoras, Pennsylvania, where the flow of the river turned from the southeast to head southwest for Delaware Bay. At this critical point New Jersey, New York, and Pennsylvania came together. The instrument continued to be used on many surveys in New Jersey and was borrowed by Surveyor General Colden of New York. James Alexander's son William succeeded his father, who died in 1756, as surveyor general, and the quadrant passed into his possession. The Jersey Quadrant had demonstrated that in the hands of a competent surveyor, a precision instrument could solve an acrimonious boundary dispute. The consequence of this satisfactory resolution was not lost on the two proprietors of Pennsylvania and Maryland.

Between 1761 and 1763, Thomas Penn and Cecilius Calvert consulted widely among the learned men of London. The scientific community was small and well connected; the center of their lives was the Royal Society's rooms in Crane Court, a narrow alley off London's Fleet

Brass quadrant of twenty-inch radius (inverted), by
Jonathan Sisson, which was similar to his larger
Jersey Quadrant. (Photograph courtesy Armagh
Observatory, Northern Ireland)

Street. Many of the clock and instrument makers were also clustered
along Fleet Street and the Strand, the main thoroughfare linking the
City of London with Westminster. The two streets were divided by the
grim Temple Bar gate with the grisly remains of Townley and Fletcher,
the Jacobite rebels executed in 1745, still on display. The Strand was
also London's most fashionable shopping and hotel street, with coffee-
houses such as the Grecian in Devereux Court (now called the Devereux Arms) frequented by wits and literary men, and by scientists
such as Isaac Newton and Astronomer Royal Edmund Halley (of
comet fame). In the same lane was Tom Twining's renowned teahouse
(still selling tea today), and just around the corner were taverns such
as the George, and the Crown and Anchor, for casual meetings, convivial discourse, and overnight stays in Town.

Crane Court, Fleet Street; the meeting place of the
Royal Society.

For Penn and Calvert, well-to-do, powerful, and influential men,
making contact with scientists and academics would have been a simple business and their most logical starting point was Dr. Bradley, the
sixty-eight-year-old astronomer royal. James Bradley graduated from
Balliol College, Oxford, in 1714 and discovered astronomy through
his uncle, Reverend James Pound, who also introduced him to Edmund Halley, the then astronomer royal. In 1718, Bradley was elected
to the Royal Society and three years later accepted the Savilian Chair
of Geometry at his old university. He was a consummate and meticulous mathematician and astronomer, publishing a table of refraction in
1720 that allowed the correction of astronomical observations for the
light-bending effects of the atmosphere. In 1727 Bradley discovered
stellar aberration, explaining why a star's position in the sky seems to
vary during the year. When Halley died in 1742, Bradley was his nat-

The Devereux Arms, once the Grecian Coffeehouse, a favorite meeting place for London's wits and literary figures.

ural successor and was elevated to astronomer royal with a salary of £250 per annum. In 1747 he discovered nutation and went on to observe, collate, and catalog the positions of stars, which he listed by their right ascension and declination, and began to record the distance of the Moon from these stars for different times of the month.

Peter Daval, an amateur astronomer, a barrister, and a past secretary of the Royal Society, was also approached by the proprietors, as was John Robertson (1712–1776), the talented mathematician and first master of the Royal Naval Academy in Portsmouth. Robertson calibrated John Harrison's famous chronometer "H4" before departure on its first sea trial on November 18, 1761. Thomas Penn enlisted the assistance of Daniel Harris, mathematician and astronomer, and of Thomas Simpson (1710–1761), second master of the Royal Military Academy at Woolwich, where the art of surveying was germane to

contemporary advances in artillery. Cecilius Calvert limited his private
consultations primarily to Dr. John Bevis, physician, scientist, and
amateur astronomer, whom Dr. Bradley had personally recommended.

Dr. Bevis had an astronomical observatory at his home in Stoke
Newington, then a quiet village far beyond the sprawl of London
where, in 1731, he discovered the Crab Nebula, the remains of a super-
nova observed by the Chinese in 1054. Bevis had participated in an
ambitious survey campaign on Salisbury Plain, the great expanse of
chalk uplands in the south of England, where a parallel of latitude and
a segment of meridian had been measured carefully. On that occasion
he had used an equatorial mounted reflecting telescope, made by his
friend James Short, that he described as "a transit instrument." Dr.
Bevis was an accomplished scientist and, apart from his expertise in
astronomy and medicine, developed the forerunner of the modern electrical capacitor. In London, at the time, was that other celebrated electrical scientist, Benjamin Franklin. In 1754, for his *Experiments and
Observations on Electricity,* Franklin had been awarded the Royal Society's prestigious Copley Medal, and was elected a Fellow. He had come
to London to represent the province of Pennsylvania in its battle with
the Penn family over taxation. Between bouts with Thomas Penn and
lobbying parliamentarians, however, he pursued his many experiments.
From his riverside lodgings at 36 Craven Street, at the western end of
the Strand, Franklin entertained both scientists and radical politicians,
delighting them with tunes from his "armonica," a mechanized version
of Richard Pockrich's musical glasses. He thoroughly enjoyed London's
society and befriended many influential Whigs, industrialists, and dissenters who, like him, sought a radical reform of Parliament and a
wider and equitable relationship with the American colonies. He was
also making friends among men of science and participating in the
Royal Society's activities. Peter Collinson, the naturalist and antiquary
consulted by Dr. Colden, the surveyor general of New York, was a
close friend, and John Bevis was one of his many acquaintances. From
his frequent discussions with Thomas Penn, as a member of the Pennsylvania General Assembly, Franklin was aware of the search in London
for surveying instruments and professional advice.

In January 1761, the fame and virtues of the Jersey Quadrant were
brought to Penn's attention. He approached William Alexander (1726–
1783), then in London pursuing a claim to the title of his distant rela-

Benjamin Franklin's lodgings at 36 Craven Street,
London.

tives, the earls of Stirling. Alexander immediately agreed to write to
his widowed mother, requesting her to make the instrument available
to Reverend Richard Peters, Penn's provincial secretary in Philadelphia.
Scouring the scientific emporiums of London, Penn acquired more instruments, including a three-foot brass telescope fitted with a reticule
and a swivel that he dispatched to Reverend Peters on April 13, 1761.
He also purchased a two-foot brass zenith sector made by Watkins of
Charing Cross at the west end of the Strand, which he sent to Philadelphia in May 1761.

Penn noticed increasingly that whenever he met with astronomers,
mathematicians, instrument makers, or patrons of the sciences, the
conversation always turned to the forthcoming transit of Venus, the
first in one hundred years. Had he or Calvert known it, the two men
who would solve their boundary problems, Mason and Dixon, were

already on the high seas en route for the Royal Society's overseas observing expedition. The Scottish mathematician and astronomer James Gregory (1638–1675) had suggested that observing the planet Venus as it passed in front of the Sun would provide a method for measuring the distance to the Sun (the solar parallax). In 1716, Edmund Halley devised a practical scheme for making the necessary measurements from widely spaced locations around the planet. He recommended that observations should be made at Madras, India, or Bencoolen (Bengkulu), a British trading post in southwestern Sumatra, and from Fort Nelson on Hudson Bay. The displacement in longitude of these remote stations, some 180 degrees or half a hemisphere apart, would in effect be a very long baseline. The tiny angle subtended by the planet between the distant extremities would be the parallax.

The Royal Society was in part funding the overseas transit of Venus expeditions in collaboration with the Admiralty; in France, the Académie Royale de Sciences was similarly engaged with preparations. Despite the war, the two scientific bodies continued to share information. The great event of the transit would occur on June 6, but as the date drew near, news came that Dr. Bradley was unwell. Instead, the astronomer royal's old friend Reverend Nathaniel Bliss (1700–1764) would make the transit observations at Greenwich, aided by the new observatory assistant, Charles Green (1735–1771). The earl of Macclesfield, the president of the Royal Society and a noted astronomer, was preparing for the great event at the observatory he and Bradley had built at Macclesfield's country home of Shirburn Castle. He would be assisted by another rising star, Tom Hornsby (1733–1840) of Oxford. The Royal Society chose a twenty-eight-year-old Cambridge Fellow called Nevil Maskelyne to send to the distant island of Saint Helena in the southern Atlantic, while Bradley's observatory assistant Charles Mason and a land surveyor from Durham named Jeremiah Dixon were supposedly en route for Sumatra.

Reverend Nevil Maskelyne (1732–1811), astronomer and mathematician, was the third child of Edmund and Elizabeth Maskelyne of Purton in Wiltshire. His background was one of wealth and privilege; he had been a scholar at Westminster School, where, at the age of sixteen, he observed the eclipse of July 25, 1748, an event that affected him profoundly and was to shape his life's work. The following year he went up to Cambridge, first at Saint Catharine Hall, then at Trinity

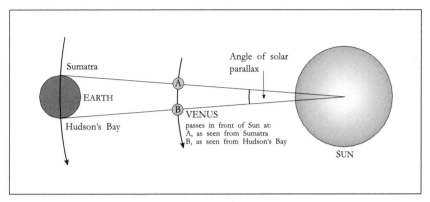

Measuring the parallax during the transit of Venus.

College. While Maskelyne was at Cambridge, his elder brother Edmond was serving with the East India Company and, during the siege of Arcot, befriended Robert Clive (1725–1774). Edmond sent for their sister, Margaret, to join him on his tour of duty specifically to introduce her to his dashing young friend. Admiration turned to affection, and Margaret became Mrs., and eventually Lady, Clive in the little church of Fort Saint George, Madras.

Nevil Maskelyne met his famous brother-in-law, the soldier who made India a British province, for the first time when Clive and Margaret returned to England in 1754. It was the same year Maskelyne graduated from Trinity and his sister bore her first child, Edward. The relationship between Nevil Maskelyne and his brother-in-law remained cordial despite their obvious differences in character—where Maskelyne had excelled, Clive's student days had been a struggle and his learning was poor, although he educated himself in the governor's library in Madras. Clive's moody and quarrelsome nature contrasted sharply with that of his younger, studious, mild, and genial brother-in-law. Both men were destined to follow very different but historic paths and would seldom meet again.

With the start of the Michaelmas term, Maskelyne returned to his college to take Holy Orders, a prerequisite for a Cambridge fellowship in the eighteenth century. In the tower above Trinity College, the inventor of the chronometer, John Harrison, was busy installing one of his famous turret clocks, oblivious of Maskelyne, his future adversary,

Reverend Nevil Maskelyne (1732–1811); engraving by
E. Scriven, circa 1800. (National Museum of American
History/Smithsonian Institution, Washington, D.C.)

strolling around the quad below. The next year Maskelyne met and
greatly impressed the astronomer royal, Dr. Bradley, and developed a
friendship that lasted to Bradley's death seven years later. Maskelyne
gained his M.A. in 1757 and in the same year was elected a Fellow of
Trinity. The following year his scientific prowess was recognized with
his election to a fellowship in the Royal Society of London.

Maskelyne studied under James Bradley, observed his methods,
and emulated his many skills. He assisted in preparing Bradley's table
of refractive indexes that were eventually published in the Nautical
Almanac in 1767. As the first transit of Venus in a hundred years
loomed on the astronomical horizon, it was natural for Bradley to rec-
ommend to the Royal Society his able young prodigy as the astronomer to lead the British overseas expedition from the island of Saint
Helena. Bradley also recommended that the astronomer for the Ben-

Weir Farm, Gloucestershire, birthplace of Charles Mason. (Photographed with the kind permission of the present owner, Mr. D. H. Taylor)

coolen (Bengkulu, Sumatra) observations should be his observatory assistant, Charles Mason.

Charles Mason, astronomer and associate of the Royal Society, was born at Wherr (now Weir) Farm in the Gloucestershire village of Oakridge Lynch in April 1728. One of four children born to Charles Mason, a baker and miller, and his wife, Anne, he attended the Tetbury Grammar School and received additional tuition from Robert Stratford, a mathematician from the nearby village of Sapperton. In 1756 he joined Dr. Bradley's staff at the Greenwich Observatory as an observing assistant on a retainer of £26 a year, an amount equivalent to that of a poor tenant farmer. However, it was the practice of the day that a scientist's work was his own to profit from; hence, his daily tasks were priced individually. He also had other sources of income, or stipends, from the Board of Longitude. Mason, a competent mathematician and adept with complex astronomical figures, was endowed with the rare capability of being able to visualize their three-dimensional shapes. His knowledge of contemporary geodesy (the study of the shape of Earth) was recondite as well as practical. As an astronomer, he

Saint Kenelm's church, Sapperton, where Mason
was christened and twice married. The author's
son Peter stands next to Rebekah's grave.

was as painstaking in his record keeping as he was accomplished in his
observing skills.

It was near Mason's home of Sapperton in Gloucestershire that he
was introduced to a local girl; love blossomed, and they married and
moved to Mason's house in Greenwich, where they produced two
lively sons. Tragically, in 1759, Rebekah Mason died, perhaps in child-
birth. She was laid to rest a few days later, close by the south door of
the little Queen Anne church of Saint Kenelm's, Sapperton. Reverend
Allen Bathurst led the service and read the prayer as the thirty-year-
old mother was lowered to her final resting place, surrounded by
grieving friends and family, including the astronomer royal, who com-
forted a distraught Charles Mason. A plain block of mellow Cotswold
stone marks her grave, where, on a brass plaque, the visitor can still
read Mason's own words:

SACRED
To the Remains of Rebekah
Wife of Cha Mason J^{un} ARS
With the Greatest Serenity of Mind
She departed this Life the 13th of Feb 1759
(at Greenwich Kent)
in the 31st year of her Age
Could the unsally'd of Heart from Dissolution save
In Vain Might Death assum'd this silent Grave
But Fate how hard!
Her able Morn in Dark Shade expire
And Noontide Sun went down with Jobs Desire

Some years later, in 1770, Mason married again, to Mary, who bore him six more children; but he ever loved his Becky. Charles Mason, ARS, was a God-fearing man: intelligent, witty, with a lively sense of the ridiculous, but given to occasional bouts of melancholia; mellifluent, meticulous, and discerning, but above all, an adventurer, a man of his time. Something of his character comes through in the pages of the journal he alone kept throughout the great North American survey. Mason was immensely curious about the natural world, even recording in his journal a visit to a large and beautiful cave that sadly was later destroyed by quarrying, reflecting on its melancholic air.

Whether it was a beautiful curtain of stalactites, the fall of a meteor, or the size of a hickory bough that caught his attention, Charles Mason admired with full reverence the glory of God's creation that daily surrounded him. His eye for a fine line and his deep love of geometric form was frequently and lyrically expressed while he was standing aloft a high hill surveying the vista of the long West Line. During the winter periods, when work was impossible, he journeyed afar and often alone, exploring the American colonies on horseback. He recorded his conversations with interesting people he met along the way and the places he visited, embellished with insight and contemporary comment. The fabulous lands far to the west fascinated and intrigued him, and he took any opportunity that arose to question experts and record their knowledge.

Mason's companion for the transit of Venus campaign, Jeremiah Dixon, is a somewhat shadowy figure. He was born in Bishop Auckland, County Durham, on July 27, 1733, the fifth of eight children in the family of George Dixon, a wealthy Quaker colliery owner at Cock-field, and his wife, Mary. At John Kipling's school in Barnard Castle he excelled in mathematics and was familiar with the noted mathematician and astronomer William Emerson. Through family connections, Dixon was acquainted with John Bird, the celebrated scientific instrument maker, also from Bishop Auckland, who constructed many of the fine instruments for the Royal Observatory at Greenwich. Dixon's prowess as an amateur astronomer was recognized by Bird, and it was almost certainly through him that Dixon was recommended to Dr. James Bradley as a promising assistant.

One cannot help feel there are facts about Jeremiah the passage of time has erased. He may have learned his trade in his father's coal mine mapping the galleries, or apprenticed to a local surveyor. During his examination at the Royal Military Academy in Woolwich, he candidly confessed to the board he had neither attended Oxford nor Cambridge universities and had received no formal training in astronomy. The chairman of the examination panel was perplexed and asked Dixon: "Then at what other seat of learning, pray?" Dixon replied, "In a pit cabin on Cockfield Fell." It can be assumed that he started his professional career as he ended it, probably surveying the medieval common fields of his home county for the Parliamentary Enclosure Acts. It was not uncommon for bright boys to come under the patronage of an aristocratic benefactor, as happened to William Bayly, the son of a Wiltshire artisan, who also became an assistant in the Royal Observatory. Dixon may have benefited from some prestigious sinecure, for by the time he was examined at Woolwich and selected for the transit of Venus expedition at the age of twenty-eight, he had been practicing his profession some ten years.

Mason was officially engaged by the Royal Society on September 11 on a salary of £200, and Dixon was recommended as his assistant. Dixon, already in London, responded promptly to the society's invitation "to accompany Mr Mason, and be under his directions." For the next two months Charles Mason and his new colleague Jeremiah Dixon were busily engaged in familiarization and training with their new equipment. The instruments for the transit of Venus observations included a 12-inch Hadley quadrant made by John Bird and two reflecting telescopes made by James Short, each of 24-inch focal length and magnifying 120 times. At least one of the telescopes was fitted with a micrometer scale. Short, from his workshops in Surrey Street, had capitalized on the improved production methods then emerging for crafting small telescope mirrors and made his fortune by selling large numbers of his expensive instruments to the wealthy aristocracy. Mason was familiar with all their scientific instruments, while Dixon, as an amateur astronomer, was probably at ease with the telescopes. The micrometer, a screw for making fine measurements, and the quadrant were new to him and required some practice during the evenings beneath the starry skies at Greenwich before he became proficient in their use. The Royal Society also furnished them with an astronomical pendulum clock, or regulator, made by John Shelton, a very precise and expensive piece of equipment requiring special attention.

Dixon was a competent mathematician but not of the caliber of Charles Mason, who had a profound understanding of geodesy, as it was then understood. The two men spent much time exploring astronomical and geodetic, especially spherical, trigonometry. Finally, in the fall, before the equinoctial gales set in and brought an end to safe sailing, Mason and Dixon left London with their baggage and scientific hoard stowed carefully in their hired carriage, and headed for Portsmouth. The wharves and quays of the great naval base were busy with men loading the accoutrements of sea warfare, for England and France were then locked in the conflict of the Seven Years' War. Scarred and battered frigates filled the dry docks, the largest of their kind in the world, where carpenters and riggers frantically repaired the damage of battle.

The two scientists reported to the base commander on November 24 and were escorted to HMS *Seahorse,* a fighting frigate moored in the harbor. However, the weather and problems in fitting out the vessel for the long voyage delayed sailing. Finally, on January 8, 1761, at two in the afternoon, the *Seahorse* made sail, turned into the choppy seas of the English Channel, and set course for the Lizard Point and their last sight of England. By evening of the next day they were well out of sight of land and changing course to the west-southwest and the Bay of Biscay. The captain, acutely aware of the danger yet wishing to pick up the northeast trades, kept well to the north of the bay, intending to steer clear of the enemy shores of France and Spain for a safer entry into the Atlantic, before turning south. At first all went well; then, at eleven o'clock on Saturday, January 10, came a cry from the fighting

tops as a sail was seen bearing down fast on *Seahorse* from the wind-
ward. The alarm was sounded and marines and gunners rushed to their
posts. The cannon were loaded, primed, and run out as the ship prepared for battle. The newcomer was the *L'Grand,* a thirty-four-gun
French frigate, somewhat larger than the lighter *Seahorse.* As the two
vessels closed, the Frenchman raked the English ship with deadly fire
from its heavy guns.

W hether Mason and Dixon stayed on deck or took shelter below is
not known, but for the two landlubbers, their first brutal experience of
war at sea was a terrifying experience. The tumultuous thunder of the
English guns, the dull thump and crack of French shot pounding their
ship, the screams of injured and dying men, the stench of gunpowder,
vomit, and blood, was beyond their wildest nightmares. The battle
raged for "1 hour 10 minutes" as each ship took advantage of wind
and sea to inflict mortal damage on the other. Suddenly the Frenchman came about, breaking off the engagement, and headed away. *Seahorse* set off in pursuit and "all the sail possible was made to keep up
with her," but the British vessel was badly mauled. Although still sea-
worthy, the superstructure was damaged and its rigging shot to pieces.
Eleven of the crew lay dead and thirty-seven others were seriously
injured, "a great many of which are mortal," so the captain came about
and headed for Plymouth to make repairs.

This attack was counter to the spirit of the unwritten protocol that
scientific expeditions were exempt from hostile engagement. The practice of the day was to fly a white flag along with the national ensign
to let a potential belligerent know the vessel was on a scientific mission. However, we don't know if *Seahorse* followed this practice. In any
case, it demonstrates the hazards scientists of that time encountered
when venturing overseas, and was a foretaste of what was to come.

Aware of the pressures of time and possibly suffering from shock
after the French attack, Mason and Dixon wrote to the Royal Society
requesting a diversion to a suitable location closer than Sumatra. The
Royal Society, however, did not appreciate their letter and replied with
"threatened inflexible resentment and prosecution with the utmost
severity of the law," and suggested, in no uncertain terms, that the two
young gentlemen best rejoin HMS *Seahorse* and continue with their
assignment.

The repairs to *Seahorse* took several weeks. Finally it was able to set off again on February 3, out into the Atlantic rollers, following the well-trodden path of southbound mariners, down through the Azores to pick up the northeast trades and a long haul towards the Brazilian coast to catch the winds that would take them to South Africa. The wearisome passage through the blistering heat of the doldrums was as depressing an experience to the scientists as it was to the seasoned veterans of His Majesty's navy; Mason, in particular, suffered from seasickness. The only relief for Mason and Dixon was that they were able to turn their astronomical skills to assisting the navigator in determining the ship's latitude and experimenting with lunar distances to find the longitude.

The delay in Plymouth had seriously prejudiced any hope of reaching Bencoolen by the beginning of June in time to observe the transit. As *Seahorse* made its ponderous way south, Mason and Dixon discussed the matter with the captain, who agreed that it was unlikely the warship could make a swift enough passage across the fifty-five hundred miles of the Indian Ocean to reach Sumatra in time. Instead of rounding the Cape of Good Hope, there seemed no alternative but to divert to Cape Town.

An east-southeasterly course across the southern Atlantic brought HMS *Seahorse* to the southern cape of Africa, where it dropped anchor in Table Bay on April 27, 1761. The suspicious Dutch authorities of Cape Town sailed out to the English warship, and its captain and his distinguished scientific guests were invited ashore to explain themselves. The Cape was then a Dutch colony, but when the authorities learned of Mason and Dixon's mission, and accepted their explanation that a minor mishap in the English Channel had delayed their departure, the astronomers and the ship's crew were permitted to land.

Permission was also given for astronomical observations to be made in Cape Town, so with the active assistance of the Dutch authorities, the Englishmen built a small astronomical observatory. The structure was wooden, twelve feet in diameter with walls five feet high, and fitted with a conical rotating roof with an aperture through which the telescope could point to any part of the sky. No doubt the design had been agreed upon earlier and was probably the model for the temporary observatories Mason and Dixon would later construct in

North America. The tiny observatory was erected behind Saint Mary's Cathedral, a location that can be ascertained precisely from their observations: latitude 33 degrees 44 minutes 42 seconds south, longitude 18 degrees 15 minutes 9 seconds east.

By May 4, the instruments were properly installed and the all-important pendulum clock, which would provide the times for the observations, was fastened to heavy timbers sunk four feet into the ground and braced with iron rods. Using the Hadley quadrant, Mason and Dixon observed equal altitudes of stars as they rose and set across the meridian. From the star's right ascensions, they were able to calculate the sidereal time and determine the rate, or "going," of the pendulum clock. Even the best clocks of the period could not keep time precisely; therefore, by observing sidereal time frequently and comparing this to the clock's time, its rate of gain or loss could be ascertained. The day for the transit of Venus was plagued by clouds that occasionally obscured the Sun, but as the morning wore on and the Sun rose in the east, the astronomers managed to measure the angular distance from the Sun's furthest edge and Venus's southern limb. In all they recorded six transit measurements on that chilly June 6, as well as measuring the apparent diameters of both the Sun and Venus.

It was by no means a perfect transit; the cloudy planet and the Sun never reached a common right ascension before both sank from view beneath the western horizon. Another opportunity would arise eight years later that would prove to be a far more spectacular affair, both for the observers and for scientific progress.

After the great event of the transit, Mason and Dixon spent a further four months in Cape Town, observing equal altitude stars and the zenith distances of latitude stars to add to the Greenwich Observatory's growing catalog of navigational stars. The two English astronomers and their curious observatory became a familiar sight and attracted much interest. It was not all work—both men enjoyed the social round and explored the country around the Cape—but eventually the ship *Mercury* dropped anchor in the bay and it was time to leave. On October 3, 1761, they weighed anchor and set sail for the tiny Atlantic island of Saint Helena, to rejoin Nevil Maskelyne.

Maskelyne's transit of Venus had been a disaster; the weather had remained cloudy and the plumb bob of his zenith sector had failed miserably. On arrival, Mason's first task was to make the necessary

Saint Helena from the sea. Illustration from Charles Darwin's *Journal of a Voyage Round the World,* 1835.

observations to determine the local rate of their pendulum clock. The local strength of gravity and the centrifugal effects of Earth's speed of rotation affect a pendulum's rate of swing (the period; or, as Mason called it, "the Vibration").

By measuring the period of the clock's pendulum and comparing this to its rate at a known location, it was possible to calculate small variations in gravity and hence determine the degree of Earth flattening. Throughout the campaign in South Africa, the length of the pendulum had been kept constant, but at Saint Helena, fourteen degrees latitude north of the Cape, the clock ticked a little faster. Jeremiah Dixon's performance as a professional astronomer and observer had been exemplary. Toward the end of the year, he returned to South Africa to make further gravity observations while Mason remained on Saint Helena, assisting Nevil Maskelyne with astronomical and tidal measurements until both left for England in December 1761.

CHAPTER 6

Mr. Bird's Contrivances

WITH THE TRANSIT of Venus over, the scientific community of London settled down to write the papers they would deliver to the Royal Society. All the astronomical data from the many observers around the country and overseas had to be collected, compiled, and checked. Maskelyne and Mason were due back from Saint Helena imminently with, it was expected, a significant amount of valuable information from the Southern Hemisphere. Mason and Dixon's inability to reach Sumatra by June 6 and their decision to divert to Cape Town was unfortunate, and a full explanation was required.

Meantime, the two proprietors of Pennsylvania and Maryland resumed their quest for quality surveying instruments. In distant Pennsylvania, Governor James Hamilton was informed at home of progress as the search went forward. He wrote to Thomas Penn requesting him to find "a special transit Instrument made in London twelve or fourteen years ago," undoubtedly referring to the Jersey Quadrant, unaware that arrangements were already in hand. In August 1761, the Council of Proprietors of the Eastern Division of New Jersey had met at the behest of William Alexander's mother and agreed to loan their precious quadrant for the proposed survey. The giant instrument was delivered to the Pennsylvania commissioners in December 1761.

At about that time difficulties arose between the two provincial camps on what correctly defined a westerly direction for the boundary line between Maryland and Pennsylvania. John Robertson, master of the Royal Naval Academy, and Dr. Bevis vehemently disagreed as to whether the proposed border should be a great circle, advocated by

Robertson, or a parallel of latitude. Governor Sharpe of Maryland was amused, commenting in a letter to Cecilius Calvert in February 1762: "I cannot but smile to see how vastly Dr Bevis & Mr Robinson [sic] differ in their definition of a true East & West Line." In April 1761 Penn had reminded his commissioners that the line should be a parallel of latitude according to law, but for curious reasons, the gentlemen in Pennsylvania seemed to prefer a great circle. Robertson, who supported this contention, must have known that a great circle, which is a section passing through Earth's center, would give his client Mr. Penn less land than he was entitled. The argument was academic; the provincial grants clearly stipulated the border was to be a parallel of constant latitude, and on this point both Penn and Calvert agreed.

There were also other, more pressing, difficulties for Thomas Penn in London. Benjamin Franklin, representing the Pennsylvania legislature, had successfully won a grudging concession from Penn through a persistent campaign of lobbying and argument. The crippling cost of defending the long frontiers from attack had forced the legislature to either negotiate a tax deal with Penn or petition the king for a change in the charter. The polite but intransigent Penn managed to equivocate for a while, but eventually conceded to Franklin that he could indeed raise a land tax. It was a weak compromise and did little to ease the growing tension between the farmers and frontiersmen of Pennsylvania's western counties and the affluent urban population in the east. When Mason and Dixon reached America, they were to see the result for themselves.

In their search for surveying instruments, Penn and Calvert were still concerned that none of the instruments they had acquired could deliver the accuracy in latitude required. Even the celebrated Jersey Quadrant could only produce one-half minute of arc, equivalent to an uncertainty of over half a mile on the ground. Penn remained closely in contact with William Alexander, surveyor general of New Jersey, and was grateful for his advice on a number of occasions and for arranging the loan of the Jersey Quadrant. In May 1762, Thomas Penn wrote to Alexander to say he had received advice that an instrument called a zenith sector would solve the latitude problem and that "I have bespoke one of Bird . . ."

John Bird (1709–1776) had his instrument workshop at the sign of The Sea Quadrant in Court Gardens, a small square at the end of a narrow alley leading off the Strand. In the cramped building, whose roof timbers shook whenever the bells of nearby Saint Clement Danes rang, Bird had become famous for making the finest scientific instruments. As a young man he had been apprenticed to Jonathan Sisson and had also received instruction from the celebrated clock and instrument maker George Graham. By the time Mr. Penn came knocking at The Sea Quadrant's door, John Bird had already invented the revolutionary slow-motion tangent screw, a device that enabled readings of a fraction of a second to be made. Bird's tangent screw was added to Sisson's iron-framed quadrant at the Royal Observatory and would later complement Bird's own eight-foot radius brass quadrant made for the observatory in 1767.

In his discussions with Bird, Penn was accompanied by his advisers, including Nevil Maskelyne, who had made recommendations for improving the instrument. The astronomer later noted: "Mr Bird has contrived one [zenith sector] . . . in which the plumb-line is adjusted so as to pass over against and bisect a small point at the centre of the instrument." John Bird estimated it would take him some two months to construct a six-foot instrument that, he said, would provide an accuracy of two seconds of arc ($\frac{1}{1,800}$ of a degree). Satisfied that Bird could build such a device, Penn instructed the instrument maker to proceed. Bird's estimate of two months to build the instrument was grossly underestimated; on November 13, Penn wrote again to William Alexander complaining that "I have pressed Mr Bird very much to finish the sector." Lord Baltimore also agreed to provide a zenith sector and purchased an old instrument made by the late Jonathan Sisson. When completed, Bird's zenith sector, with its micrometer tangent screw that read to a fraction of a second of arc, was examined by Calvert, Thomas Penn, and Dr. Bevis, who all proclaimed its excellence despite the cost's being three times that of Sisson's old instrument.

Among their shopping list of instruments, the proprietors also required an astronomical transit instrument. It was suggested that Dr. Bevis's equatorial telescope, used on Salisbury Plain, would be most suitable. The proprietors met to examine the instrument, but were disappointed with what they found. Of further concern were the results Governor Sharpe of Maryland was having in testing Sisson's zenith sector and the other telescopes delivered to America. Sharpe reported in September 1762 that none of the instruments gave adequately repeat-

John Bird (1709–1776). (Courtesy National Maritime Museum, London)

able results or were capable of sufficient resolution (the ability of a telescope to differentiate between two distant objects), which was vital if the survey was to be a success. Fortunately, Thomas Penn had commissioned from John Bird another instrument in addition to the six-foot-radius zenith sector. This was "a transit and equal altitude" instrument of a similar design to that described by Pierre-Charles Le Monnier; it would prove to be second only in practical value during the North American survey to Bird's very fine zenith sector.

The exact details of John Bird's transit and equal altitude instrument are known because in 1912 it was discovered lying beneath the floorboards in Philadelphia's Statehouse and is now on permanent display in Philadelphia's Independence National Historical Park. The instrument was used, among other things, for determining the direction of the meridian (the direction of true north). It consisted of a thirty-three-inch-long telescope of moderate magnification, mounted

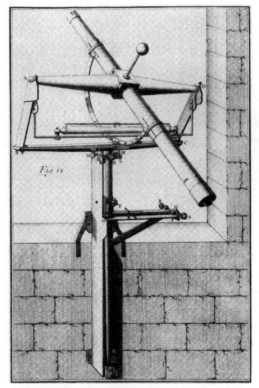

Transit and equal altitude instrument by
George Graham. (Illustration from Charles-
Pierre Le Monnier's *Histoire Céleste*)

on a horizontal, or trunnion, axis, and capable of being tilted in the
vertical. A graduated semicircular scale of ivory was attached to the
underside of the telescope and a long, sensitive spirit level hung from
the trunnion axis supports just above the semicircular scale. Elevation
was measured on the scale where it touched an index mark on the
hanging level. By turning the vertical axis through ninety-degree steps
and adjusting the screws until the bubble in the spirit level was centered, the instrument could be leveled precisely.

To find the direction of true north, the transit's telescope was
pointed toward a suitable star as it rose toward the meridian, at which
point it would reach its highest point, or altitude. Shortly before it
reached the top of its climb across the sky, as the star crossed the telescope's horizontal wire, the transit's vertical axis would be clamped

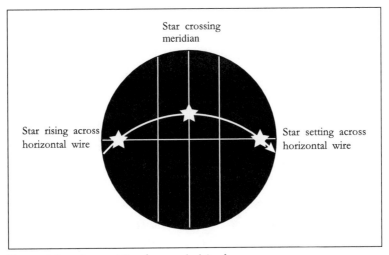

Star crossing
meridian

Star rising across
horizontal wire

Star setting across
horizontal wire

Determining the meridian by equal altitudes.

and the time noted. The star would be tracked as it crossed the meridian and began to set. When the star again crossed the horizontal wire
(i.e., at an equal altitude), the time was again noted; the mean of the
two times gave the moment when the star crossed the meridian.

The most precise of the astronomical instruments acquired by the
proprietors for the North American campaign was John Bird's six-foot-
radius zenith sector. This instrument consisted of a tall stand, probably eight feet high, from the top of which was suspended from a pivot
a six-foot-long telescope tube. At the base of the stand was fastened
the instrument's engraved ivory scale, which was a sector with a radius
of six feet—hence the name.

The scale was quite short, probably covering a sector of arc no
more than ten degrees either side of the center line. A micrometer was
attached to the telescope that allowed angular measurements to be
read to a hundredth of a second of arc ($\frac{1}{360,000}$ of a degree), although its
precision was probably little better than the two seconds of arc John
Bird originally estimated. The instrument was set vertically with the
aid of a precise plummet arrangement. During the transit of Venus
measurements on Saint Helena in 1761, Nevil Maskelyne's sector had
suffered from a serious fault caused by a defective suspension design.
Consequently, he devised an improvement, which John Bird had perfected and incorporated in the new instrument, so that "the plumb-line

is adjusted so as to pass over against and bisect a small point at the centre of the instrument." The purpose of the instrument was to measure
the zenith distances of stars lying in the meridian; hence *zenith* sector.

From the zenith (the point in the heavens directly above the observer), the angular distance to a star as it crossed the meridian was measured. The eyepiece of the instrument was so low to the ground that
the observer had to lie on his back to see through the eyepiece and
operate the delicate tangent screw. By modern standards, it would have
been a tedious, frustrating, and very tiring occupation, but such discomfort was accepted as part of an astronomer's lot. Having identified
the star and observed its zenith distance, the star's declination (angle
above the celestial equator) would be found from Dr. Bradley's tables of
star positions. To find the astronomical latitude, the measured zenith
distance was either added or subtracted to the declination, depending
upon whether the star lay to the north or to the south of the zenith.

Another instrument used extensively was a quadrant, an ancient
astronomical device similar in appearance to a modern sextant frequently featured in historical maritime dramas. The instrument was
used primarily for measuring vertical angles to the stars. The famous
Danish astronomer Tycho Brahe (1546–1601) built his own giant-sized
quadrants and a huge sextant at his observatory at Uraniborg during the
1570s. The smaller mariner's quadrant was invented in 1730 simultaneously, but independently, by Thomas Godfrey (1707–1749) of Philadelphia and John Hadley (1682–1744), the vice president of the Royal
Society of London. It is not unreasonable to believe that two different
persons, three thousand miles apart, invented the quadrant in the same
year. Navigation problems were uppermost in the minds of scientific
men of the time and the advances in instrument making meant that
the invention was inevitable. The two inventors each claimed the
accolade, and an angry Godfrey wrote to the Royal Society in 1734
claiming rights to the invention. His application was rejected, probably unfairly because he was a mere colonial artisan, while Hadley was
a mathematician and Fellow of the Royal Society who, among many
achievements, perfected the reflecting telescope, opening a new chapter in precise astronomical observation.

Like Godfrey's, Hadley's quadrant was in reality a double reflecting octant with an engraved scale covering forty-five degrees of arc.
Mirrors doubled the angular aperture, giving an effective measuring

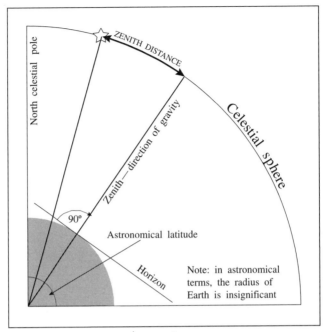

Measuring the zenith distance of a star.

arc of ninety degrees; hence the name quadrant, or quarter of a circle. The quadrant, with which Hadley's name became synonymous, was fitted with a horizontal bubble level to assist mariners with their latitude observations, and from it, in 1758, John Bird developed the mariners' sextant. By using the Hadley quadrant on its side, rather than vertically, horizontal angles between two distant marks could be measured with a reasonable accuracy. Mason used this method for measuring the width of wide rivers by triangulation, and the principle is still used today.

Another instrument available was the true quadrant, essentially a ninety-degree sector of a circle engraved on a scale. These were used on land and for astronomical observations to measure vertical angles to celestial bodies to find latitude. A siting telescope, or alidade, was fixed to a pivot at the right-angled corner of the quadrant with a precise level laid along the top edge of the scale. An eighteen-inch-radius John Bird quadrant on display in London's Science Museum is fitted with a graduated horizontal plate as well as a level. This instrument was manufactured for the Royal Society and was actually used by

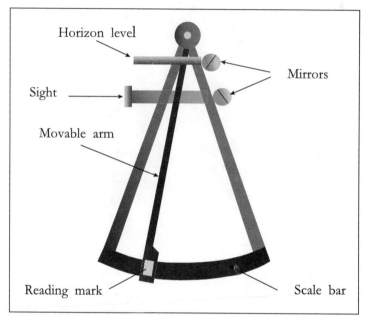

Horizon level

Mirrors

Sight

Movable arm

Reading mark

Scale bar

Schematic of a Hadley pattern quadrant.

Charles Mason some years later. The Jersey Quadrant was probably very similar, but was never used; rather, Mason relied on his eighteen-inch-radius Hadley pattern instrument, which he used frequently.

For linear measurements, the North American survey expedition was equipped with 22-yard-long Gunter, or surveyor's, chains. Edmund Gunter (1581–1626) designed his famous measuring chain based on the dimensions of an acre (10 chains long × 1 chain wide = 4,840 square yards). The chain was decimal, made up from 100 links, each 0.66 feet, or 7.92 inches, long. Gunter's chain was eventually adopted as the exclusive legal measure for North American property surveys and remained in common use until very recent times. Mason and Dixon also used measuring rods they called "levels," precision-cut lengths of softwood tipped with brass. A standard builder's level was used to keep them horizontal. To measure a line, the levels would be brought together so their ends met perfectly, either butt to butt or, on a slope, supported on stands or stakes and the ends connected using a fine plummet.

To ensure the measuring chains and levels remained in calibration, Dr. Bevis advised Calvert to commission John Bird to construct a

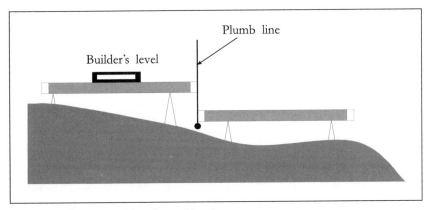

Measuring distances with softwood levels.

3-foot-long precision brass standard. At the time of the survey, the English standard measurement units were the foot and the yard. Official master standards were kept under lock and key by the Exchequer and in the Tower of London; a copy was also held by the Royal Society. At an estate sale in 1790, General William Roy, engaged in assembling instruments for Britain's new mapping agency, the Ordnance Survey, bought a 42-inch-long brass standard fitted with a micrometer scale that read to $\frac{1}{1,000}$ of an inch. This brass standard had once belonged to George Graham and had Jonathan Sisson's name engraved on it, but in fact it had been made by a young John Bird when apprenticed to Sisson. Engraved on the standard were the comparative lengths of the Exchequer and Tower of London standards and that of the French half *toise* (1.07 yards). A duplicate of this standard was provided to the Académie Royale de Sciences in Paris, and it is probable that John Bird used this very standard to manufacture the one supplied to the proprietors.

A critical component for astronomical observations is time. In 1760, small, precise, portable timekeeping clocks were not available; instead, astronomers used regulators, improved versions of the pendulum clock invented by Christiaan Huygens in 1656. For the astronomer, these had the further advantage that the rate the pendulum swung back and forth could be used to measure small variations in gravity. The North American survey was equipped with just such a clock, made by a Mr. Jackson of Philadelphia, as well as a small "alarm clock" for timing astronomical observations.

For their mathematical and trigonometric calculations, the surveyors used seven-figure logarithmic tables. John Napier invented logarithms, a tabular method for multiplication and division, in 1614; in 1624 his colleague, Henry Briggs, published a set of natural logarithms (log tables), and later developed tables of trigonometric logarithmic functions (trig tables). The slide rule had also been invented and perfected between 1654 and 1683 by Seth Partridge and Henry Coggeswall. However, there is no mention by Mason in his journal of using such a device or that other curious invention, Napier's bones, the forerunner of the slide rule and shunned by most mathematicians of the time. Among the veritable library of books and tables required for the work were the latest star almanacs and ephemera, tables of star corrections supplied by the Royal Observatory, and sundry texts and epistles on all matters germane to the work in hand. The library, in its wooden sea chest for protection against the heat, wet, cold, and humidity, would accompany the surveyors throughout their travels.

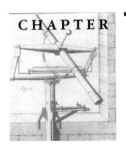

CHAPTER 7

"Persons Intirely Accomplished"

SAFELY BACK in England from the transit of Venus campaign, Maskelyne and Mason had much mathematical work to complete, checking the computations, collating the many observations, and preparing learned papers. Mason and Dixon's own paper was titled "Observations Made at the Cape of Good Hope." Mason was also collaborating on a paper with Thomas Hornsby (1733–1810), the up-and-coming Oxford don and accomplished astronomer, who had observed the transit of Venus from Lord Macclesfield's home, Shirburn Castle, near Oxford. Mason and Dixon were familiar faces around Crane Court and tales of their African exploits were eagerly sought; the storm caused by Dixon's letter to the Royal Society and the blunt reply had blown over, but was not forgotten.

On the long voyage from Saint Helena to England, Maskelyne had conducted more longitude experiments by lunar distances and was becoming obsessed with the method. He was convinced that lunars would solve the mariner's longitude problem, as was Mason, who had prepared the original set of tables. Maskelyne decided to publish a mariner's guide to the lunar method together with the necessary tables immediately upon his return. Shortly before, on March 27, 1762, John Harrison's chronometer, number H4, had returned to England from Jamaica at the end of its first longitude sea trial. The longitude solutions provided by Harrison's "watch" were phenomenal; in fact, the instrument was so accurate as to be almost unbelievable. Maskelyne was interested in the "mechanicks" alternative to his own laborious lunar method, but was skeptical, and for good reasons. Isaac Newton himself had expressed severe doubts that a mechanical solution could ever be accurate, or reliable; Maskelyne's own experience with astronomical clocks and watches reinforced this belief. Harrison's H4 time measurer was a radical piece of technology and lay within the great void between classical astronomy and precision engineering; it had no precedent. There was also the barrier of rank and education; Maskelyne was minor aristocracy, university educated, and numbered among the intellectual elite of London. John Harrison (1693–1776) was a carpenter and clock maker who lived and worked in a remote Lincolnshire village.

Harrison's lifelong love of clocks and watches began with the gift of a pocket watch while he was recovering from a childhood attack of smallpox. His early education was only rudimentary, but his intense interest in science led him to study mechanics and physics. His passion was building exquisite pendulum clocks constructed entirely from wood. A few examples of his all-wood turret clocks, commissioned by the aristocracy to adorn their homes and stable yards, are still working today.

Harrison's home of Barrow-upon-Humber was not far from the seaport of Hull, and it was probably there, sometime before 1728, that he first learned of the £20,000 longitude prize. Despite the doubts of "university educated Men," Harrison knew instinctively he could devise a clock so reliable and accurate that it could be used by a mariner to find longitude at sea. Walking all the way to London, Harrison took his first design and ideas to George Graham, the country's leading clock maker. Graham was so impressed with Harrison that he encouraged him to build a prototype and even loaned him a sum of money to start. It took Harrison seven years to construct his first marine clock, designated H1, a giant contraption of brass and steel weighing over seventy-two pounds. H1 was presented to the Board of Longitude, whose members were impressed enough to give it a trial at sea. With an advance from the board, Harrison returned to Lincolnshire to improve the design. The result was H2, another huge device, but which never went to sea. Instead, Harrison was convinced he could do much better. He set about constructing his third marine clock, H3, on which he labored for seventeen years. In 1753 he had a pocket watch made for him by his friend, John Jeffreys, and was so inspired by its compactness that he set the H3 clock aside and began on the world's first chronometer.

John Harrison from an engraving by Tassaert, 1768.
(Courtesy National Maritime Museum, London)

Designated H4, the "watch" was a miracle of compactness, a mere five inches in diameter. Harrison was very proud: "I think I may make bold to say that there is neither any other Mechanism or Mathematical thing in the World that is more beautiful or curious . . . than this my watch or timekeeper for the Longitude." H4 went to Jamaica on its first sea trial in 1761, in the care of his son William. During the course of the voyage, the clock lost a mere three seconds, well inside the rules for winning the longitude prize, but the Board of Longitude was not totally convinced. They wanted another sea trial to prove the first was not a fluke, and, by way of encouragement to Harrison, granted him a sum of £1,500.

Nevil Maskelyne, however, was certain in his own mind that lunars were the only reliable and economical solution to the longitude problem. Nevertheless, he was also aware that Harrison and his clock-work designs had impressed some of the best instrument makers of

London, including the influential James Short, and these same men were also his colleagues in the Royal Society.

It was through his associate membership in the society that Charles Mason first became acquainted with Benjamin Franklin. As a mechanically minded man, Franklin was curious about Harrison's precision watch. Mason, on the other hand, was a proponent of the lunar distance method for finding longitude. Nevertheless, the two men struck up a friendship that endured until Mason's death. On July 13, 1762, shortly before Franklin returned to America, the scientific community learned of the tragic death of Dr. Bradley, the sixty-nine-year-old astronomer royal, at his home in Chalford, Gloucestershire. Mason, deeply saddened when he heard the news, was not surprised, as Bradley had been unwell for some time. Nathaniel Bliss was nominated as Bradley's successor to the royal post.

Reverend Nathaniel Bliss was born the son of a "Gentleman" and lived at Bisley, a few miles from Dr. Bradley's home. Like Bradley, he was educated at Oxford, where he gained his B.A. and M.A. from Pembroke College. In 1742 Bliss succeeded Edmund Halley as Savilian professor at Oxford and was elected a Fellow of the Royal Society. He was also a close friend of George Parker, the earl of Macclesfield, and was a frequent visitor, together with Bradley and Hornsby, at Shirburn Castle. It was through no small effort of the earl that Bliss was appointed astronomer royal. Bliss's sinecure as Savilian professor passed to Mason's collaborator, Thomas Hornsby, a worthy heir and future astronomer in charge of Oxford's Radcliffe Observatory. It was also about this time that Thomas Penn and Cecilius Calvert received letters from their American commissioners informing them of the failure of their surveyors in setting out the eastern boundary of Maryland along the Delaware Tangent Line and requesting professional assistance.

Within two months of the signing of the Treaty of Paris in February 1763, ending the Seven Years' War, Jérôme Lalande (1732–1807), professor of astronomy at the Collège de France, arrived in London. His objective, apart from renewing old acquaintances, was a spying mission to inspect for himself Harrison's chronometer number H4. Like the British, the seafaring French were desperate for a solution to the longitude problem. Lalande managed to get a sight of H4 at the end of April. On May 9, he was joined by two compatriots, Ferdinand Berthoud (1727–1807), the finest watchmaker in France, and the mathe-

The Royal Observatory, Greenwich, circa 1800, from an engraving by Thomas
Shepherd. (Author's collection)

matician Charles Camus (1699–1768). The three scientists planned
another visit with the suspicious John Harrison at his London home in
Red Lion Square, where they were permitted to inspect the early pro-
totypes H1, H2, and H3, but mysteriously H4 was nowhere in sight.

Lalande and his colleagues from the Paris Observatory had also
observed the transit of Venus both at home and abroad, and were eager
to exchange information with the London astronomers. It was either at
this time, or possibly before the Seven Years' War, that Charles Mason
was introduced to the famous French astronomer, and the two men
developed an enduring professional acquaintance that would prove useful in the years ahead. Lalande was, like Mason and Maskelyne, an
advocate of the lunar distance method; the three of them spent many
hours out at Greenwich discussing Mayer's lunar tables and Bradley's
and Mason's improvements.

The transit of Venus expedition had been a famous affair, comparable with Edmund Hillary's conquest of Everest or the first lunar land-
ing, and the exploits of all involved, including Mason and Dixon, were
well known. From the "scientifik curious" of London, Thomas Penn
learned that Mason and Dixon were "lately returned from the transit,"
and from Nathaniel Bliss he ascertained that both men could be made

available. The two astronomers-cum-surveyors (the term geodesist did not appear until the nineteenth century) appeared to be ideally qualified candidates to resolve the difficult Maryland-Pennsylvania boundary issue.

In late spring 1763, Penn arranged an introduction to Mason and Dixon, probably through John Bird, to whom he was now a familiar figure and valued customer. In a series of early meetings Penn established their interest, discussed the subject with Cecilius Calvert, and arranged further meetings with Mason, Dixon, Maskelyne, and Bliss. Penn and Calvert needed to be certain that the two surveyors were capable of solving the difficult task that had confounded the best surveyors in America. Penn's advisers—John Robertson, Daniel Harris, and Thomas Simpson from Woolwich—assisted in the practical examinations of the two young men. Peter Daval, an astronomer and barrister, was particularly useful in giving learned opinion on the legal issues of the colonial boundaries and their practical resolution. Calvert's consultant and Bradley's friend, Dr. Bevis, provided valuable insight on the current shape of Earth, as it was then known, and the values for degrees of latitude in the Pennsylvania region.

The meetings between the two surveyors and the proprietors and their advisers were sporadic, depending heavily on the availability of one party or another during their normal business affairs. When satisfied that Mason and Dixon were competent, conversation turned to the difficult technical challenges of the boundary survey itself and exploring the complexities of the geodesy. On July 30, 1763, Calvert was able to write to Governor Sharpe in Maryland with the good news that the "geometrical surveyors" had arrived in London and that he and Mr. Penn "attended with Mathematicians have had meetings, at which times many Questions have been propounded & solved which are delivered to the Surveyors," adding that "Messrs Dixon and Mason, allowed by the best Judges here as persons intirely accomplished and of good character."

In considering the offer from the two proprietors, Mason and Dixon had to weigh the difficulties they might face, due in part to the strained political situation existing between Britain and her American colonies, and the dangers inherent in the American wilderness. In North America, the Seven Years' War had culminated some three years earlier, yet tensions between the old enemies remained and there were plenty of reports of outbreaks of violence between colonists and the Indians. However, gratuitous violence was more common in eighteenth-century England than now, no less so than in London, where gentlemen retained "minders" (bodyguards) to accompany them after dark. Indeed, as Mason and Dixon attended their meetings and cogitated, the audience in Covent Garden's Theatre Royal stormed the stage armed with swords and cudgels protesting the abolition of post-interval half-price tickets. This fierce reaction during Thomas Arne's *Artaxerxes* was just one example of mob violence and a reminder of the growing social unrest fomenting in England.

State violence toward malefactors was often more atrocious than the crime itself. Just forty years before, a woman was burned alive in Smithfield for heresy, and at Tyburn, just beyond the town limits, the worse of Newgate Prison's inmates were hanged in public on Fridays, often in batches of six at a time. Capital crimes included what today would be regarded as petty; stealing sixpence from a farmer's boy or defacing Westminster Bridge attracted the same punishment as murder or arson. At such times the London mob gathered, as many as twenty thousand for a good hanging, and the scene took on the air of a fair. The mob, a motley collection of ne'er-do-wells, pickpockets, idlers, and the curious, also had a benevolent side to their macabre behavior, an example of which illustrates the common man's contempt for the law. The month Mason and Dixon returned to London was the occasion for the manifestations of the famous Cock Lane Ghost that plagued the home of a twelve-year-old girl in West Smithfield. Crowds paid a penny to inspect the scene of the trouble (allegedly caused by a poltergeist). Dr. Samuel Johnson was one of many investigators of the mystery and pronounced the affair a hoax perpetrated by the girl's father. The man was tried for fraud and sentenced to a year in Newgate and some time in the pillory. Instead of throwing rotten fruit at the miscreant as he hung from the crossbeam, the mob cheered and collected a subscription for him and his poor family.

Major crimes such as highway robbery, piracy, or treason were still punishable by burning or disembowelment, but in Lalande's homeland the punishments could be even worse. For a feeble attempt at assassinating Louis XIV in 1757, Robert François Damiens was, in public, torn limb from limb by a team of four horses; he was still alive when only one arm remained attached to his body. Mason and Dixon's view of the danger posed by the Americas must be tempered somewhat by the times in which they lived. Such cruelty and barbaric behavior was the norm, and they were probably more concerned with disease or injury.

Both men had been out of the country for some eighteen months. While Dixon was a bachelor, Mason was a widower and had to consider the welfare of his two young sons, William and the curiously named Doctor Isaac. Once more the two boys faced the prospect of a long separation from their itinerant father. It was usual for the families of mariners and merchants to suffer long periods of separation, and wives were never certain if their husbands would ever return safe from the perilous sea. Apart from the hazards of uncertain navigation, there were pirates to contend with, and even ship's crews were known to rob the passengers. Eight years previously the crew of the *Palatine,* en route to the New World with a band of emigrants, mutinied, robbed the passengers, and left them to drift at the mercy of the sea. The ship was lost and entered into the legends of the ghost ships, every so often appearing wraithlike off the coast of New England, crewed by its hapless spirits.

However, for Mason and Dixon there was the prospect of a fat fee, at least £600 each and maybe more, for neither knew how long the work would take. What part Jeremiah Dixon took in the negotiations is not known; he probably left much of the money matters to Mason, returning to see his family in Durham and enjoying a period of glory among his old friends. He was back in London in July, probably lodging at Mason's Greenwich house, less than an hour by carriage from the center of London, when disturbing news arrived from America: an Indian chief by the name of Pontiac had gone on the warpath.

Despite the real chances of danger or death, the degenerating political climate, and not before further lengthy discussion and pecuniary negotiation, on Thursday, August 4, 1763, Charles Mason and Jeremiah Dixon signed their contract with the proprietors. The next few weeks were spent packing the precious instruments, settling their affairs, and concluding their consultations with the panel of experts. Finally the day came for Mason to say farewell to his suffering family; he would not see them again for many years. Mason and Dixon set off from London in company with Thomas Penn, traveling in style in his fine coach on the long and hazardous journey to Falmouth, the traditional embarkation point for the Americas. Out on the River Fal, the packet boat tugged at its moorings, awaiting its cargo of emigrants. At the top of the spring tide on the morning of Saturday, September 3, 1763, the boat slipped its cable and set sail, bound for the New World.

 **8**

The Southernmost
Point of the City

IN 1756, England and Prussia had gone to war against their old adversaries, France and Spain. In Europe it became known as the Seven Years' War, but the battles conducted in colonial America come down to us as the French and Indian War. The conflict that raged across much of European North America began in earnest almost immediately. In the early years of the North American campaign, the fighting favored the superior French forces. George Washington and his colonial patriots were forced to surrender Fort Necessity, near present-day Uniontown, Pennsylvania, and the British army under command of General Edward Braddock, supreme commander in North America, was slaughtered on the Monongahela River. Oswego and Fort William Henry also fell to the French and their Indian allies. A steady buildup of British and colonial troops during 1758 led to a series of counterattacks. In July, a marine-style assault led by Lord Jeffrey Amherst against Louisbourg led to British control of the Saint Lawrence River, and the capture of Fort Ticonderoga by General William Johnson secured Lake Champlain. In the same year, British forces finally took the formidable French bulwark in the west, Fort Duquesne, celebrating by renaming it Pittsburgh in honor of Prime Minister William Pitt. General James Wolfe stormed the Plains of Abraham to take Quebec in 1759; the following year, Montreal also fell to the British army. This last event signaled, more or less, the end of the campaign in North America.

In February 1763, the Anglo-German and Franco-Spanish belligerents signed the Treaty of Paris that ended the Seven Years' War. France acknowledged, however reluctantly, England's sovereignty over the American mainland east of the Mississippi (with the exception of New Orleans and Louisiana). In return, England granted to France a handful of concessions in the West Indies and fishing rights off New-foundland. However, many ordinary people, and the emerging leaders of English Radicalism, saw the treaty's concessions to France in the West Indian islands as a poor bargain and would have preferred to return to the French the wilderness of Canada rather than lose the lucrative Caribbean plantations. On the other hand, the government saw the annexation of Canada as an effective foil against the growing unrest in the colonies. Benjamin Franklin's popular vision was for Canada and the American colonies to become autonomous nations within a Greater British Empire. As it was, within a dozen short years of the Treaty of Paris, the days of the powerful colonial proprietor, and of British America itself, were no more.

Throughout the conflict in America, native Indians bolstered the armies of both sides. The British cause was supported by the Six Nations Indians, or Iroquois League, an alliance of eastern woodland Indians forged sometime during the late sixteenth century when two great Indian chiefs, Hiawatha and Dekanawidah, cemented the confederacy of the Onondaga, Mohawk, Oneida, Cayuga, and Seneca tribes. The sixth member of the league, the Tuscarora, joined in 1722. The French forces relied heavily on the support of the Six Nations' traditional enemies, the Algonquin, the Huron, the Cherokee, and the Ottawa, who, even before the war had started, were wreaking havoc on settlers. George Washington, on a reconnaissance during the winter of 1753–1754, recorded a gruesome atrocity on the western marches of Pennsylvania and Virginia:

> We met . . . 20 Warriors, who were going to the Southward to war, but . . . they found 7 People killed and scalped, all but one woman with very light Hair, they turned about and ran back, for Fear the Inhabitants should rise and take them as the Authors of the Murder: They report that the People were lying about the House, and some of them much torn and eaten by Hogs; by the Marks that were left, they say they were French Indians of the Ottaway Nation, Etc. that did it.

Despite the treaty with France, tension in the colonies remained high. Native American rights and property were continuously violated, often brutally. The pacifist Quakers were generally more successful in their dealings with the native people than other colonists, yet even in Pennsylvania, atrocious retribution was not unknown. In Britain, the defense bill had risen from a peacetime budget of £6.5 million to over £15.5 million at the peak of the Seven Years' War. This, together with the reimbursement of provincial war costs known as the Massachusetts Settlement, had impoverished the Exchequer. To add to the burden of colonial defense, Pontiac, chief of the Ottawa, embittered by the defeat of the French forces he had supported and resolute in opposing further British expansion, led his warriors in an uprising. In 1762, it is said, he secured the agreement of all the major tribes from Lake Superior south to the Mississippi to mount a concerted assault on the line of British forts.

On May 5, 1763, not too far from the British fort of Detroit, Chief Pontiac addressed his amassed warriors: "It is important for us, my brothers, that we exterminate from our lands this nation which seeks only to destroy us." He condemned the treatment of the Indians by the British while lauding the beneficence of Louis XV. Two days later, the Indians struck with devastating force; eight of the twelve forts were overwhelmed or wiped out. Pontiac himself led the attack on Fort Detroit. From north to south, the rampaging Indians plundered the frontier and massacred some two hundred settlers. Defending the colonists from the marauding Pontiac, to which neither Maryland nor Pennsylvania contributed, raised yet more questions in Parliament. Why should the British taxpayer pick up the cost of defending His Majesty's subjects on the far side of the ocean? The costly war, its unsatisfactory settlement, and the prospect of more taxation conspired with outright dislike of Prime Minister Lord Bute, who had ousted Pitt the previous year, to bring the government down.

A close friend of George III, Bute's downfall was also due, in no small part, to the new political awareness fueled by such political newspapers as John Wilkes's *North Briton.* The "champion of liberty" and father of English Radicalism was a thorn in every government's side and he was repeatedly expelled from Parliament for seditious behavior; yet the people loved him. Wilkes's support for the American cause during the 1770s was widely acclaimed. His name became associated with the radical Chevalier de la Barre, executed for sedition in 1766 at the tender age of eighteen, and the pair became immortalized in Major John Durkee's new town in Pennsylvania, Wilkes-Barre.

Pontiac and hundreds of angry warriors were still terrorizing the western marches when the Falmouth packet arrived in Philadelphia on the flood tide of Tuesday, November 15, 1763. Disembarking from the packet boat, after a ten-week passage across the turbulent North Atlantic, Charles Mason and Jeremiah Dixon were met on the quay and shown to their rooms in the bustling city. That evening the two companions, grateful to be rid of the heaving deck, terrible food, and squalid conditions in the sailing ship, strolled delightedly around the wide streets of the chilly metropolis, savoring the exotic delights of colonial America.

♪   The next morning Mason and Dixon were closeted with the "Commissioners appointed by the Proprietors of Pennsylvania . . . " led by the Honorable James Hamilton of Philadelphia. There was the irascible Benjamin Chew (1722–1810), chief secretary, Reverend Richard Peters, the provincial secretary, and Reverend John Ewing (1732–1802), Presbyterian minister and provost of the College of Philadelphia. The middle-aged Benjamin Franklin, a stalwart among the scientific and philosophical congregation and a member of the legislature, was deeply interested in the work, although he himself was not an astronomer and was not present on this occasion. After the introductions, the men got down to business; the legal situation was explored and the geodetic principles of the survey discussed. The question of whether the West Line would be a great circle or a parallel of latitude had been resolved between the proprietors, but it was no doubt aired once more at the commissioners' meeting. Apart from the technical issues, there were many other details to cover; hiring men, logistics, observatory materials, procedures, and, of course, a money supply for paying the wages.

Pontiac's rebellion was a source of worry; the great chief had scored some impressive victories, culminating with the battle of Bloody Run. Despite a defeat a few days later at Bushy Run and Lieutenant Colonel Henry Bouquet's relief of Fort Pitt, Pontiac had demonstrated the potential of the Indian alliance. However, the commissioners were confident the worst of the trouble was over and reassured the two surveyors. In fact, it was only the beginning of a long period of unrest among the Indians; along the western marches, for hundreds of miles, angry native tribes defied the white man. Settlers farming the fertile silts of the valleys were abandoning homesteads and fleeing eastward;

even in the East, the white population was frightened, and there were calls for retribution on every Indian alive.

After their first meeting, Mason and Dixon returned to their lodgings to write a letter to Horatio Sharpe, the governor of Maryland, advising His Excellency of their arrival in America and to prepare his Maryland commissioners. Along the way, they met people in the streets and in the tavern, where they learned that unlike God-fearing white Europeans, the Indians were not "real men" and should be treated as animals. The more fanatical claimed "were they [the Indians] not the Canaanites whom God had commanded Joshua to destroy?" The devout Mason and Dixon, a Quaker, were puzzled and shocked by the fierce hatred and bigotry on the streets. Philadelphia was a strange city, a mixture of British and European styles and people, black slaves attending their masters and mistresses, but of the indigenous Indians there was no sign.

A week after arriving in Philadelphia, the precious scientific instruments were brought ashore from the Falmouth packet. There were logistical preparations to attend to; contracting carpenters, organizing supplies, buying winter clothing, and fitting out their field operations room in the Statehouse. It was not until Friday, November 25, that the zenith sector was carefully unpacked and inspected for damage after its long sea voyage from England. The following Monday the transit instrument was checked. Both were found to have survived undamaged.

On Wednesday, the commissioners from Maryland arrived in Philadelphia, led by the capable Governor Sharpe accompanied by his personal secretary, John Rideout, and John Leeds (1705–1790), the astronomer and surveyor. Thursday was the first full meeting attended by the commissioners of both sides. After formal introductions, the gentlemen from Maryland brought in Lord Baltimore's "Compound Instrument," probably James Short's telescope loaned by Dr. Bevis. Friday and Saturday were taken up with more meetings, discussions, and examination of instruments. John Bird's beautiful zenith sector was inspected minutely, while Mason extolled its virtues; such an exquisitely accurate instrument had never before been seen on American soil. Bird's "transit and equal altitude instrument" was compared with Dr. Bevis's so-called transit telescope. The two English surveyors condemned the latter out of hand as totally inappropriate for the task, preferring the more portable, less complex, and far more precise Bird transit. As Sharpe reported in his letter to Calvert after the meeting, "it seems after all that has [been] said of the transit Instrument [Dr. Bevis's instrument] cannot be thereby truly or precisely described there being no Movement that Messr⁵ Mason & Dixon could shew or the Commissioners discover to bring & keep the Telescope in the plane of a Parallel of Latitude: It was however delivered by our Commissioners to the two Gentlemen to be used as they should see occasion. . . ." Curiously, after all the trouble Penn's commissioners had taken to acquire loan of the Jersey Quadrant, there seems to have been no sign of the thirty-inch-radius giant.

As the discussions progressed, it became clear to Mason and Dixon that the task before them was greater than originally anticipated. The work consisted of establishing two boundaries; the West Line parallel of constant latitude separating Maryland from Pennsylvania, and the eastern boundary of Maryland, the so-called Tangent Line dividing it from the three counties of Delaware. There were three legally fixed physical locations from which Mason and Dixon could work; the southernmost point of the city of Philadelphia, the belfry of the courthouse in New Castle (center of the twelve-mile radius), and the Middle Point of the transpeninsular line dividing Delaware's three lower counties from Maryland's territory in the south of the Delmarva peninsula. This last point had been established by the American surveyors in 1760, in accordance with Lord Hardwicke's ruling. The Tangent Line, which ran slightly west of north from the Middle Point, had been the line that had finally defeated them and resulted in Mason and Dixon's appointment.

Before Charles Mason and Jeremiah Dixon arrived in Philadelphia, the commissioners had agreed, on the advice of the city's officials, that the legal origin for the West Line survey, "the southernmost point in the City of Philadelphia," was to be the north wall of a house on the south side of Cedar Street (now South Street) near its junction with Second Street. Exactly fifteen miles south of this point, according to Lord Hardwicke's ruling, the West Line dividing Maryland from Pennsylvania would commence. The best maps of the provinces available and John Sennex's definitive legal map showing the lines stipulated by Lord Hardwicke were spread out and studied. Mason, Dixon, and the commissioners spent many hours poring over the maps and documents while local experts, knowledgeable of all the lands thereabout, were asked for guidance. Reverend Peters, having been involved with the original surveys, was particularly well informed and provided good advice. About this time Joel Bailey, a surveyor from Chester County, joined the team. He would prove to be a stalwart right-hand man to Mason and Dixon, making and repairing equipment and even assisting with the observations.

On Monday, December 5, Mason engaged a gang of carpenters to build an observatory to his design, close to the agreed location of the house on Cedar Street. The next day the disappointing Sisson sector was set up alongside John Bird's instrument for inspection. Mason pointed out its many imperfections, noting that "the Nonius [vernier] would not touch the middle part of the Arch [scale]." While the carpenters hammered away building the observatory, the two surveyors were sworn in before the commissioners. On December 9, they received their initial instructions, copied by Mason to Thomas Penn in London on December 14:

1st to settle the Latitude of the southernmost point of the City of Philadelphia by the Sector.-

2nd to find a Point by the Sector, 30 or 35 miles west from this Place, having the same Latitude as the southernmost Point of this City.-

3rd from this Point so found to measure 15 miles horizontally due South, which done to observe the Latitude of the South End of the said line by the Sector, and to proceed to run the Parallel of Latitude thru this last Point which is to be the North Boundary of Maryland and South Boundary of Pennsilvania.-

4th on the 15th June next, (if we receive no further orders from the Commissioners,) we are to begin the tangent Line, as those already run for Tangency are so irregular differing from each other in the Middle about 200 feet.-

5th When we judge we are within 10 days of finishing the said tangent, we are to inform the Commissioners that they may meet us at the tangent Point or thereabout.-

As our instruments are in very good Order, and not in the
least damaged by the Voyage, we hope by the end of next
Summer, to give a satisfactory Account of all the above Work
mentioned in our instructions.

On first glance, it would appear that Mason expected to complete,
within six months, not only the preliminary work, but also the parallel of latitude separating the two provinces. Unless Mason was overly
ambitious, or very badly informed, it has to be concluded that what
was meant was that the work on the West Line would commence, but
would not be completed. In fact, the commissioners suddenly were
unclear how far the boundary should run, for news arrived from Britain that changed everything. On October 7, 1763, partly in response
to Pontiac's uprising, King George III issued a royal proclamation. Its
wording was emphatic:

> No Governor or Commander in Chief in any of Our other
> Colonies or plantations in America do presume for the present,
> and until our further pleasure be known, to grant warrants of
> Survey, or pass Patents for any Lands beyond the heads or
> sources of any of the Rivers which fall into the Atlantic Ocean
> from the West and Northwest; or upon any Lands whatever,
> which, not having been ceded to or purchased by us, as afore-
> said, are reserved to the said Indians, or any of them.

The terms of the proclamation effectively brought to an end all
settlement west of the Appalachian Mountains. The British government appointed Sir William Johnson and John Stuart as general super-
intendents to oversee Indian affairs and to enforce the proclamation's
prohibitions. All matters concerning native land rights and trade,
west of the mountains, had to be conducted through the officially appointed officials. In the end, the colonists would have other ideas as
the pressure of the expanding population pushed the frontier ever
westward, but for the time being lip service was paid to the sweeping
proclamation.

This apparent sop to the belligerent Pontiac and his warriors by an
arrogant government out of touch with its people gave rise to bitter
resentment. One of the first reactions came as the observatory on Cedar
Street reached completion and Mason installed the instruments "proper
for observing." Horrific news arrived by express from Lancaster, a town

about sixty miles west of Philadelphia. A band of frontiersmen had launched an unprovoked dawn attack on the little Conestoga Indian village of Shawanee Creek. The men, mostly young unmarried Irish-Scot immigrants from the townships of Donegal and Paxton, became known as "the Paxton Boys."

December 14, the day of the attack, was a freezing cold day and snow fell in heavy flakes. Most of the villagers were already out working for local farmers or selling their wares, and only six Conestogas—three men, two women, and a ten-year-old boy—were at home when the Paxton Boys struck. "These poor defenceless creatures were immediately fired upon, stabbed, and hatcheted to death; the good Shebaes, among the rest, cut to pieces in his bed. All of them were scalped and otherwise horribly mangled, then their huts were set on fire, and most of them burnt down." The kindly and venerable village elder, Shebaes, was in his eighties and had participated in negotiating the land treaty with William Penn in 1701. One of the mothers had hidden her little child under a barrel, warning it to be silent. One of the villains fired his rifle through the barrel, breaking the child's arm, yet still the child kept silent.

Leaving the scene of their bloody handiwork, the men headed for town, where a group of them knocked at the door of Robert Barber. He did not recognize any of them, but it was a harshly cold day, and he invited them in to get warm and gave them breakfast. The men asked Barber why the local people allowed the Indians to live nearby. He replied that the Indians were inoffensive and offered no threat. They asked him what he thought would happen if the Indians were killed. Mr. Barber sternly replied that anyone who did such a thing could expect to be punished, just as if they had killed white men; the men scowled, for "they were of a different opinion." After they left, Barber's two young sons came in; they had been looking at the strangers' horses, and told their father that "they had tomahawks tied to their saddles which were all bloody, and that they had Christy's gun." Christy was their playmate, the little boy whose wrecked body lay amid the ashes of his home. Shortly after, a messenger arrived, breathless, and told Barber about the massacre down the road. Mr. Barber hurried out of his house and rushed to the village; what he found sickened him. The murdered Indians lay hacked and mutilated all around in the smoldering ruins of their homes, "like half-consumed logs."

The magistrates of Lancaster were shocked by the ferocious barbarity of the "white savages." As a precautionary measure, they rounded up the remaining survivors and installed them in the town's new workhouse-cum-jail. Governor John Penn (a grandson of William Penn) and James Hamilton of Philadelphia issued a proclamation instructing judges, sheriffs, and "all His Majesty's liege subjects in the province" to arrest the murderers and their accomplices. The Paxton Boys had no respect for magistrates or governors and their reputation for gratuitous violence was a deterrent to any who might turn them in, added to which the Boys were supported by a large minority of the population.

Mason and Dixon may well have wondered what they had got themselves into. To add to their gloom, the weather was bitter cold and icy rain lashed against the windowpanes of their lodgings. After two days and nights of persistent rain and snow, the surveyors were ready to commence work. They began their first round of observations on the clear but freezing evening of December 16 when Mason "brought the Instrument into the Meridian by making several stars pass along the horizontal wire in the middle of the Telescope."*

Observing on average six stars each bitterly cold night, the two men spent nine nights, including Christmas, observing zenith distances of latitude stars with the "plane of the Sector facing the EAST." Three nights were lost when clouds obscured the heavens; the surveyors gratefully retired to the warmth of the local inns and caught up on the latest news and views on the Indian situation. On Christmas night, the tenacious surveyors used the transit instrument in tandem with the zenith sector to observe equal altitudes of beta Aurigæ in order to calibrate their clock. The equal altitude observation, which yielded the sidereal time, involved fixing the vertical angle of the transit instrument and noting the time a rising star crossed the horizontal wire of the telescope. Keeping the vertical angle fixed, the star was tracked as it crossed the meridian and the time noted when the same star set across the horizontal wire. The mean of the two times was the moment when the star crossed the meridian. Dr. Bradley's star tables provided the right ascension for the star, and, with a few calculations, the side-

---

*See "Setting the Zenith Sector" in the Appendix.

real time was deduced. The difference in the sidereal time measured by the sector against that observed with the transit was just half a second. This result rendered two important pieces of information; that the instruments could be correctly aligned in the meridian (north-south line), and that they were able to replicate the all important sidereal (star) time accurately.

On December 28, wrapped in furs and blankets against the bitter cold, and probably visited or even assisted by Philadelphia scientists, they began the tedious process of repeating the observations, turning the zenith sector through 180 degrees to mean out any error. This procedure is still used by modern surveyors, who will "change face" when observing survey control with a theodolite. Back in the warmth of their lodgings, the observations were corrected using the declinations for the stars provided by Dr. Bradley; each observation was laboriously adjusted for aberration, deviation (nutation), atmospheric refraction, and precession.

While Mason and Dixon busied themselves with the astronomical observations and complex calculations, to the west the Paxton Boys busied themselves with their cruel deeds. On December 28, the gang, swollen to fifty strong, rode into Lancaster and broke into the jail. A Philadelphia pamphlet, published anonymously because "so much had fear seized the minds of the people . . . " that the writer was afraid to give his name and address, tells of what happened next:

> When the poor wretches saw they had no protection nigh, nor could possibly escape, and being without the least weapon of defence, they divided their little families, the children clinging to their parents. They fell on their faces, protested their innocence, declared their love to the English, and that in their whole lives they had never done them injury. And in this posture they all received the hatchet. Men, women, and children were every one inhumanly murdered in cold blood.

After their horrific crime, the Boys casually remounted their horses and, whooping and hollering, rode out of town. One of the first people on the scene was Lancaster resident William Henry, son of the celebrated inventor, who wrote to a friend of what he found:

> The first notice I had of the affair was that, while at my father's store near the courthouse, I saw a number of people running

down-street toward the jail, which enticed me and other lads to follow them. At about six or eight yards from the jail we met from twenty-five to thirty men, well mounted on horse, and with rifles, tomahawks, and scalping-knives, equipped for murder. I ran into the prison-yard, and there, oh, what a horrible sight presented itself to my view! Near the back door of the prison lay an old Indian and his squaw, particularly well known and esteemed by the people of the town on account of his placid and friendly conduct. His name was Will Soc. Around him and his squaw lay two children, about the age of three years, whose heads were split with the tomahawk and their scalps taken off. Toward the middle of the jail-yard, along the west side of the wall, lay a stout Indian, whom I particularly noticed to have been shot in his breast. His legs were chopped with the tomahawk, his hands cut off, and finally a rifle-ball discharged in his mouth, so that his head was blown to atoms, and the brains were splashed against and yet hanging to the wall for three or four feet around. This man's hands and feet had been chopped off with a tomahawk. In this manner lay the whole of them—men, women, and children—spread about the prison-yard, shot, scalped, hacked, and cut to pieces.

The word that reached Philadelphia the next day painted a scene of the most brutal savagery. The provincial populace was divided in its views; the Quakers were shocked and appalled as were most decent folk, yet a large minority supported, or at least found some justification, for the actions of the Paxton Boys. In Lancaster itself, the Episcopalian minister wrote in vindication of their deeds as "bringing Scripture to prove that it was right to destroy the heathen"; it was nothing less than the word of God Himself supporting the Paxton Boys.

The next morning, Philadelphia was buzzing with a rumor that the Paxton Boys were on their way to the city, threatening to attack the Quaker population and kill every Indian sympathizer. Mobs of their supporters openly mocked the governor outside his residence and denounced his proclamations. On Province Island, a few miles down river, a large number of Christianized Indians were placed under the protective custody of the military when word came that the Boys intended to attack and slaughter every one of them. The Paxton Boys' march through the Pennsylvania countryside was "like that of a band of maniacs," threatening both Indians and peaceable white folk. David Rittenhouse (1732–1796), from his plantation in Norriton, witnessed their passing, and wrote to a friend in Philadelphia:

> About fifty of these scoundrels marched by my workshop. I have seen hundreds of Indians travelling the country, and can with truth affirm that the behaviour of these fellows was ten times more savage and brutal than theirs. Frightening women by running the muzzles of guns through windows, hallooing and swearing; attacking men without the least provocation, dragging them by the hair to the ground, and pretending to scalp them; shooting dogs and fowls: these are some of their exploits.

The rumor of the Paxton Boys' advance on Philadelphia proved to be unfounded and the city stood down its forces. In the early hours of January 4, as Mason and Dixon concluded their night observations, the Indian refugees under escort from Province Island filed silently past the observatory, heading for sanctuary in the Moravian Brethren's meetinghouse. The governor had decided that he could no longer offer the protection they needed and placed them under the protection of Sir William Johnson, the Crown's agent for Indian affairs. At daybreak, news of the Indians' exodus spread and angry mobs gathered at the meetinghouse. Jeering and cursing the wretched Indians, the mobs threatened them with burning and hanging. The military escort had its work cut out, valiantly keeping the mob from the terrified Indian families, as the sick and aged were herded into wagons and the sorry procession set out, bound for distant Perth Amboy, in New Jersey, where two ships waited to ferry them to New York.

To Mason and Dixon, the angry scenes and bitter hatred were unlike anything they had witnessed before; London mobs were genteel compared to the wild Pennsylvania frontiersmen and the wrathful colonists. The governor issued proclamation after proclamation, threatening the severest penalties for anyone who molested the Indians. A huge reward of £200 was offered for the apprehension of the ringleaders, but public sentiment was inflamed to such a degree that the government was powerless.

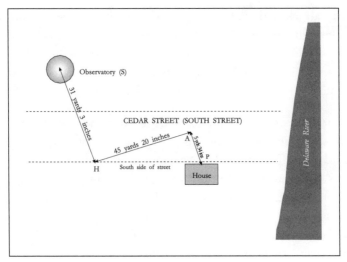

Southernmost point of Philadelphia.

Mason and Dixon's work in the troubled city was nearly done. After completing the astronomical observations, they were able to calculate the latitude for the zenith sector within their cozy observatory. All that remained was to relate the observatory's position to the legal origin by measuring the meridian distance (S to H plus A to P) to the house front, a distance of 37.15 yards, equal to 1.1 seconds of latitude. The final result for the latitude of the southernmost point of the city of Philadelphia was 39 degrees 56 minutes 29.1 seconds north; the boundary separating Pennsylvania from Maryland was to lie exactly 15 miles due south of this point.

CHAPTER 9

Fifteen Statute
Miles, Horizontal

ACCORDING TO LAW, the West Line separating Pennsylvania from Maryland was required to follow a parallel of constant latitude, exactly fifteen statute miles south of the house on Cedar Street. On the advice of Reverend Richard Peters, Penn's provincial secretary, Mason and Dixon decided not to proceed directly south, which would have involved two difficult crossings of the wide Delaware River as well as working through the province of New Jersey. Instead, they chose first to head due west and establish a point that corresponded to the same latitude as Cedar Street, then turn due south. Leaving the carpenters to dismantle and pack the observatory, Mason and Dixon set off in company with Joel Bailey on Saturday, January 7, 1764, to reconnoiter the area near the forks of the Brandywine River where, according to Peters, surveyors from New Jersey had established similar positions in 1730 and 1736.

Conscious that somewhere nearby the Paxton mob was gathering more recruits and terrifying the country people, they hurried as best they could along the muddy lanes. Thirty-one miles west of Philadelphia, "at the forks of the Brandiwine," they came to Mr. John Harland's plantation, where the earlier surveyors' marks still stood. Using their Hadley quadrant to check the latitude, they found that the site suited their purpose admirably. After negotiating terms with the affable Mr. Harland, they returned to Philadelphia to load up the dismantled observatory and pack their equipment.

While it was never their intention to measure the distance from Philadelphia to the Brandywine, it occurred to them that the geographic

93

information they found in Pennsylvania was sadly lacking. One important piece of information missing was the true linear equivalent of a degree of longitude. As the charter for Pennsylvania stated that the breadth of the province was to extend five degrees from the Delaware, it would be necessary, at some point, to ascertain the value. Mason and Dixon were quick to recognize that such a piece of geographical information would also be of value to the Royal Society. They saw the opportunity and, before they left Philadelphia, Jeremiah Dixon wrote to his friend John Bird in London, with a proposal for the Royal Society that he and Mason "measure a Degree of longitude, upon a parallel at Philadelphia." This letter was to affect profoundly later events when the proposal changed to the measurement of a degree of latitude.

Once the observatory frames, tents, stores, and the less fragile instruments were loaded into wagons, the survey party set off. The all-important zenith sector was carefully laid on a feather mattress above the springs of "a single Horse chair," a two-wheeled chariot. The midwinter weather was icy cold as the caravan made its ponderous way along the deep-rutted lanes that led to the Brandywine. On arrival at Harland's farm the surveyors were made comfortable in the house while the hired hands were billeted in the barn. The first task was to erect the sector's temporary observing tent in Harland's backyard. For three freezing nights the surveyors shared the discomfort of peering at the stars through the tall zenith sector while lying on the ground. At last they were satisfied that for all practical purposes, they were close enough to the same latitude as Cedar Street to start the serious measurements.

The post set up by the New Jersey surveyors in 1736, when establishing the temporary lines dividing the contending parties, stood nearby. Dixon instructed the carpenters to erect the portable wooden observatory next to this post. While the building was completed, Mason and Dixon started their zenith sector observations in the garden tent. Six frigid nights were spent patiently observing with the "Sector's plane set east"; then, when the observatory was complete, they moved in and began observations with the sector's "plane set west." The observatory was constructed 9.5 yards south of the tent, equivalent to 0.3 seconds, which would have to be deducted from the latitude observed from the tent.

The following days were bitterly cold and it snowed so hard that work was impossible. On January 27 disturbing news arrived from

Philadelphia. The band of Indian refugees who had passed by Cedar Street, bound for Perth Amboy, had been refused passage to New York on the orders of its governor. Mr. Fox, the missionary commissioner in charge, had no alternative but to return with the suffering Indians to Philadelphia "in full confidence that the Lord in his good providence, for wise purposes best known to himself, had ordained their travelling thus to and fro." Their return journey had been terrible, the weather dreadful, the elderly and "the little children suffered pitiably" crossing the frozen rivers, crawling across the treacherous ice on hands and knees.

The pitiful band reached Philadelphia on January 24 and were immediately escorted to the barracks. Again they were mobbed and jeered, molested, and threatened. Their situation in the city further deteriorated when news arrived that the Paxton Boys were on their way. The governor, reacting to the serious state of affairs, put Benjamin Franklin in charge of the defense of the city. He had eight heavy cannon installed on a rampart hastily erected in front of the barracks. The citizenry were called to arms, and even the pacific Quakers hurried to the barracks in defense of the Indians.

At the Harland plantation, a safe thirty miles west of the troubles, the weather had cleared sufficiently to allow the surveyors to resume work. They had hardly done so when more bad news arrived from Philadelphia. On February 4, six hundred of the Paxton rioters arrived at the city's outskirts, calling for the Indians to be handed over. Learning of Franklin's defensive preparations, they waited until the next night, then began to close in. The whole of Philadelphia had been roused; church bells rang, bonfires flared, and signal cannon fired. Additional cannon were mounted at the barracks and all able-bodied men were ordered to the Statehouse, where arms were issued, as the city prepared for the assault. The governor sent a delegation to the rioters to find out what they wanted:

> They asserted, insolently, that there were among the Indians some who had committed murders, and that they must be given up. Some of the ringleaders were then taken into the barracks and asked to point out the murderers. Covered with confusion, they were obliged to admit they could not accuse one Indian there. They then charged the Quakers with having taken away six and concealed them.

When this also proved groundless, and without any hopes of a victory by arms, the mob withdrew. An unsteady calm settled on the city.

The road west from Philadelphia to the Susquehanna, home to most of the rioters, passed uncomfortably close to the Harland plantation. Fortunately, the activities of the English surveyors roused no suspicions, and by February 28 their night observations were complete. During the process, Mason had turned the zenith sector through 180 degrees and, using both the sector and the transit instrument, twice observed equal altitudes of the star Capella to find the meridian and local sidereal time. A pendulum clock, specifically manufactured for the survey by Mr. Jackson of Philadelphia, was installed in the observatory, and its "going" was meticulously recorded together with the temperature. Later, these measurements would provide corrections to adjust the clock's timekeeping for any variation in the length of its pendulum.

The latitude of the observatory was determined to be 39 degrees 56 minutes 18.9 seconds north, which was 10.5 seconds less than the latitude of the house on Cedar Street. Mason calculated that this 10.5 seconds of arc was equal to 16.23 chains (357 yards), using the estimated value of a degree of latitude supplied by Dr. Bevis in London. However, Mason knew this value to be questionable: "After measuring the 15 Statute miles Horizontal and finding the arch [arc] in the Heavens corresponding, if it does not agree to 69.5 miles to a degree we should account for the 10″.5 accordingly."

Having established the latitude point at Harland's place, which was marked with a monument that became known as the "Stargazers Stone," Mason and Dixon prepared to measure the fifteen miles south to establish the latitude of the provincial border. Mr. Loxley, one of the carpenters, delivered a batch of twenty-two-foot-long softwood "levels." The levels would be used with their Gunter's chain to measure precisely the critical distance. It was still bitterly cold and snowing heavily; thick clouds frequently interrupted the night observations. Wrapped in furs, without any special gloves or snow boots, they persevered until eventually they managed an observation of the polestar "transiting the Meridian." On Monday, March 5, they set out a marker point to the north, but because of the poor conditions, Mason had doubts about its accuracy. The inclement weather persisted; for the next ten freezing days and nights, the surveying gentlemen betook themselves of Mr. Harland's hospitality.

For the Harland family, out in the wilds of Pennsylvania, it was tremendously exciting. Mason and Dixon entertained their hosts with tales of their travels to strange, far-flung regions of the world and the latest gossip in London. The political situation back home and in the colonies featured prominently; Prime Minister Grenville had forced through the Plantation Act and the Currency Act. This last had serious effects on the colonial economy, already at breaking point, as the temporary wartime paper currency was withdrawn from circulation. A string of customhouses staffed by British officers had been set up to collect the new colonial tax. A new vice admiralty court threatened to deprive the disenfranchised colonists of their right to trial by jury.

The British government also raised the specter of a new tax, the first that would actually impinge on American domestic affairs. The tax, Harland said, would be levied on all manner of common things; newspapers, legal fees, bills of lading, and even on playing cards and dice. Benjamin Franklin was back in London, once more clashing with Thomas Penn, petitioning for a reversion of the province to a Crown colony. He was also representing colonial interests and had incautiously advised the British government that the colonists would object strongly to any new tax, but would understand the need and accept the inevitable. Harland was not so sure. Trouble was brewing; the colonists were Englishmen, and an Englishman's right was to be taxed only by his elected representatives. The colonists of America had no vote in the British Parliament.

Mason was an Anglican, while Dixon and probably the Harlands were Quakers; so conversation was lively. The two young Englishmen certainly endeared themselves to their new friends. Eventually the weather cleared sufficiently for them to prove the meridian alignment. With a heading mark for the southward line, they hired four axmen to start cutting open a vista through the woods.

The next evening, on March 17, one of those regular but spectacular astronomical events occurred, an eclipse of the moon, when Earth lies exactly between the Moon and the Sun and the shadow of the spherical Earth is seen to cross the lunar landscape. The Harland family listened intrigued as Mason and Dixon discussed their preparations in front of the parlor fire. The evening was cold and brilliantly clear as Mason set up one of the big brass reflecting telescopes to observe the details of the eclipse. As the sky grew dark, the entire family turned out to watch the eclipse begin. After Mason had completed his scientific observations, he allowed the family a rare chance to peep through the eyepiece at the top end of the powerful Newtonian reflector. It was a perfect evening for observation: "The edge of the Sun's Shadow on the Moon's disk was the best defined I ever saw, the air was so clear it was remarkably distinct from the penumbral shade." Mason recorded the local apparent time when the eclipse ended; "8 hours 21 minutes 59 seconds p.m." This is the first reference to recording local apparent time, determined earlier in the day by solar altitude observations, just as a surveyor or astronomer would today.

The importance of observing the local apparent time of a lunar eclipse was that the same phenomenon would have been observed in Europe. The difference between the local apparent time and the time of the eclipse in Europe yielded the difference in longitude. Mason received such observations, made by the Paris observatory, in the infrequent letters that arrived from home. In his notes for July 6, 1764, Mason refers to "the difference of the Meridian from Paris by the Lunar Eclipse of March 17," which enabled him to compute a reasonably precise longitude for John Harland's backyard.

While Mason and Dixon lodged with the Harlands, the axmen were busy cutting down trees and clearing the bush to open the southward vista. For six days a week, starting at seven each morning with a break for a midday meal of bread, cheese, and strong ale, the men worked until sunset; but on Sundays all rested. This was Quaker country, and while it was pardonable to work on a Sunday, or even on Christmas night, in the big city, in the countryside the folk were less liberal minded.

On the morning of Monday, April 2, with a clear vista open before them, Mason and Dixon began measuring the 15 miles south. At first they used Loxley's 22-foot-long levels, but their quality did not please Mason, so he reverted to using the 16.5-foot (one rod) levels he had brought from England. Where the ground allowed, the distances were measured with the 22-yard-long Gunter's chain that Mason checked daily against the levels to ensure they remained in calibration.

After nearly two and a half weeks chaining down the vista, they arrived at a tree on the south side of a field belonging to Mr. Alexander Bryan. Throughout the measurement process, the surveyors meticulously recorded the name of every landowner whose property they traversed. They had measured 14 miles 66.7 chains, and to this distance Mason added the 16.23 chains (10.5 seconds of latitude) that the observatory in Mr. Harland's plantation was south of Cedar Street, giving an overall southward distance from the parallel of Philadelphia of 15 miles 2 chains 93 links. To allow for this excess over the statutory 15 miles, they set up a post 2.5 chains north to mark the location for the next observatory site.

Mason, Dixon, and the crew returned to the Brandywine, spending a few days with John Harland and his family, before packing the instruments and the observatory for transportation to Mr. Bryan's field. On April 21, leaving the carpenters to erect the observatory at the new site, the two surveyors made the short journey on horseback to Philadelphia to present their status report to the commissioners. They were back in Bryan's field on April 25, but then the weather turned bad; seven days of solid rain and heavy cloud stopped all work. On May 3 the weather improved, and for the next eleven nights the surveyors took turns beneath the zenith sector, lying on the hard floor of the observatory, patiently observing the zenith distances of the stars that passed the lens.

To be certain there was no mistake in measuring the critical fifteen miles, Mason and Dixon remeasured the distance all the way back to John Harland's farm. Every bay (complete measured section) of the tedious process was checked and compared with its previous value. Both men were experienced and careful measurers, and it can be deduced from the errors Mason discovered as they remeasured the distances that some of their assistants were allowed to make measurements unsupervised. This was intentional and by way of a training period for the whole team, as it would not have been practical for Mason or Dixon to do all the observing and measuring work themselves. Mason and Dixon were helped practically by at least three assistants, themselves surveyors: Joel Bailey, Jonathan Cope, and William Darby.

After spending some days remeasuring the questionable bays, the task was completed to their satisfaction. The preliminary chain-and-level measurement from the Brandywine to the tree in Mr. Bryan's meadow was 1,179.40 chains. Mason deducted 71 links from the total to allow for the "small inclinations of Hills, etc."; how he arrived at this odd figure is uncertain, unless he allowed 5 links correction per mile. To this corrected distance, he added the 16.23 chains the

Brandywine observatory was south of Cedar Street to give an overall distance of 1,194.92 chains (14.9 miles).

Saturday, May 19, saw them again closeted with the commissioners of Pennsylvania and Maryland at the courthouse in nearby New Castle. Mason and Dixon met with the commissioners on two more occasions, spending the intervening time reobserving the latitude at Harland's farm at the fork of the Brandywine. On June 9 their observations were complete, and the next week was spent poring over seven-figure log tables computing the results. The difference in latitude corresponding to the 14.9 miles that separated the Brandywine from Bryan's field was calculated from the stellar observations to be 0 degrees 12 minutes 55.8 seconds. By proportions, Mason determined that one degree of latitude equated to 68.223 statute miles and not the 69.5 miles previously estimated by Dr. Bevis. Knowing this discrepancy, Mason calculated that the 16.23 chains he had allowed for the 10.5 seconds the Brandywine observatory was south of Cedar Street should have been 15.92 chains, and the distance from the observatory to the 15-mile point was 7.91 chains. Here a stout oak post was dug into the ground, painted white and marked with the word "West" carved into its western face.

The final latitude for the critical point, which had taken some six months of hard work throughout the winter season, was presented to the commissioners on June 12, 1764. The value for "the Post mark'd West" was 39 degrees 43 minutes 18.2 seconds north latitude, and it lay exactly 15 miles south of the southernmost point of Philadelphia, as required by law. Mason wrote in his journal:

> The Point 15 miles South of the Southernmost Point of the City of Philadelphia is situated in Mill Creek Hundred in the County of Newcastle, in a Plantation belonging to Mr Alexander Bryan. The Middle of the Front of Mr Bryan's House, bears from the point 37° 52' Northwesterly distant 23.38 chains (each chain 22 yards). It is close by the East side of a small Run, the Head of which is due North distant 5.00 chains. From the Point to the Middle of a small rivulet called Muddy Run, on a due South course is 7.15 chains.

Today a geodetic surveyor would approach the derivation of a parallel of latitude exactly the opposite way to that used by Mason and Dixon. They *measured* the 15 miles, then observed the latitude; now we

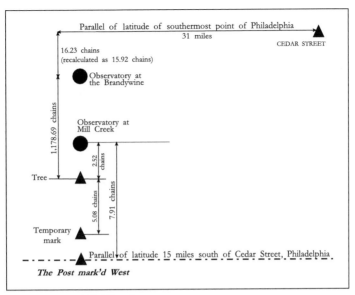

"The Post mark'd West."

would *calculate* the latitude directly. This is possible because we know the Earth's shape, but Mason did not. It is also apparent that he had made an error. Assuming the value for the house on Cedar Street as absolute, the latitude for a parallel 15 miles due south is in fact 39 degrees 43 minutes 26.4 seconds and not 39 degrees 43 minutes 18.2 seconds; Mason and Dixon had chained 829 feet too far south. How could this have happened? Either Mason and Dixon were incompetent surveyors, which they certainly were not, or there must have been other causes. Neither had measured such a long distance before, and although they measured the distance twice and made an allowance for the slopes, they could not have been aware of the enormous difficulties they would encounter in their work.

The cause of the error was probably a combination of factors, but one thing is certain: the correction for the "Hills etc." was insufficient to account for such a large amount. The chance that they made a gross error in their measuring is miniscule; they would have had to lose 12 whole chains, or 50 levels. The measures themselves may have been very slightly longer than modern standards, but certainly not the 8 inches per chain required to account for the whole error. The same effect, overmeasuring, is also evident from their later work, although the error is smaller.

A number of factors were at work, some unknown to the surveyors, and others known and for which they attempted to compensate.
The cumulative error attributable to their zenith sector alone, which
John Bird claimed to be accurate to 2 seconds of arc, might have produced an uncertainty of some 200 to 300 feet. Then there was the difficulty of setting the sector precisely vertical. From all indications, the
plumb line's alignment was better than 10 seconds of arc, equivalent
to a ground error of some 1,000 feet. Mason was aware of these problems and minimized their effects by turning the instrument, "the plane
of the Sector," through 180 degrees to mean out the errors. Another
source of error is attributable to slight variations in the strength of
gravity, creating an effect surveyors call "the deviation of the vertical."
This was known to exist in 1764, although its magnitude was uncertain and could not be allowed for.

Recent precision work on the Mason-Dixon line, to determine its
position in a modern geodetic system using the satellite-based Global
Positioning System, detected errors of these magnitudes. It has to be
remembered, when comparing Mason and Dixon's latitudes and longitudes with modern measurements, that their observations were astronomical and not geodetic. The distinction is important; the only way
of comparing like-for-like would be to recompute Mason and Dixon's
work, allowing for deviations in the vertical, and then transforming
the results into a modern geodetic system. Some critics have suggested
unreasonably that Mason and Dixon's achievements were disappointing
or inadequate. But many others hold Mason and Dixon to be excellent
surveyors; Mason, in particular, is often described as brilliant. As for
John Bird's zenith sector, no instrument exceeded its precision for
another hundred years.

CHAPTER 10

The Tail of Ursae Minoris

DURING THEIR prior discussions with the commissioners in December 1763, it had been agreed that once Mason and Dixon had established the "true latitude," that is, "the Post mark'd West" in Alexander Bryan's field, their next task was to begin the West Line boundary survey. However, June 15 had also been set as the date for starting on Lord Baltimore's eastern boundary, and it was to this that Mason and Dixon turned their attention. For the most part, the boundary was the Tangent Line running from the Delaware peninsular Middle Point to where it grazed the western half of the twelve-mile radius centered on New Castle's courthouse. The difficult problem of setting out this complex line had led to Mason and Dixon's appointment.

The starting point for the main West Line firmly fixed, the surveyors departed Bryan's field, leaving the hired hands to pack the equipment. The zenith sector, brass telescopes, and other instruments from the observatory went to a Captain Rice's home for safekeeping; only the transit instrument was retained.

In the days that followed, a large company of men—including a steward, tent keepers, cooks, chainmen, and laborers—two wagons, and eight draught horses mustered in New Castle in preparation to move south. Until the advent of modern satellite surveying systems, it was usual for major surveys working through tough terrain to consist of a large party.

While they waited for the team to assemble, Mason and Dixon caught up with their infrequent letters from home. They read that the earl of Macclesfield had died at Shirburn Castle on March 17, the same

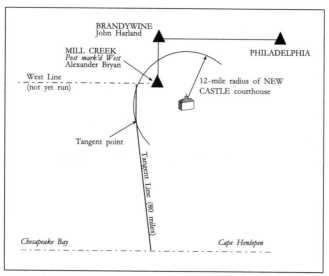

The Delaware Tangent Line.

day as the eclipse; it was a great loss to science and to the Royal Society, of which he was president. The new president of the society was to be James Douglas, the earl of Morton (1702–1768). They also read that their colleague, Nevil Maskelyne, had sailed with Charles Green to establish the longitude of Barbados in preparation to again test John Harrison's chronometer. On the long passage to the tropics, Maskelyne had taken a copy of Mayer's latest tables to make further experiments with the lunar distance method of finding the longitude.

Shortly after daybreak on Monday, June 18, the caravan of men and equipment set off along a dusty track. Mason and Dixon were in no hurry and left their lodgings in Newark, Delaware, the next morning to trot after the lumbering procession. The night was spent in Dover, then early the next morning the procession was off again. Two further days were spent on the south road before the wagons, pack-horses, and men arrived at the Nanticoke River. A tented camp was erected near Galestown, where more laborers were recruited, bringing the crew to thirty-nine strong. Early on Monday, June 25, the survey team paddled their canoes across the wide Nanticoke before setting off on a seven-mile march across country to the Middle Point marker stone. That evening Mason and Dixon set up the transit instrument.

The Tangent Line was to be a segment of a great circle, the short-est distance between two points on the spherical Earth. Mason and Dixon's method for establishing the Tangent Line has been a mystery; however, a careful study of Mason's observations has unraveled the whole procedure. The secret was their ability to run a dead straight line for over eighty miles from the Middle Point all the way to the tangent point, something never before done. It was like trying to aim for the Empire State Building from Philadelphia without deviating more than a foot or so. Their method was as complex as it was tedious.

First, a marker was placed about one-half mile distant from the Middle Point in the direction of the Tangent Line as shown by the posts left by the recent, unfinished American survey. Mason observed equal altitudes to find the meridian (true north) and the sidereal time in order to calibrate their pocket watch. The procedure was by now familiar to most of the men; the vertical axis of the large transit instrument was tightened and the time recorded as a star rose across the telescope's horizontal wire. The star was tracked as it moved slowly westward and the time was again noted as it set, recrossing the horizontal wire. The mean of the two times was the instant when the star crossed the meridian. This was repeated three or four times with dif-ferent stars to determine the rate at which their pocket watch gained, or was fast, against sidereal time. An example from Mason's journal illustrates the method:

Time by Watch

Star	Rising	Setting	Mean	RA of Star	Watch Fast
Alpha Lyrae	18:54:38	19:58:50	19:26:44		
Alpha Lyrae	18:55:40	19:59:54	19:27:47		
Alpha Lyrae	18:56:44	20:00:57	19:28:50		
			19:27:47	18:28:58	0:58:49

With an accurate rate for their watch, the surveyors then placed a candle at the marker half a mile away and aimed the transit's telescope at it. This direction had to be maintained exactly for the next eighty miles. For a permanent guide, Mason chose a tiny star in the constel-lation of the Little Bear. The transit's telescope was tilted up from the distant candle flame and then Mason waited until about 4 A.M., when "the star in the Tail of Ursae Minoris" (delta Ursa Minor) crossed the wire of the transit. The time of the event was corrected for their watch's error to give the right ascension of the "mid-Heaven," the sidereal time when the star crossed the Tangent Line.

On June 26, the surveyors, like the Wise Men of old, set off to follow the star. That same day they reached the third milepost set by the earlier American survey party. As the team went forward, they measured the distance (offset) from their line to every fifth milepost of the American line set out in 1762. This method was almost certainly advanced by Jeremiah Dixon, ever the practical land surveyor. The weather turned hot and it rained frequently, turning the dust to sticky mud that clung to their boots. They reached the Nanticoke River on Saturday, June 30, and measured its width by setting out a baseline on the northern shore and measuring the angles with the Hadley's quadrant from the southern shore. The instrument was used on its side, in the same manner a modern surveyor uses a sextant to measure horizontal angles. For two weeks, Mason and Dixon led their large team forward, passing the twenty-fourth milepost on July 13. Each night was spent observing equal altitudes to find sidereal time and to check their alignment with delta Ursa Minor. Mason's journal is noticeably vacant of his usual detail; the work of running the line would have been more familiar to Dixon. Perhaps Mason the astronomer did the night shift while Dixon supervised the day work.

On Saturday, July 14, Mason gave "the overseer of the Ax Men a proper direction" to follow, then he and Dixon left to visit the Speaker of the Maryland House of Delegates, Colonel Robert Lloyd, forty miles away in Talbot County. It made a pleasant, civilized weekend break with time for some intellectual conversation and a decent bottle of claret. After this diversion, and for the next five monotonous weeks, they pushed the line forward, crossing the broad Choptank River on July 25, where Dixon celebrated his thirty-first birthday amid the trees and fields of Delaware. Eventually they arrived at the sixty-ninth milepost on the southern shore of the tidal Bohemia River. It had been a dreary, humdrum survey routine unworthy of comment. On August 18, they sent two letters by express courier to Governors Sharpe and Hamilton, requesting they advise their commissioners that the first phase of the work would be completed within ten days.

They reached what was judged to be the tangent point on August 25. Cutting away the undergrowth, Mason recovered the markers left by the 1760 survey party when measuring the 12-mile radius from New Castle's courthouse. Extending the markers forward to where they intersected the new line, Mason discovered they were 22.51 chains (495 yards) too far west of the 12-mile post. The local "Chain Carriers" measured this distance and, to make certain it was correct, Mason himself measured it "and made it within a Link of the same." From this, it can be reasoned that the local men did much of the measuring alone, or at least with minimal supervision. The American surveyor Joel Bailey, who was not in the team on this occasion, frequently assisted with the stellar observations and many of the complex survey tasks.

The distance from the new line to the last marker of the third American line was 17.25 chains (380 yards). Dixon's proposal was to use the unprecedented straightness of their new line to adjust the position of the slightly meandering American line. Mason and Dixon drew up a table of offset distances that they calculated would achieve this and bring the original mileposts into the line of the true tangent. On September 4, starting at the north end of the new line, they began the elementary job of setting out each one of the offsets. The entire task was completed by the twelfth. One of the wagons suffered badly crossing over the rough land and was sent on to Philadelphia for repairs and to collect more tents. The wagon had still not returned by the time they set off south, but it finally turned up at Mr. John Twiford's house, on the banks of the Nanticoke, on September 13.

The wagon master brought news back from the city that Benjamin Franklin was returning to London. This time the distinguished gentleman was going as the Pennsylvania assembly's official agent to work with their London resident, Richard Jackson. The financial strain of defending the lengthening frontier, the internal tensions within the province, and the apparent ineffectiveness of the Penn administration had prompted the assembly to act. Franklin's objective was to seek a change in the charter, making Pennsylvania a royal province in order to secure the aid of British troops and an injection of money for the ailing colony.

Twiford's house was not far from the great Pocomoke Swamp and headwaters of the Pocomoke River. In company with some of their men, Mason and Dixon took the day off to go exploring. Charles Mason was impressed: "There is the greatest quantity of Timber I ever saw: Above the Tallest Oak, Beech, Poplar, Hickory, Holly and Fir; Towers the lofty cedar: (without a Branch), till its ever green conical top seems to reach the clouds." Mason was at heart an explorer, a man of his age. He concluded: "The pleasing sight of which; renewed my wishes to see Mount Lebanon."

On Monday, September 17, Mason went to the tenth milepost and "began to find a direction for the Visto that should pass through our offsets." His purpose was to check the alignment of the true tangent. The method he used for this final check is still a common procedure among engineering surveyors. He set out three precisely aligned marks as near as possible parallel to the line of the tangent. The center mark was near the tenth milepost, another mark half a mile north, and the other mark a mile to the south. From the center mark, he projected the line southward until he arrived at the Middle Point stone; the check line missed the stone by 2 feet 2 inches too far west. Returning to the tenth milepost, they ran the same line northward and at each milepost measured the offset distance to the Tangent Line.

Fall was well advanced and the weather turned cold and foggy. For three days it was so thick that work was impossible. Unbeknownst to the surveyors as they groped through the effluvium of the marshes, John Bird in faraway London had received Dixon's proposal to measure a degree of longitude and raised the issue at a meeting of the Royal Society. Bird also discussed the proposal with Thomas Penn. On October 25, the society recorded in its minutes that Lord Morton, the president, had "mentioned to the Council that Mr Penn had made an Offer to the Society of directing Messrs. Mason and Dixon . . . to measure a degree of Longitude, upon a parallel of latitude between Maryland and Pensilvania without any Expense to the Society if the Society would direct the method of doing it." The society readily accepted the offer and passed a vote of thanks to Penn. Lords Morton and Cavendish, along with society members Canton, Raper, Short, and Maskelyne, were instructed to form a committee to draw up the necessary instructions.

Meanwhile, in Delaware on November 2, Mason and Dixon had a short meeting with the commissioners at nearby George Town to discuss progress before resuming work. The 12-mile-radius post was reached on November 10, where the offset from the line was found to be 16 feet 9 inches east of the post. Another table of offsets was compiled and the error proportioned over the whole length of 80 miles. This was then compared with the measurements; the greatest difference was a mere 3½ feet at the thirty-mile post, which entirely satisfied Mr. Mason.* The final check on the alignment of the Tangent Line was to measure the angle at the tangent point between the Tangent Line and the courthouse belfry in New Castle. If the line were a true tangent, then the angle would be a right angle. Mason wrote that "it was so near a right angle, that, on a mean from our Lines, the above mentioned Post is the true tangent Point."

The two surveyors again met with the commissioners on November 21 at Christiana Bridge for a four-day session, which included much social interaction, to discuss the commissioners' concerns over the rate of progress. The commissioners decided that the West Line should be the next priority and that it should proceed as far as the Susquehanna River. Once that section was complete, the surveyors were to return to complete Lord Baltimore's eastern boundary, connecting the tangent point with the West Line parallel of latitude. The work was taking longer than originally anticipated and winter was upon them. There was nothing more to be done until spring, so the laborers and hands were laid off for the winter and Mason and Dixon returned to the Brandywine to spend Christmas with their friend John Harland and his family. Their last job of 1764 was to write to the "Honorable Proprietors" in London, informing them that the elusive Tangent Line had been successfully completed.

The clever thing about the method used by Mason and Dixon in solving the difficult Tangent Line is its simplicity; they did not resort to any complex trigonometry. Instead, Mason's genius was to run a very straight line for over eighty miles, using a single star as his guide. The error at the end was simply proportioned back along the length of the line. Had the American team done the same with their second line, Mason and Dixon's services may never have been required. However, the great West Line, which did require enormous skill, would have undoubtedly defeated the local surveyors.

---

*See "Running the Tangent Line" in the Appendix.

CHAPTER 11

Fine Sport
for the Boys

SITTING IN FRONT of the roaring log fire of John Harland's farm-stead reading letters from home, Mason was distressed to learn that Nathaniel Bliss had died, after serving just two years as astronomer royal. He had not been well for some time and had spent his last days in Oxford rather than London. A number of candidates had received sponsorship for the vacant post, including James Short, the Surrey Street instrument maker and mathematician; Tom Hornsby from Oxford; John Michell, the Cambridge astronomer who first conceived of black holes; and Reverend Nevil Maskelyne. Mason's replacement, Charles Green, had taken charge of the Greenwich Observatory while the choice for Bliss's successor was debated.

The year 1764 had been a busy one for Nevil Maskelyne; he had been appointed by the Board of Longitude to test John Harrison's chronometer. On March 18 he had sailed on the *Princess Louise* in company with Charles Green, bound for Barbados. Arriving early in May, the two astronomers determined the longitude of the island in preparation for the arrival of the *Tartar*, bearing John Harrison's son William with the experimental "watch." On the voyage out, Maskelyne had experimented with Mayer's latest lunar tables, was delighted with the results, and let everyone in Bridgetown know it, much to young Harrison's anger. Testing and observations had gone on for several weeks until Harrison and the precious H4 chronometer departed for England, leaving Maskelyne behind to complete his longitude observations from the eclipses of Jupiter's satellites. The astronomer's final value for Barbados was just 9 minutes 47 seconds of longitude east of H4's position, a mere eleven statute miles, well within the one-half of a degree needed to claim the rich longitude prize.

With the Christmas and New Year festivities at the Harland homestead over, Mason set off alone to explore the countryside. Departing from the Brandywine on Thursday, January 10, he headed west for the town of Lancaster, some thirty-five miles distant. "What brought me here was my curiosity to see the place where was perpetrated last Winter the Horrid and inhuman murder of 26 Indians, Men, Women and Children, leaving none alive to tell." Mason was troubled by the Paxton Boys' massacre of the Conestoga the year before. There was a Scottish Highland regiment quartered at the town's barracks, but for some unrecorded reason they did not act to prevent the atrocity or intervene, allowing the villains to escape unmolested. Mason was particularly appalled by this nonchalant and despicable disregard for human life on the part of His Majesty's troops, "no honor to them."

Drunk on liquor and inspired by a vague religious fervor, the Paxton Boys' motive was one of the worst kinds of bigotry, coupled with a loathing for any degree of authority over their wild lives. Tacit support for their bloody crimes came from many who were frightened of Indian uprisings, and the rumors of Indian atrocities committed at distant, nebulous places. Many justified their raw bigotry with biblical quotes, a "horrid perversion of scripture and religion, to father the worst of crimes on the God of Love and Peace." Benjamin Franklin, himself no lover of the Indians, was so disgusted by the brutality of the massacres that he was impelled to published a pamphlet entitled "The Christian White Savages" in condemnation of the Paxton Boys' doings.

Scarcely a year had passed since the massacre and the memory of those terrible days were still vivid. Mason spent several days in Lancaster, unraveling the facts and exploring the town. Before leaving his lodgings at the hotel, he wrote a letter to a Mr. Kingston, then set out for Pechway, Pennsylvania. As he trotted along the road, he met Samuel Smith, the retired sheriff of Lancaster County, and they rode along in company talking and swapping travelers' tales. The subject of the boundary survey naturally came up and Smith told Mason another story of frontier violence. In 1736, the folk living on either side of the disputed border between Maryland and Pennsylvania were at open war. Loyalists of both camps confronted one another across the line and raided one another's homes and property. On the banks of the Susquehanna a Maryland farmer called Cresiep found his home besieged by fifty Pennsylvanians. Inside the house fourteen members of his family, friends, and workers were taking shelter. Despite calls for surrender, the Marylanders would not give up without a fight, and a fierce gun battle ensued. The wooden house was set afire and the occupants had no choice but flee the burning building. As they rushed out, one of Cresiep's men was shot down and killed by the Pennsylvanian frontiersmen.

At the time, the animosity between the two proprietors, the Penns and the Calverts, was at its height, although diplomatic relations had not been broken off, and the wrangle had passed to the English Court of Chancery for resolution. The local settlers on either side of the line were aware of this, but found it clearly insufficient. Ostensibly, the northern province was Quaker while the southern was Catholic, and both professed religious tolerance. Yet there was little or no toleration. Fierce loyalty to Pennsylvania and the Penn family opposed fierce loyalty to Maryland and the Calverts. Man's craving to wave a patriotic flag and defend a cause, however unjustified, prevailed.

Leaving old Sam Smith at Pechway, Mason made his way back to John Harland's plantation. On Monday, February 11, restless as ever, he set out once more, this time heading his horse northeast toward New York. He crossed over the Schuylkill River to stay the night with Mr. McClean, the "commissary for the lines" (the survey's paymaster) in his Philadelphia town house. The thirteenth was the sixth anniversary of Becky Mason's death and a melancholy day for Charles. Home thoughts from abroad turned toward distant Gloucestershire and the little family he had not seen for nearly eighteen months.

The next morning, he set off across the frozen quarter-mile-wide Delaware River; there were no bridges in those days. Halfway over, the ice fractured and his horse broke through the thin crust into the freezing river below. He managed to recover the horse without harm, but it had been a close call and a timely warning to take greater care in the future. Passing through "Prince Town" in New Jersey, he visited the new university campus and "the most Elegant built Colledge I have seen in America." He spent that night at a hostelry in Brunswick, passing the evening in convivial companionship and learning more about the colonies. After an early breakfast next morning, he set out for Elizabeth Town, where he took the ferry across the river to Staten Island. From the north shore, he embarked on the sailing ferry for the long trip across the Upper Bay to New York City. A few days were spent in the bustling city enjoying the culture and society of the metropolis, and no doubt visiting The Theatre, in Nassau Street, before leaving Manhattan for a journey across the East River to explore Long Island. From the island he recrossed the rivers on his way back to Staten Island and the "Eastern road," before swinging south to ride down the frozen lanes to Perth Amboy. This was the town where, a year earlier, the refugee Indians from Philadelphia had been turned back by New York authorities.

Traveling along, Mason passed through Freehold, where he turned off and headed for the little market town of Mount Holly. It was Sunday, February 24, and the citizens of Mount Holly were at worship. As Mason passed a Quaker meetinghouse, a raucous bunch of boys emerged, gleeful to have escaped the solemnity of Sunday worship. Mason's horse shied at their frolicking and he gave it a smart tap on the head with his whip. The creature immediately collapsed to the ground "as if shot dead," and poor Charles was thrown: "I over his head, my hat one way wig another and whip another, fine sport for the boys." With as much dignity as he could muster Mason picked himself up, recovered his stunned horse, and led him, "very serene," past the Friends who were now pouring out of the meetinghouse. Mason was highly amused by the episode but he had also sustained a nasty hip injury that kept him in bed for the rest of that day and all of the next. On Tuesday he set off once more, his hip still smarting from the fall. He crossed over Raccoon Creek and the Delaware River and headed toward New Castle, then back to rendezvous with Jeremiah Dixon at their lodgings in Newark, two miles south of Alexander Bryan's field and the "Post mark'd West."

Unknown to Mason and Dixon, whose letters from home could take up to three months to arrive, the choice of Bliss's successor as astronomer royal had turned into a political conflict. The battle lines were essentially drawn between those who supported John Harrison's claim to the longitude prize and those who did not. The dispute was also politically aligned, tempered by social leanings and aspirations. On one hand were the powerful Tories, representing solidity and the landed classes; on the other were the more or less radical, middle-class Whigs. Alexander Small wrote to Benjamin Franklin, now living at his old lodgings in Craven Street, about the astronomer royal affair in early December:

Mr Short is a Candidate for Greenwich but having opposed Lord Morton [president of the Royal Society] in the £5000 affair [Harrison's prize money] Lord Morton now opposes him and gives it as a reason, that Mr Short is a Scotch Man though he acknowledges that he is the fittest for it of any Man. These two [James Short and John Michell] who would have done honour to the place, being thus laid aside, I believe the Tory Interest, at present all powerful, will get it for an Oxonian, who never made an observation. What Candide Patrons we are of the Sciences!

James Douglas, the earl of Morton, was Scottish aristocracy, so his reference to James Short being a Scot was not an ethnic slight. Lord Morton was a Tory; he owned vast tracts of land and, as a young nobleman, had been a Jacobite sympathizer. Short, on the other hand, was a mild-mannered but landless artisan and scientist and a natural candidate for the Whig cause. He was also well educated, having attended Edinburgh University, where he studied mathematics and science and mastered the art of making mirrors for reflecting telescopes. He was an eminently suitable candidate, but was not from Oxford or Cambridge.

Traditionally, Oxford University was a Tory bastion, whereas Cambridge inclined toward the Whigs. As Sir William Browne wittily wrote on George I's donation of the bishop of Ely's library to Cambridge University:

The King to Oxford sent a troop of horse,
For Tories own no argument but force:
With equal skill to Cambridge books he sent,
For Whigs admit no force but argument.

Whether Alexander Small in his letter to Franklin had mistakenly thought Maskelyne an Oxford man, or if he was in fact referring to the Oxford don Thomas Hornsby, he was, either way, being particularly ungenerous to both candidates, as they were each accomplished astronomers. Nevertheless, it is true that Lord Morton was a strong supporter of Nevil Maskelyne and went to great lengths to promote his candidacy. Ultimately the post went to the Cambridge man, and so it was that as Charles Mason was fording the chilly waters of Raccoon Creek, Reverend Nevil Maskelyne was being sworn in as the fifth astronomer royal.

CHAPTER 12

"From the Post Mark'd West"

MODERN SURVEYORS have developed techniques that exploit the capacity of theodolites to measure horizontal and vertical angles with great precision. Unlike their modern counterparts, Mason and Dixon did not possess an instrument that could produce a consistently accurate angle for the full 360 degrees of a circle. The scale arcs of scientific instruments were hand-divided and engraved onto brass, silver, or, more often, ivory. (The invention of the circle-dividing engine by Jesse Ramsden in 1777 would totally revolutionize the technology, costs, and availability of precise measuring instruments.) The accuracy of the scale arc of Mason and Dixon's zenith sector says much about John Bird's consummate skill as an instrument maker. Instead of relying on less than precise measuring circles, Mason the astronomer used the night sky as his theodolite with such proficiency that the results compare more than favorably with modern techniques.

The method Mason and Dixon devised for running the Pennsylvania and Maryland border was a clever combination of astronomy and land surveying techniques. The shortest distance between two points on Earth's surface is a great circle, but the West Line dividing the two provinces was required by law to be a parallel of constant north latitude, exactly fifteen miles south of Philadelphia. Together, Mason and Dixon contrived a complex procedure; first, they would establish the true latitude (derived at the "Post mark'd West"), then run a series of great circle segments, each ten minutes of longitude, or approximately eleven miles long. At the far end they would reobserve the latitude and correct for any error. With either end of the great circle fixed, they then computed offset distances from the great circle to the true latitude.

Mason calculated that the greatest offset distance between the great circle and the true latitude, halfway along the segment, would be 17.14 feet. The observations and calculations required expert knowledge of spherical trigonometry, as well as accomplished astronomical skills. In their lodgings at Newark, Mason meticulously wrote out the complicated procedure in his journal. Using spherical trigonometry (in which, unlike plane trigonometry, the sum of the angles in a triangle exceeds 180 degrees) Mason calculated that the line of a great circle should lie at an angle 89 degrees 55 minutes 51 seconds west of true north. To find this angle (or azimuth) from the night sky, the surveyors first chose a low elevation star that would cross the proposed line. The instant when the star would be in the required position was found by adding the 89 degrees 55 minutes 51 seconds to the star's right ascension. Equal altitudes from the transit instrument provided the sidereal time and the error of their clock; local sidereal time equals the right ascension of a star when it is on the meridian. Allowing for the clock error, the transit's telescope was pointed to the star at the instant calculated when it would be in the right position. The transit was locked so it could not move in the horizontal and the telescope was tilted downward to point along the vista. Half a mile away, a chainman holding a lantern was directed to the left and right until, when he was on the line, a peg was hammered into the ground. The whole laborious procedure was repeated for different stars until the surveyors had a small cluster of marks.*

All of Saturday, March 2, was spent in the Newark homestead poring over seven-figure log tables, computing the complicated mathematics, and preparing a table of star positions and times. The weather outside was miserable; sheets of icy rain and sleet lashed against the window shutters, heralds of the equinoctial gales. The survey team, billeted around the small iron-making town, observed Sunday as a day of rest, and Mason and Dixon accompanied their host family to worship in the Newark church. Monday dawned, cold and overcast, the rain falling in an unceasing torrent. Rain, sleet, and snow kept the sur-

---

*See "Setting Out the West Line" in the Appendix.

veyors and their team indoors for the next two weeks. Conversation around the homestead fire turned to the proposed and, for the colonists of British America, contentious Stamp Bill then being read in the House of Commons. The Bill would impose colonial taxation on a variety of common and everyday goods, such as newspapers, and even on legal costs. While taxation of any sort was unwelcome, the fact that the colonists had no say in the matter lay at the heart of the popular unrest and increasing resentment towards Britain.

On the night of Wednesday, March 20, the surveyors hazarded a few hours outside, riding over to Mr. Bryan's field to observe five equal altitude stars before the clouds returned and hid the heavens from view. Next morning was the vernal equinox, when the sun crossed the celestial equator into the Northern Hemisphere, heralding the arrival of spring; it snowed hard and the wind howled. Venturing out of the house at nine o'clock on Sunday morning, Mason measured the depth of snow; it "was two feet nine or ten inches deep in general, where the wind had not least effect to heap it." A few observations of the star Regulus were attempted on Wednesday, but the snow was still too deep for any further progress. On Saturday, March 30, two chain carriers, Darby and Cope, arrived at the house to join the survey team, exhausted from struggling through the snow from the Lower Counties. The snowfall slowly eased, but the sky remained too cloudy to make any observations.

Finally, on April 4, after a month of awful weather, the night sky cleared and Mason and Dixon ventured out to begin the observations for determining their direction west. The low-elevation stars Procyon, beta Leonis, Alcyone, Aldebaron, and alpha Aries were observed sequentially. The clock was calibrated against meridian altitudes of Regulus, beta Leonis, and Procyon. Then, with the all-important times calculated, three marks were set out half a mile to the west; all fell within eighteen inches of one other. At long last, Mason and Dixon were ready to start the West Line boundary survey "from the Post mark'd West."

Friday, April 5, dawned chilly but clear as they set up the transit instrument and sighted the center of the cluster of marks. The Gunter's chain was laid out and, while Mason kept the chainmen on line, Dixon led the way forward across the new crops in the fields. By Monday they had reached White Clay, 1 mile 58 chains from the "Post mark'd West." They crossed Little Chistiana Creek at 3 miles 25 chains and passed Mr. Price's house at 3 miles 49 chains. A few black slaves and their overseers watched the survey party pass slowly across their fields as the border separating the two provinces took shape. Pressing on, they crossed over the Greater Elk and Lesser Elk Rivers. On Saturday, April 13, they arrived at the road between Octorara and Christiana Bridge, 12 miles 9 chains from Bryan's field, and the end of the first ten-minute great circle segment. It was time to check the latitude.

The zenith sector arrived on its special carriage from the storehouse at Mr. Bryan's plantation and Mason prepared for the zenith distance star observations. Operating the giant instrument was a trial of patience and skill; the observer had to lie on his back to peer through the eyepiece of the six-foot telescope while operating the delicate tangent screw. Often only one zenith distance was managed; on other occasions, three or four stars might be observed. The number of stars in Dr. Bradley's tables was limited, no more than four hundred in the whole firmament, and of these only a handful would pass the zenith sector's field of view. Latitude observations began on April 16, using a group of just four stars, and were complete by Mason's birthday nine days later. Mason and Dixon then passed the frosty nights of April 25 to the twenty-seventh observing equal altitudes with the transit instrument to find their clock error against sidereal time in preparation for setting out the next eleven-mile great circle section.

They were now well and truly out in the wilds, having forsaken warm homes for draughty tents, damp beds, and camp cooking. As far as is known, neither Mason nor Dixon had any experience setting up or running a survey camp, and its arrangements can only be assumed. The camp was run under the sharp eye of Moses McClean, an experienced camp boss, probably a former army quartermaster. The surveyor's tents, including those of the local surveyors, were set apart from those of the crew. All the cooking was done outside, over a campfire between the tents. Breakfast was ready by sunup, to get the most from the day's work, and lunch was a furtive meal of cold meat and perhaps a jug of beer. The main meal of the day was taken in the evening, when all the men got in from their labors. Game was plentiful in the forest, and elk and deer, which some of the men hunted, supplemented the provisions they carried with them. The forest was also home to predators such as wolves and bears, and the camp boss made sure a careful watch was kept at night. Mason and Dixon did not go on their expedition without some creature comforts, including various spices for their meals and some delicacies and treats, as well as a few books for pleasure and the Bible for meditation. With exception of the Quakers, all the men drank hard liquor, and it was the job of the camp boss to make sure they did not drink to excess.

Although there is no mention of the subject by Mason, it is almost inconceivable that the American surveyors were restricted to mundane work. It can be safely assumed that Joel Bailey operated all the instruments at some time or another and shared the task of booking the readings and reducing the observations. Jonathan Cope and William Darby, although described as "chain carriers," were, if not from the start, competent measuring surveyors and undertook tasks unsupervised. At the end of each day's work, all the surveyors would get together to go over the measurements and compile their notes for computation. Both Mason and Dixon took turns with the calculations, but the more complex astronomical and mathematical work was probably left to Mason alone.

The calculations for the latitude at the end of the first section showed that the zenith sector's position was 43 yards too far north of the true latitude for the West Line. The deviation from their course over the 11-mile section was less than 0.13 degrees. Using trigonometry and arithmetic proportions, Mason drew up a table of offset distances to move the line they had measured to the true latitude for the provincial boundary.* This complex and tedious procedure would be repeated time and again as they moved ever westward. Content with the results of their first great circle section, the surveyors set out on the next leg of the West Line.

Obliged to keep the commissioners informed of progress, Mason and Dixon sent letters by express horse courier on Tuesday, April 30, advising that the survey team expected to reach the Susquehanna River within twelve days. The meandering Octorara River was crossed twice before they reached the eastern shore of the Susquehanna River, 23 miles 67 chains from the "Post mark'd West" in Bryan's field. To

---

*See "Adjusting the 10-Minute (11-mile) Segment of the West Line" in the Appendix.

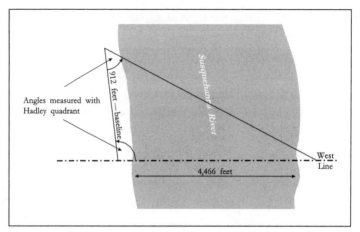

Measuring the distance across the Susquehanna River.

measure the width of the great river they resorted to plain trigonome-try. A baseline 912 feet long was set out along the top of the west bank and, using their 18-inch-radius Hadley quadrant, they measured the subtended angles.

A few miles later brought them to the end of the second 10-minute arc. The zenith sector was once more erected within its tent and another round of observations began. Each night from May 12 to the nineteenth the surveyors took turns lying beneath the sector's eye-piece, measuring zenith distances, save for two nights when it was just too cloudy to work. One evening Mason idly tried a trigonometric experiment; by doubling the length of the great circle arc to 20 min-utes, or 22 miles, he found that the maximum offset halfway would be 24.68 yards. This distance would be outside of the 8-yard cut, or "Visto," they were blazing through the trees, and would necessitate more cutting. It was a good idea and would speed up the work, but the idea was put aside for the moment.

The warm evening of May 19 was spent taking equal altitudes and setting out three wooden pegs about one mile to the west, on the far side of the Susquehanna. The marks were checked and all fell within a seventeen-inch cluster. Returning across the wide and sluggish river in a canoe one sultry afternoon, Mason was astonished by the sudden and dramatic onset of an electrical storm, the like of which he had never seen before. Dark, ominous clouds filled the sky, enveloping the forest and river in gloom. About a mile and a half east of the river, wide streaks of blue lightning "about a foot in breadth to appearance" flashed from the inky black sky into the verdant forest. "This was the first Lightning I ever saw in streaks continued without the least break through the whole . . ."

The storm passed, and, after a brief respite caused by the cloudy weather, it was back to lying beneath the sector for another five nights of patient observation, plagued by various insects and bites from the ubiquitous mosquito. Sunday, May 26, and the following day were spent computing the results of their observations, calculating a new table of offsets, and observing evening equal altitudes with the transit instrument. In addition to their regular star observations, the night of May 26 was an opportunity for Mason to observe a stellar eclipse, when the Moon passed in front of the star Regulus in the constellation of Leo. It was a pleasant evening—the temperature had risen to fifty-five degrees Fahrenheit—but high cloud prevented observing the "immersion," the moment when the star disappeared behind the Moon. A little later, when the clouds broke sufficiently for a clearer view, "the Emergence from the moon was observed with Certainty, with a Reflector [Short's reflecting telescope] that magnified about 70 times." Mason knew that Charles Green would record the same phenomenon in London, as would Lalande's astronomers in Paris. Later, the times for the event would be compared against local apparent time and the difference would yield the longitude of the Susquehanna River.

The Susquehanna marked the limit of their instructions, and they could not proceed further west without the commissioners' consent. On May 28, the surveyors broke camp and carefully packed the delicate instruments into the wagons. With the tables of offsets at hand, the distances from the great circle lines to the true latitude were laid off at every mile and marked with a fresh post. Progress in this repetitive task was excellent and the survey team was back at John Harland's plantation for the evening of the last day of May. After a good night's sleep in a proper bed, Mason, Dixon, and the crew were up early for breakfast, ready to travel the twenty-five miles across country to Newark and the tangent point to complete the commissioners' instructions.

The line north from the tangent point to where Maryland, Pennsylvania, and the Three Counties (Delaware) converged, some three miles northwest of Newark, was to be a meridian or true north line.

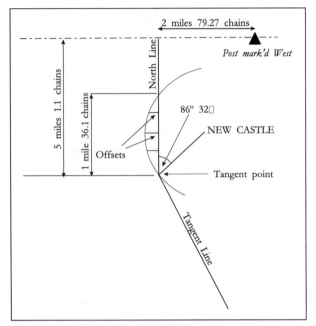

Setting out the North Line from the tangent point.

On the warm summer evening of Saturday, June 1, 1765, Mason set up the transit and equal altitude instrument at the tangent point marker ready to start work. To locate the meridian he and Dixon observed the polestar and a star in the tail of the Great Bear called Alioth. Four other stars were observed to check the direction and a mark was set out accordingly, indicating due north. The next day, Sunday, was observed in peace, reflection, and writing letters to the commissioners and to people at home. Expresses were also sent to Annapolis and to Philadelphia, informing the provincial governors that they expected to complete the North Line within a week.

The first section of the North Line was a chord of the twelve-mile circle around the New Castle courthouse belfry. Mason used the Hadley quadrant to measure the angle between the meridian and New Castle and found it to be 86 degrees 32 minutes. It was a simple matter of trigonometry to calculate the distance from the tangent point to where the line cut the circle to the north. From the "properties of the Circle" Dixon then calculated the offset distances from the meridian line to the circle.

The chaining parties set out across the fields and farms on Monday, June 3, passing close by the front door of Mr. Morgan, who was now unambiguously a citizen of the Three Counties. At 2 miles 78 chains north they passed Mr. Golespier's meetinghouse, then on the left the house of John Rankin, now a Marylander. On June 6 they arrived at the parallel of latitude 15 miles south of Philadelphia; they were 2 miles 79.27 chains west of the post in Mr. Bryan's field. The distance from the tangent point to the West Line was 5 miles 1.50 chains "horizontal measure," to avoid any possible confusion. They drove a post into the ground "marked W on the West Side and N on the North Side." The post stood in a field belonging to Captain John Singleton, who now found that his tobacco plantation lay in three provinces: Maryland, Pennsylvania, and the Three Counties (Delaware).

From June 7 to the sixteenth, Mason and Dixon waited at their lodgings in Newark for news that the commissioners were ready to assemble, whiling the time away checking their calculations and socializing. They also wrote a very long letter to Nevil Maskelyne, among other things congratulating him on his appointment as astronomer royal. They pointed out the opportunity at hand, and the excellence of the flat terrain, for measuring both a degree of longitude, as originally proposed, and, more importantly, a degree of latitude. They commended to him that the Royal Society support the bold proposal and agree to their proposed fee of £200.

At length, on Monday, June 17, the commissioners rendezvoused with the surveyors at nearby Christiana Bridge in New Castle County, bringing with them seven cut stones to mark the border. After a pleasant day digging holes and supervising the setting up of the markers, the commissioners and the two surveyors retired to the nearby tavern. Seven months had passed since they last met; it was time to bring the commissioners up to date on their progress and settle the accounts. Mason and Dixon explained in detail the methods they had employed on the West Line, all of which met with the commissioners' approval. They then turned to the next phase of work. The gentlemen from Pennsylvania and Maryland agreed that the West Line should proceed westward, but were also mindful of the British government's prohibition restricting any further westward colonial expansion. A compromise was reached, however, and the Englishmen were accordingly instructed "to continue the Parallel of Latitude (in the same manner

Engraving of one of the Tangent Line stones, circa 1900,
by an unknown artist. (Courtesy Stock Montage, Inc.,
Chicago, Illinois)

we have run it to the River Susquehannah) as far as the country is
inhabited, etc."

Before leaving Christiana Bridge and returning to the Susquehanna,
Mason and Dixon wrote a letter to Cecilius Calvert and Thomas Penn
in London on the same subject of their letter to Maskelyne. They explained to the proprietors the business of measuring a degree of longitude and a degree of latitude, and requested their permission "to use
their Instruments; and the indulgence to do it in their Provinces."
Such measurements, the first of their kind in North America, would
further advance knowledge of the shape of Earth and complement the
work of the French Académie Royale de Sciences.

CHAPTER 13

The Pencil
of Time

THE MORNING OF the summer solstice in 1765 dawned bright and clear as Mason and Dixon mounted their horses and set off from Christiana to join up with the hired hands at the Peach Bottom ferry. Riding slowly through the heat of the day, they passed along the dusty country roads, then turned north. Peach Bottom village, its ferry long gone, can still be found at the end of a lane nestled along the rocky shores of the Susquehanna a few miles north of where the West Line crosses the broad river. The survey team and the wagons with the victuals, stores, and tents; the tree cutters and chainmen; and the stewards and cooks assembled in the village the next morning to set up camp by the river.

During their sojourn in New Castle County, Mason and Dixon had devised a new stratagem for setting out the direction for the West Line. As they did not have a precise means of measuring horizontal angles, Mason used the night sky as his compass. However, an alternative method for setting out an accurate horizontal angle is to construct a large right-angled triangle on the ground. In this way a small angle can be calculated in terms of the sides of the triangle; the longer the triangle's sides, the more accurate the result.

When the surveyors first reached the Susquehanna, the latitude observed with the zenith sector had been 580 links too far north of the true line. In order to correct this, and bring themselves back into the line, they resorted to arithmetic proportions and a long, thin triangle. First, they set out a radius of 1.187 miles westward across the wide river from the point where the zenith sector had stood on May 19.

Mason then calculated that the length of a 10-minute great circle arc would be 11.37 miles and, by proportion, the error of 580 links was comparable to 60.5 links at the distance of 1.187 miles.* This distance of 60.5 links was set out on the ground at a right angle to the "direction found by the stars." Satisfied with the result, Dixon gave orders for the chaining crew to follow the new direction westward.

The country to the west of the Susquehanna was well populated by settlers, many of them German immigrants. As Mason and Dixon passed the homes, the farmsteads, and even a schoolhouse, they meticulously recorded each one: "At 30 Miles 42 Chains Mr James McKenleys House 3 Chains to the North." The passage of the surveying team was a sight worth seeing and the homesteaders were frequent visitors, lured by the shouts of the men and Dixon's curt instructions. Rumors of the famous pair flew before them and a sense of relief followed, knowing that the years of border hostility and bloodshed were passing away. Some of the backwoodsmen may have been less than elated by the results, but the fact that Mason and Dixon were independent and "famous astronomers," coupled with the sheer size of the survey team, meant that trouble from that quarter was unlikely. There was no sign of the hostile Agnews, the Blacks, or the Eddy boys, nor was there any sign of big Tom Hooswick, who twenty-two years before had brutally relieved Lord Baltimore's surveyors of their equipment.

The end of the third section was reached on July 3, some 37 miles 17.98 chains from the "Post mark'd West." Rather than setting up the zenith sector and wasting precious days finding the latitude, Mason decided to employ the new stratagem and press on. In his journal, he explains in great detail this clever piece of eighteenth-century logic, which was to become a standard routine for the work and a principle that has survived down to the present time. These days a surveyor might describe Mason's process as trilateration rather than triangulation. Until the advent of electromagnetic distance measuring instruments in the early 1960s, measuring the angles of a large triangle (triangulation) was the only method used to cover large tracts of ground. Excluding the more exotic theodolites, the best instruments

---

*See "Running the Sections from the Susquehanna" in the Appendix.

in common use are accurate to about 5 seconds; at a range of 20 miles this tiny angle represents a distance of some 30 inches. Modern distance measuring systems can be even more precise than this. By measuring the sides of a large triangle (trilateration) rather than its angles, a more accurate result is possible. Mason and Dixon did not use trilateration in the modern sense of the term, but they did use some of its elements that allowed angles to be set out by offset distances with great success. The trusty transit instrument was set up and aligned on a point established using the new method, and, with this direction to aim for, the chaining party once more set off west.

For the next eleven miles, as they chained through the eight-yard-wide vista cut from the virgin forest, they passed only two isolated pioneer farmsteads. The wagons loaded with the stores and precious instruments went by a different route and caught up with the advance party on July 11. The next day they crossed the road leading from York Town to Baltimore, 48 miles 64.5 chains from Bryan's field. It was midsummer; the daytime temperature had climbed steadily to nearly 90 degrees Fahrenheit, and the nights were hot and sultry. Whenever possible the surveyors shunned the stifling heat of the tents, preferring to sleep beneath the stars despite the incessant chirruping of cicadas and other night noises. They were still many miles east of any potential Indian trouble, but the forest was home to bears and other predators; a night watch was maintained and the campfire was kept burning.

On Friday, July 12, Mason and Dixon stood the crew down while they determined the latitude; this would be the acid test for the new method of running the line. Every sweltering night from July 12 to the twentieth the two Englishmen took turns lying beneath the giant zenith sector, patiently adjusting the tangent screw micrometer, measuring the zenith distances of the stars as they passed overhead. The transit instrument was also set up, alongside the tall sector, to observe equal altitudes of stars crossing the meridian, by which means they measured the error of their watch. At these times, with so many observations to make, all the surveyors from the team were employed. Mason then calculated the times when suitable stars would cross the azimuth (the angle from true north) for the next section of the line. On Saturday, July 20, he had sufficient information to set out the first line point, a quarter mile west of the sector.

After Sunday breakfast, Mason held a morning service, leaving the rest of the day for relaxing pursuits. On Monday he processed the zenith observations, but instead of calculating the latitude directly, which would have been straightforward, he compared each star's zenith distance with that recorded at the observatory in Alexander Bryan's field. By modern practice, this is strange, but it tells us a lot about the astronomer Mason. His goal was consistency; the "Post mark'd West" was the absolute, the datum point, and by using the original observations for comparison, he ensured that his work remained consistent with the latitude derived at Mill Creek. Even if he did not know their magnitude, Mason was aware that inconsistencies were present in their zenith sector and that deviant effects could manifest themselves as errors.

Mason corrected each stellar observation for the effects of nutation, aberration, and precession using the tables supplied to the team by the astronomer royal. The spread of the zenith distances was less than two seconds of arc; after averaging the results, the surveyors discovered they were just fifty-six feet south of the true parallel. Knowing this error, Mason and Dixon were able to compile a new table of offsets from their present location back to the twenty-sixth milepost. The instruments were packed into the wagons on July 23 and the direction fifty-six feet south of the true latitude was laid out for the fifth stage and the next great circle line.

At 49 miles 7 chains, they passed John Lawson's lonely homestead, half a mile east of Gunpowder River. For the next 10 miles they crossed and recrossed the Gunpowder as it meandered through the forest and across new-made fields. Saturday evening brought some light relief as Mason and the crew celebrated Jeremiah Dixon's thirty-second birthday in the wilds of Pennsylvania. At 58 miles 58 links, a house appeared among the trees, 50 links to the north; it belonged to a homesteader named Valentine Vant, who now owed his taxes to Pennsylvania. Shortly thereafter they crossed the road from York to Baltimore at modern Lineboro. On the west and final bank of the Gunpowder they came to the end of the fifth section, 60 miles 57.18 chains from their starting point. Mason calculated that they were 28 feet north of the parallel. Again, they set out a half-mile extension of the line and an offset that would produce the critical angle of 8 minutes 18 seconds north of west.

It was July 30 when they set forth on the sixth section; beneath the dusty trees it was hot and humid. A cluster of homes and farms passed by, their owners' names revealing German and British roots; Rinot, Hoarish, Stophel, Fight, Staphel, Rinoman, and Worth. Sunday, August 4, was a well-earned day of rest spent in worship and gossiping with the local homesteaders. Darby and Cope, the two foremen, kept an eye on the young hires as they flirted with the country girls while the Sunday luncheon was spread out on the grass beneath the shade of the trees.

The survey progressed past Mr. Hiltibrand's house, at 70 miles exactly, and shortly after crossed the narrow Piney Run River, which "empties into the great River Potowmack." On August 7, 71 miles 43.18 chains west of Mill Creek, they called a halt and set up the zenith sector in preparation for determining the latitude. The hot weather had turned sultry and the noontime sky grew inky black; from the southwest a thunderstorm closed in and the heavens opened onto the surveyors below. Mason and Dixon bellowed orders to the chainmen, while Joel Bailey yelled at the hired hands to get all the instruments under cover as livid streaks of lightning rent the sky and thunderclaps boomed around the empty forest. Heavy rain beat down, turning suddenly to hailstones. The assiduous Charles Mason, the water streaming from his cocked hat, collected one chunk of ice and measured it. "The hail intermixed with pieces of ice; one piece of an irregular form measured one inch and six tenths in Length, one inch two tenths in breadth and half an inch thick."

That night and for the next ten hot and humid nights, the zenith stars Vega, Deneb, and delta and gamma Cygni were observed, wheeling slowly from east to west across the object lens of the six-foot zenith sector. Equal altitudes of Vega and Deneb yielded the sidereal time and their watch error. Line marks for the next direction west were set out on August 16 as the stars Hamel, Eta Pleiades, and finally Aldebaron "passed the direction, or Azimuth of 90° 04′ 09″," toward the east. The same stars were again observed the following night and a new mark set out "so near it could not be bettered."

Mason computed the latitude from the zenith observations, again directly comparing the results with those observed at Mill Creek. The answer showed they were 4.58 seconds of arc (6.94 chains) too far north, and a new table of offsets was calculated back to the forty-eighth milepost. At the point where they had changed direction on July 30, the offset to the true latitude was found to be 3.23 chains south, a satisfactory result that vindicated their new method of proceeding. Mason's journal notes and diagrams became quite complex, yet the process remained the same: a combination of arithmetic proportions and spherical trigonometry, all laboriously computed with seven-figure log tables in the sweltering summer heat, the whole time tormented by insects and clouds of mosquitoes.

With a new direction and a known offset, they started out on the seventh segment of the line. By the evening of Tuesday, August 20, Alexander Bryan's field in Mill Creek lay 72 miles 77 chains to the east. Only one lonely house was spotted that day, belonging to Stephen Grise, 154 feet to the north. Next morning they crossed the Monocracy road, passing Michael Miller's place and Henry Bower's house a scant 700 feet apart; their clearly visible chimneys would have made Daniel Boone feel claustrophobic. Mason's written description was a map in words; later, this word map would be transposed into a strip plan of the whole enterprise. The U.S. Geological Survey has mapped the United States in detail, and on its 1/24,000 scale maps it is possible to plot with certainty the ancient site of every home, farm, Quaker meetinghouse, school, and church that Mason and Dixon recorded.

Over Willollowey's Creek and passing the Davis and McCewn places in Harney, Maryland, the survey team reached Rock Creek on August 23, 78 miles 66 chains down range. Although it was summer, the creek just below the point where Mash Creek joined it was over 130 feet wide. Six miles to the north, and 98 years in the future, General Robert E. Lee would suffer his catastrophic defeat and tens of thousands of young Americans would make the ultimate sacrifice. But when Mason and Dixon were chaining peacefully through the Pennsylvania forests, Gettysburg wasn't even a settlement.

Sunday was a day of rest spent in worship with the farmers, in idle gossip, and in flirting with the local girls who had come to watch the famous survey pass their homes. Setting off early on Monday morning, the chaining party passed four homesteads within the space of a mile. At noon Mason called a halt, a hundred yards west of Matthew Elder's house, and set up camp. Sitting beneath the dappled shade of a large tree, their backs against its warm trunk, Dixon read out the logs and antilogs while Mason computed the direction for the eighth great circle section. A new line extension was run as before and the offset laid out. After breakfast the next day, as the Sun cleared the eastern horizon, they were off again, leaving the cooks to clean up and the wagoners to follow as best they could.

The 22-yard Gunter chain, under the direction of Darby and Cope, was laid out on the cleared ground. While Darby held it firm at the zero end, Cope snaked the chain to get it straight and flat to the ground and marked his end with a chaining arrow. Dixon measured the slope with either an inclinometer or, perhaps, the Hadley quadrant, which was fitted with a spirit level. Standing alongside Cope, Dixon consulted a set of correction tables and measured on an inch or so to correct the slope to the true horizontal distance, then resited the chaining arrow. With Cope on the front end and Darby at the other the chain was pulled forward, Dixon remaining by the arrow. The same process was repeated and then Darby handed the first chaining arrow to Dixon, who kept the tally, by which means they kept count of the number of chain lengths measured.

Up ahead the cutters were hard at work, opening the eight-yard-wide vista and clearing the brush away, their shouts and bawdy country humor echoing through the great forest. The felled timber was a boon to the settlers along the line, providing lumber for their homes and fuel for the coming winter. Near Liberty Mills, Pennsylvania, the crew reached the foot of South Mountain, the first in an endless series of Appalachian ridges that seem to have been scraped across the landscape of North America by a giant comb.

South Mountain signaled the start of Mason and Dixon's first hill section; where the slopes became too steep for normal chaining, the 16.5-foot levels had to be used. These levels, similar to those used on the Tangent Line and each one rod in length (i.e., four to a chain), slowed progress a little but preserved the accuracy. The party crossed the endless ridges to reach 94 miles 63.68 chains west on September 6, 1765. Twelve days and nights were spent making zenith and equal altitude observations and processing the results. Mason computed that they were 85 links south of the true parallel and prepared another table of offsets back to the seventy-first milepost. With a new direction for the line, the party set off on the next twenty-minute arc, proposing to change direction halfway by the now customary offset method.

One Saturday, clear of the mountains and in a flat and fertile land, they camped near the home of Staphal Shockey. Over supper, Mr. Shockey, in his mellowed German accent, told Mason and Dixon about a cave some six miles to the south that was worth a visit. The two Englishmen took the following day off and rode south into Maryland on a sight-seeing expedition. The cave was at the end of a short, steep lane and was indeed worth the trip. Mason was much moved by the solemn beauty of its stalactites and stalagmites:

> The entrance is an arch about 6 yards in length and four feet in height, when immediately there opens a room 45 yards in length, 40 in breadth and 7 or 8 in height. (Not one pillar to support nature's arch): There divine service is often (according to the Church of England) celebrated in the Winter Season. On the sidewalls are drawn by the Pencil of Time, with the tears of the Rocks: The imitation of Organ, Pillar, Columns and Monuments of a Temple; which, with the glimmering faint light; make the whole an awful, solemn appearance: striking its Visitants with a strong and melancholy reflection: That such is the abodes of the Dead: Thy inevitable doom, O stranger; Soon to be numbered as one of them. From this room there is a narrow passage of about 100 yards, at the end of which runs a fine river of water: On the sides of this passage are other rooms, but not so large as the first.

This beautiful limestone cavern near Cavetown, Maryland, survived to the 1950s, when it was destroyed by quarrying. On Monday, after their brief spelunking excursion, it was back to work chaining the line westward. They crossed the Antietam River; then, at the end of the great circle section, Mason changed direction. On Sunday the surveyors again went sight-seeing, traveling down to William's Ferry on the Potomac (at the site of modern Williamsport), where the "Conecocheague falls into the said River, about seven miles to the south of our Line." They boarded the ferry and crossed to the "Virginia side" where they found a log fort, refreshment, good company, and a warm welcome in the tavern.

The last point of the eleventh 10-minute section, which also marked the limit of their instructions, was reached on Monday, October 6. The days were still pleasantly warm, but the nights were becoming chilly.

The surveyors had to dress warmly for the next fourteen nights while lying beneath the zenith sector and taking equal altitudes with the transit instrument. By October 21, they had collected enough zenith distances to compute the latitude: they were 12 chains 84 links too far south. Another table of offsets was computed back to the ninety-fourth milepost. The sidereal time of the "mid-heaven" was determined for the instant the star Hamal would cross the line toward the east. At eight o'clock, two-and-a-half hours after sunset, Hamal rose across the line on the precise azimuth, and a mark was placed 52.68 chains east of the transit instrument. Two more star crossings that chilly morning confirmed the direction exactly. The next night they repeated the process, and all three marks agreed within four inches. Dixon took an ax and blazed a tree 5 feet 11 inches to the north so that the mark could be recovered when, and if, the commissioners agreed to extend the line west.

Mason was concerned about the westerly direction they may have to take the next season and was worried they would be forced to cross the Potomac River. If this were so, then they would have two problems. Measuring across the wide river at an oblique angle would be difficult; but more importantly, the Potomac formed the border between Maryland and Virginia. If it transpired that the true latitude they were following crossed south of the Potomac, Penn's legal boundary of constant latitude would be impossible and Maryland would become divided. The political and legal ramifications would be dire. On Friday, October 25, they approached Captain Evan Shelby, a local magistrate and expert on the region. Shelby, a somewhat dubious character, was pleased enough to assist the astronomers; he even agreed to look after their precious instruments over the winter period. The next morning they all set off for North Mountain to spy out the land, but when they reached the summit it was so shrouded in mist that nothing could be seen. The captain accompanied them again the next morning, when the air was crisp and clear. From the summit, they saw the northern loop of the great river, about ten miles distant. Much to Mason's relief, they estimated that the West Line would pass some two miles north of the Potomac, near Hancock, Maryland.

After a morning service, Sunday was passed in a leisurely stroll through the woods of South Mountain, from where they saw in the far distance, straddling the West Line, the purple heads of the Allegheny

Mountains. On Monday they bid farewell to Captain Shelby, entrusting to him the custody of the proprietors' instruments for the winter period. Turning their backs to the west, they set out to lay off all the offsets they had calculated from the great circle segments to the true parallel of latitude all the way back to the Susquehanna. They arrived back at Peach Bottom on November 7; they had done very well, averaging ten mileposts per day, excluding Sundays. The work was straightforward; so, just like their modern-day counterparts, they probably turned the dull exercise into a lighthearted contest between two competing crews—the Astronomers, led by Mason, versus the Land Surveyors, led by Dixon—the prize being a night of free drinks in the Peach Bottom tavern. The next day Darby and Cope assembled the hands to be paid off and discharged for the winter. With instructions to report on April 1, 1766, for the next season's work, the men departed on their separate ways.

CHAPTER 14

"King of the Tuscarawa"

MASON AND DIXON received instructions by letter to report to the commissioners at York, Pennsylvania, on Saturday, November 16. After dismissing the men for the winter, the two surveyors spent a few days at Peach Bottom, checking their calculations and enjoying some fishing in the Susquehanna. Crossing by ferry, they set off on a twenty-five-mile ride across country to York to spend a few days recuperating and enjoying the civilized but austere pleasures of the provincial town. To the east of York, the Amish Mennonites, who had arrived from Rotterdam in late 1727, were already busy creating their own special America.

The gentlemen commissioners assembled on time and sat in session for three days. The surveyors gave a detailed account of their progress, settled accounts with Mr. McClean, the commissary, and explained their methods of establishing the line of constant latitude dividing Maryland from Pennsylvania. Without doubt, "their Excellencies" were pleased to learn that Mason had devised a way to speed up the rate of progress by reducing the time spent in lengthy astronomical observation. The original estimate for the work was grossly optimistic, and the objectives changed so much that costs had risen dramatically, as Benjamin Chew was quick to point out. During the meeting, Mason and Dixon learned that the commissioners were anxious to replace the wooden stakes on the Tangent Line with permanent stone markers before the winter set in. For this reason the meeting was adjourned. The surveyors departed York, heading for Mr. Twiford's plantation at the south end of the Tangent Line.

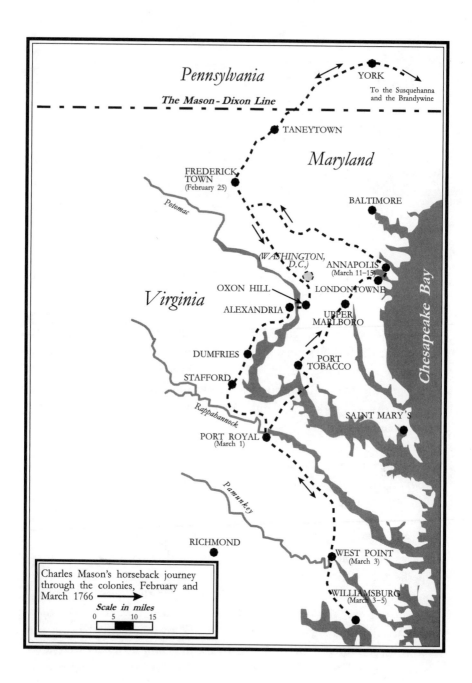

Pennsylvania

The Mason-Dixon Line

YORK

To the Susquehanna
and the Brandywine

TANEYTOWN

Maryland

FREDERICK
TOWN
(February 25)

Potomac

BALTIMORE

(WASHINGTON,
D.C.)

ANNAPOLIS
(March 11–15)

Virginia

OXON HILL

LONDONTOWNE

ALEXANDRIA

UPPER
MARLBORO

Chesapeake Bay

DUMFRIES

PORT
TOBACCO

STAFFORD

Rappahannock

SAINT MARY'S

PORT ROYAL
(March 1)

Pamunkey

RICHMOND

WEST POINT
(March 3)

Charles Mason's horseback journey
through the colonies, February and
March 1766

Scale in miles

0   5   10   15

WILLIAMSBURG
(March 3–5)

136

They were at John Twiford's home for Saint Nicholas' Day, but there was no sign of the promised stone markers. Twelve days passed while they idled on the banks of the Nanticoke—not that Mason minded, for it was one of his favorite spots. Finally, the twenty cut marker stones from England arrived by barge. Seven of the heavy markers were dropped on the south bank and the remainder were off-loaded near Twiford's house. Another thirty stones were left near the bridge over the Choptank River (Greensboro). Mason and Dixon engaged a local contractor to assist with the heavy manual work, and Joel Bailey was called in to help as well. Mason divided the labor force into two or three working parties, one probably led by the indispensable Bailey. With their stock of line markers loaded on a wagon, the eager parties set off. It took only half a day to dig each hole, drop in the stone, and witness the position before moving on to the next location. By the last day of December 1765, all the markers had been set in the ground and 50 miles of the boundary between Maryland and the Three Counties officially established. On New Year's morning 1766, Mason and Dixon left the cold, windswept fields of the Three Counties and headed for the warmth and joys of cosmopolitan Philadelphia, the theater, and some decent food.

The two English surveyors had now been in North America for two years and were familiar with Philadelphia, having spent all told some twenty-five days in the city. They were also well acquainted with many of its leading figures: gentlemen of rank and consequence, some of whom were also commissioners for the line. They knew, of course, the grumpy lawyer Benjamin Chew (1722–1810), the chief secretary and later chief justice of Pennsylvania, who was never happy with the progress or the mounting costs of the survey. A native of Maryland, Chew had studied law in London as a young man before returning to settle down in Philadelphia with his wife, Elizabeth. He was a close friend of the Penn family and through that association, was amassing a huge fortune in colonial America. At the time, Chew was a staunch ally of British rule, though this changed after the Revolution, and an ardent supporter of colonial proprietorship, especially that of Thomas and Richard Penn. Their interests were uppermost in his mind and his advice on, and jurisdiction over, the legal issues were invaluable.

Avaricious and haughty, Chew was a stark contrast to the other commissioners with whom Mason and Dixon were familiar. There was the
kindly Reverend Richard Peters, Penn's provincial secretary, and Reverend John Ewing, mathematician and provost of the College and
Academy of Philadelphia, both keen observers of the natural world.

Mason and Dixon were invited into the sanctum of the American
Philosophical Society, then meeting occasionally at the Statehouse. At
these intellectual gatherings, they met the astronomer-surveyors John
Leeds and the outstanding David Rittenhouse. Other notables who also
showed great interest in their work were the amateur astronomers William Smith and John Sellers. With such an august and interesting circle
of acquaintances, the prospect of good conversation, a hot meal, or a
night's entertainment was always at hand. These occasions also provided an opportunity for Mason and Dixon to experience how wealthy
Americans could employ an entire family of black slaves as their domestic servants. The Englishmen's views on this practice is not known; no
doubt with a twinge of conscience they accepted the situation as normal. There is an apocryphal account that suggests Jeremiah Dixon, if
not opposed to slavery, was vehemently against its barbarity. The story
goes that he saw a man beating his African slave in the street; Dixon
knocked the man to the ground and wrested the whip from his grasp
and beat him with it. When Dixon returned to England, the slaver's
whip was one of his many souvenirs.

Between social activities and the pleasures of the city, Mason and
Dixon found time to send letters home and to their clients, the two
proprietors in faraway London, informing them of the survey's progress. We do not know if Mason sent money home for his children's care
and education, or if he had arranged with Penn and Calvert to provide
advances from London. We can be sure, though, that the boys' well-
being was always uppermost in his mind, and he would have secured
a regular income for the relatives who cared for them before leaving for
North America.

That winter, the consequences of the new Stamp Act were all the
talk in Philadelphia and hostility was growing fast. An emergency
Stamp Act Congress had assembled at New York in October to discuss
the unfair tax and the worsening situation. There had been riots in
Boston, where the governor's mansion was attacked and burned down.
Mobs were roaming the streets, hunting down the despised officials

and burning the hated stamps. The colonists felt betrayed by the British Parliament and there was rebellious talk in the taverns. The call for independence was becoming ever more common. In London, Benjamin Franklin had realized his error in misjudging the reaction of colonial America. In a complete turnabout, he was now lobbying hard against the Stamp Act and seeking support for its repeal amongst the Whig faction. Mason, too, was growing increasingly sympathetic toward the colonists' plight and beginning to consider settling down in America with his distant family.

After a week in Philadelphia, Mason grew tired of the city and returned to the Brandywine to spend some time with the Harland family, leaving Dixon behind to spend more of his bachelor vacation amid the delights of the city. Six weeks passed at the Harlands' before Mason's itchy feet and insatiable curiosity set him off once more, alone, on a journey of exploration, during which he "proceeded for curiosity to the Southward to see the country." It was midwinter and very cold; the midday temperature seldom rose above 40 degrees Fahrenheit, bitter winds swept across the bleak fields, and the dark, deep woods filled with snow. Turning his long-suffering horse to the west, Mason headed for Nelson's Ferry to cross the Susquehanna on the old road between Liberty Square and Airville, Pennsylvania. The ferry was located in a tight defile, where the river, normally 1,500 yards across, narrowed to 100 yards. Mason could see the river was of a great depth and asked the ferryman how deep it was. "Well," said the man, "170 Fathoms of Line with a very heavy weight, has been let down; but no bottom could ever be found." It was well into the afternoon by the time Mason reached the western shore and trotted along the empty road towards the Blue Ball Tavern in the borough of York.

He passed Sunday in company with William Lawson and his family, on the fringes of York. The next morning he left the province of Pennsylvania, crossing the West Line on his way to Taneytown, Maryland. Tuesday, February 25, found Mason heading south for Frederick Town and lodgings for the night. The next day, Mason kept to the north side of the Potomac for some fifty miles, as far as Oxon Hill, where he crossed over by the pulling ferry. On the Virginia side he found a tavern and passed a pleasant evening enjoying the pleasures of provincial Alexandria. He breakfasted early the following morning before riding down through sleepy Colchester and on to Dumfries;

that day he covered a lazy twenty-five miles. The next day was another casual ride, to Stafford to visit the new courthouse.

As in Britain, the roads of rural America were entirely unpaved and could be treacherous mires of thick mud in the winter. The farm and freight wagons, and what few coaches ventured abroad, were forced to keep to the ways in between the fields and woods, the horse teams "struggling in mud up to their knees." The Philadelphia stage took three or more days to travel one hundred miles to New York. Mason, on his horse, avoided the worst patches of the road by using the grassy verges or following the shortcuts of other riders through the fields, and could quite reasonably cover forty or fifty miles in a day. The mail express riders, who changed their mounts in stages, could travel some seventy miles on a good day.

March 1 saw Mason trotting along the north shore of the Rappahannock, which he crossed west of Port Royal at the last bridging point before the river drained into the vastness of Chesapeake Bay. He had reached latitudes some 150 miles south of the Brandywine and the temperature was more pleasant, reaching fifty-five degrees Fahrenheit during the day; it was also less wet. In the milder climate with the onset of spring, in a land cultivated and populous, Mason, a rustic at heart, was delighted to see new crops springing up and "green peas in the fields five or six inches high." On Monday, March 3, he crossed the Pamunkey at Claybourn's Ferry, probably where the little town of West Point now stands. He stopped for lunch at an inn by the riverside. Sitting by the inn's door, entranced by the view before him, he opened his journal and began to write. "This is a beautiful situation on the Bank of the River: opposite the door in a Right Line over the River is a causeway of a Mile in Length, thro a mark [salt marsh] that is overflowed at High Tide about three feet, and if taken in, I think it would be very rich pasture."

It was a long ride, some sixty miles, and he was very tired by the time he reached the welcoming sight of Williamsburg, "the Metropolis of Virginia." The next morning he rose late and, over breakfast, wrote a leisurely letter to his friend Robert Williams, a schoolmaster and amateur astronomer from Tetbury who had a pretty teenage daughter called Mary. After a casual lunch, Mason strolled around the bustling town, making small purchases as would any tourist. He had personal contacts in the town and that evening was invited to a reception in King William's Courthouse in honor of the visiting "king of the Tuscarawa [Tuscarora]." The presence of a great chief of the Six Nations was an occasion of pride and importance for the town. The sturdy old man had traveled some six hundred miles from his distant home on Lake Erie. The British authorities had peacefully resettled the Tuscarora from their traditional home in Virginia to the western lands. Now the king was paying a rare visit to those few of his relatives who had remained in Virginia. Indian leaders and dignitaries, who supported the British cause at the time, enjoyed considerable respect among the city's leading lights, and even wore European dress on formal occasions with the white man. Even so, the pressures of westward colonial expansion, despite the 1763 royal proclamation, were posing a threat to the natives and their ancient ways. To the west, in fact, tensions were high and there was war between the tribes. In December, good news had come that Pontiac was suing for peace, and arrangements were in hand for a treaty conference. But the old alliance of the Six Nations was breaking down; if an unsatisfactory peace was declared, it could result in traditional enemies joining forces to oppose any further European expansion west of the proclamation line. The king of the "Tuscarawa" was in Williamsburg not just on a social visit, but delivering a warning. Mason was curious to meet the old man and to learn something of the lands to the west through which, one day soon, he would have to pass. Advance knowledge of the reception he might receive at the hands of the Indians, and an understanding of their traditions, could even save his life.

After the reception, Mason left the civilized pleasures of Williamsburg and headed slowly back toward Port Royal. As he approached the town from the east road, dark storm clouds billowed up and lightning flickered ominously. At "3h 29m P.M. The sun Shining in my face I saw a streak of Lightning from 10° altitude down to the Horizon." It is interesting that Mason should record this event on March 6 so precisely. He knew his pocket watch could not be so reliable, but he was a diligent man. The sun at that instant was just twenty-five degrees above the distant horizon; the lightning flash was incredibly bright. Before the storm broke he found night lodgings. The next day he crossed over the three-mile-wide Potomac River by Hoe's Ferry to the Maryland shore. That night he spent at an inn on the outskirts of Port Tobacco. Before turning in, Mason took an evening stroll down to the river quay to inspect the ships berthed in the busy port. Hard against the quayside lay the *Alice,* a sea-stained trader just in from Senegal. Her burden, a "Cargo of choice healthy SLAVES," was being processed, ready for auction.

An Englishman traveling alone, among a population increasingly resentful of the mother country, of its taxes and proclamations, tells of a brave and resilient man. How did Mason handle this potentially dangerous situation? He was a genial soul for one thing, a man with presence, though occasionally dour. He was not aristocratic, but a country boy from the solid English yeomanry. He found conversation easy, but equally enjoyed his solitary ambles. Most of all, he enjoyed the company of Americans wherever he met them, and maybe shared a little of their rebellious nature.

From Port Tobacco, Mason followed a muddy track and sauntered northward, reaching an inn half a mile east of the village of Upper Marlboro, Maryland, just as darkness fell. Sunday and Monday were spent in Londontowne, sheltered against the heavy rain and snow, before he was able to push on to his next stop, Annapolis, "the Metropolis of Maryland."

He spent March 11 and 12 walking around the busy seaport, the streets behind the waterfront looking then much as they do today. Strolling past Stewart & Richardson's store in Church Street or dropping in for a drink at Bryan's Tavern, Mason caught up with the latest news from home. He learnt from jubilant merchants and "taverners" that the British government was in turmoil and the hated Stamp Act was about to be repealed. He sent his visiting card to the governor's house and next day was ensconced with His Excellency, Governor Horatio Sharpe. Sharpe was an opponent of the Stamp Act and several months before had convened the Maryland Assembly specifically to appoint representatives to attend the Stamp Act Congress in New York. Like so many eighteenth-century gentlemen, he was also a keen follower of science and an accomplished amateur astronomer. It was Sharpe who had been amused when the first master of the Royal Naval Academy, Dr. John Robertson, disagreed with the learned Dr. Bevis on the proper definition of east and west. Sharpe and some colleagues had also tested Sisson's zenith sector and examined the unsatisfactory telescopes sent out by Lord Baltimore in the year before the arrival of the "geometrical surveyors."

Thursday and Friday were passed in pleasant discourse with the governor. Mason produced his journal, over which the two men pored, while Mason explained his methods and sipped the governor's sherry. During their meetings, Sharpe informed Mason there was to be a meeting of the commissioners across the bay in Chestertown on the twentieth, to discuss the next season's work. Mason decided that Jeremiah Dixon could attend the meeting without him, and explain to grumpy Mr. Chew why progress was slow, while he returned directly to North Mountain to start preparations. Bidding the governor farewell, Mason departed the genial atmosphere of Annapolis on March 15, shortly before news arrived that the Stamp Act was officially repealed. All across British America there was jubilation; toasts were drunk to victory and batteries of cannon fired peals of thunderous acclamation. The hated Stamp Act and its insidious conditions imposed on the disenfranchised American colonists was gone, but another bill had been enacted in its place. The artful Declaratory Act gave the British Parliament unilateral power to legislate in the colonies "in all cases whatsoever."

Returning via Frederick Town, Mason arrived at Captain Shelby's plantation in time for the vernal equinox, when night and day are of equal length. While he headed north from Frederick, Dixon was heading south from Philadelphia to meet the commissioners at Chestertown on the banks of the Chester River. At the meeting Dixon learned that the commissioners required the boundary survey to proceed all the way to the Allegheny Mountains, the limit set by the proclamation of 1763. With these new instructions, he headed west posthaste to join Mason at Captain Shelby's home. Exactly on schedule, the chain carriers, the foremen Darby and Cope, and surveyor Joel Bailey turned up with all the hired hands, ready to start work from the point where they had left off nearly five months before. Rain returned with a vengeance and the wagons, with all the camping gear, were stuck somewhere to the east in the morass of the road.

CHAPTER 15

From Hence;
to the Summit

BEFORE FINISHING for the winter break, Dixon had blazed a tree next to their azimuth marker so it could be found easily the next spring. Early on April 1, the point was recovered, undisturbed next to its tree and two-thirds of a mile east of where the zenith sector had last stood. From the marker, they measured a distance of 74.36 links south to place them on the required latitude for the border. The transit instrument was erected, sighted along the line, and work began on the next section of the West Line. The cutting crew started clearing the trees and bush from the vista and the chaining party prepared to follow hard on their heels.

Eight miles south of North Mountain lay Fort Frederick and to the north Fort Loudon, where companies of British and provincial troops were on hand in case of Indian trouble. A few days later the summit of North Mountain was reached, without incident, 119 miles 18 chains from the "Post mark'd West." The steep inclines of the hills were measured with the levels rather than the Gunter's chain, which slowed progress a little. On April 6 heavy snow began to fall, changing to a cold and persistent rain that brought work to a standstill. The spring thaw had turned the tracks and roads into quagmires of deep mud, delaying the arrival of Mr. McClean, the commissary, with all the wagons, tents, and stores needed by the crew. In the meantime, the surveyors and their men stayed on Captain Evan Shelby's plantation, waiting for a break in the awful weather.

Captain Shelby was in the habit of setting his watch against the sundial in his garden. His sundial was quite sophisticated, with the equation of time engraved around its face. Late one afternoon, during a break in the clouds, Shelby and Mason compared their pocket watches against the sundial. Mason calculated local mean time and noticed that his own pocket watch was sixteen minutes slower than Shelby's. That evening, as Mason pointed out the different constellations to Shelby, they saw a bright meteor streaking down from the northwest "in a vertical with beta Aurigae." A few minutes later "At 8h 21m a small star set over the trace [the great circle visto] as did the comet [meteor] at the above time." The next morning, April 10, the two men again compared their watches; Mason's pocket watch had lost another two minutes against Shelby's or Shelby's had gained two minutes on Mason's.

The heavy rain returned during the night and persisted, sometimes as freezing sleet or as driving snow. On April 14 the wagon team arrived, exhausted and caked in mud. The trek west from Philadelphia had taken nearly three weeks; twice as long as expected. The foul weather had turned the unmade roads into mires of slush and mud in which the heavy wagons sank up to their axletrees. McLane's story was a woeful tale of bogged-down wagons, straining horse teams, and tired and angry men. A day or so later the weather improved sufficiently to allow work to restart, but rain and snow continued to hinder their progress. On Tuesday, April 22, Mason measured four inches of snow that fell on their camp during the night. Despite the miserable conditions, a fair rate of progress was kept up. By the next afternoon they had reached the end of the great circle section, 129 miles 12.4 chains from Alexander Bryan's field.

In the comparative shelter of their cold, damp tent, Mason and Dixon computed the logarithms for the spherical trigonometry: "Here P, the Pole: OAB the true Parallel. S, the Sector at the North Mountain SCK."* They worked out that an angle of 0 degrees 14 minutes 14 seconds south of their last direction should put them back on course for the next 11-mile section. This tiny angle was set out on the ground as a long thin triangle and the transit instrument aligned along its great circle side. Once more, the chaining crew set off westward into the forest.

---

*See "Starting Point for the 1766 Season" in the Appendix.

Near Hancock, Maryland, Mason and Shelby's estimated course for the West Line, seen from North Mountain the preceding October, was substantiated when the survey team passed a scant 1½ miles north of the Potomac River. A few miles later they reached the foot of steep Sidelong Hill. The slopes proved too much for the heavy wagons in the slippery conditions, forcing them on a long detour south. Leaving the wagons behind, the survey party set off for the summit, a mile distant, then down into the valley. After wading through the freezing waters of five creeks they arrived tired and weary at the foot of Town Hill. It was the end of the ten-minute section and a party of hands was sent back to collect the zenith sector from Captain Shelby's store. It took them four days to make the round-trip in the treacherous conditions.

One hundred forty miles from the post in Mr. Bryan's distant and soggy field, the zenith sector was again erected in its tent and the weary process of night observations began. Mason and Dixon spent the next twelve miserable nights lying beneath the tall instrument, making repeated sightings of the same five stars. However, the nights were getting slightly warmer, and the days, when the sun shone briefly between the heavy rain clouds, reached seventy degrees Fahrenheit. The oak and hickory trees were burgeoning into leaf, heralding the long-awaited advent of summer.

Equal altitudes were observed with the transit instrument on May 13, to calibrate their clock in preparation for setting out the next section. Mason selected three stars that would cross the great circle, and worked out the times they would pass directly over the vista. At the appropriate instant, each star was sighted through the transit; then, with the aid of a candle lantern, markers were placed thirty-four chains to the west. All three marks fell within an eight-inch cluster. Mason then computed the latitude from the zenith sector observations and, for the sake of consistency, compared each observation against that measured in Bryan's field. Despite twenty-two miles of tough terrain and the most foul weather, they were just twenty feet south of the true latitude. Mason and Dixon drew up their customary table of offset distances back to the point from where they began, then prepared to set out the next section.

The transit and equal altitude instrument derived its name from the fact that it could be used to observe the transit of a star across the meridian. Transit also means turning the telescope over to face the reverse direction; in American survey parlance, a theodolite is still called a transit. Unlike a modern theodolite, the telescope of Mason and Dixon's instrument, being so long, had to be lifted off its bearings and turned around to face the opposite direction. The capacity of John Bird's instrument to transit has, in the past, led to a belief that Mason and Dixon possessed yet another instrument: a compass transit, or circumferentor. This instrument, of French design, was in common use for general surveying and mapmaking and would have been familiar to Dixon. However, they were not employed on the line because they were neither accurate enough nor necessary. On May 17, Mason used their instrument's transiting capability to set up a tall post well to the east, so that it could easily be seen from the top of Town Hill. The transit was then transported to the top of the hill, aimed toward the new marker, then turned to face west.

The surveyors were now well into the densely forested slopes of the northern Appalachians, a strange country of steep parallel hills that stretched, ridge upon ridge, beyond Cumberland, Maryland. Further west, the ridges piled upward to form the barrier that divided the east flowing rivers from the west, marking the limits of the 1763 proclamation. But that was thirty miles distant. Meantime, from the peak of Town Hill they chained down to the valley floor, then climbed laboriously to the summit of Ragged Mountain. Then it was down into the next valley and up to Little Warrior Mountain. Down and up to Great Warrior, where they changed their direction 0 degrees 8 minutes 18 seconds north of west. The next peak in the endless series of ridges was Flintstone Mountain; then came Evitt's Creek Mountain, followed by Nobbly Mountain, where they crossed the road from Cumberland, whose fort lay just a few miles to the south. The last ridge crossed, before the divide, was Will's Creek Mountain, where the chaining crew was obliged to wade through its cold, swift stream.

Some distance behind, Commissary McLane and the wagons with the zenith sector and the supplies were making their ponderous way forward, the horse teams winding across the faces of the steep intervening ridges. The first of the Allegheny range was crossed on Wednesday, June 4; the east side of Savage Mountain marked the end of the 10-minute section, 165 miles 54.88 chains from the "Post mark'd West." John Bird's portable zenith sector, laying snug in its special wagon, arrived on Sunday, June 8. It took seven warm and cloud-free nights to collect sufficient observations and determine they were 241 feet south of the true parallel. One of Mason's favorite time-stars, Capella, could not be seen because it was "passing the Meridian with the sun, and the weather in general a little hazy in the day time, prevented our making any observation of that Star." Capella rose in the early hours of the morning, about a hand's span in front of the Sun (a stretched hand at arm's length makes an angle of about 15 degrees). The optical quality of their instruments was sufficiently good to allow sightings of the brightest stars during daylight.

In the shade of their tent at the foot of Savage Mountain, Mason and Dixon drew up the table of offset distances back to the 140th milepost. The next day they joined Joel Bailey and some of the men on a two-mile trek to the peak of Savage Mountain to see what lay ahead of them. Mason fully noted the magnificent view before them:

> From hence; to the summit of the next Ridge called the little Meadow Mountain: I judge by appearance to be about 5 or 6 miles: Between this, (Savage or Allegany Mts.) and from the said little Meadow Mountain, runs Savage River; which empties into the North Branch of Potowmack: This is the most Westernmost Waters, that runs to the Eastward in these parts [i.e., the limit of the 1763 royal proclamation].
>
> Beyond the Dividing Mountain (Savage), the waters all run to the Westward; The first of Note (which our line would cross if continued) is the little Yochio Geni, running into the Monaungahela, which falls into the Ohio or Allegany River at Pittsbourg (about 80 miles West, and 30 or 40 North from hence) called by the French Fort Duquesne.
>
> The Ohio is Navigable for small craft by the accounts I have had from many that have passed down it; and falls in to the River Mississippi (about 36.5 degrees of North latitude; Longitude 92 degrees from London); which empties itself in to the Bay of Florida [Gulf of Mexico].
>
> The lands on the Monaungahela and Ohio are allowed to be the best of any in the known parts of North America: The Rivers abound with variety of Fish, and quantity almost incredible. At present the Allegany Mountains is the Boundary

between the Natives and strangers; in these parts of his Bri-
tanic Majesties Collonies.

From the solitary tops of these mountains, the Eye gazes
round with pleasure; filling the mind with adoration to that
prevading spirit that made them.

The land into which they now ventured was indeed very beautiful
in a vast and untamed way, yet the British government had forbidden
its passage to white men, other than for trade. Mason wondered if the
boundary survey would ever continue beyond Savage Mountain; nevertheless, he was prepared, and took the precaution of becoming acquainted with the geography beyond the mountains. The survey crew
and the folk he met during his winter travels all attested to the excellence of the western lands, the abundance of the rivers, and their potential for inland navigation. The proclamation of 1763 had done nothing
to dampen the colonists' dream of settlement west of the Alleghenies,
and Mason was beginning to understand its mysterious allure.

On June 18, an 18-inch square, 5-foot-high wood post was set 3
feet into the ground. It marked a spot on the true parallel of latitude
for the border, 3.66 chains north of the zenith sector's position. A *P*
for Pennsylvania was carved on its north face and an *M* for Maryland
was marked on the south. Mason and Dixon had also reached the westernmost limit of their commission for 1766. All that remained was to
cut open an 8-yard-wide clearing, or vista, back eastward and to set
out the distances to the true latitude from their tables of offsets. The
precious instruments, less the zenith sector, were carefully packed and
shipped 15 miles to Mr. Stumblestone's home in Will's Creek for winter storage.

On Sunday, June 22, before heading back east, Mason, Dixon, and
a few of the men took the day off to pay a visit to nearby Fort Cumberland. On the way to the British fort they crossed the road cut
through the mountains by General Braddock's ill-fated expeditionary
force to reach the Monongahela eleven years before. As he examined
the military road, Mason recalled a line from Rebekah's grave in far
away Gloucestershire—"But fate how hard!"—mournfully adding how
Braddock had "made through the desert a path, himself to pass; and
never; never to return." In July 1755, Major General Edward Braddock, the officer commanding all the allied forces in North America,

led 1,400 British troops and 700 Provincials in an attack against the
French at Fort Duquesne. His aide-de-camp, the young George Washington, unwisely suggested that the general divide his forces at Fort
Cumberland, and Braddock, even more unwisely, accepted the advice.
On Wednesday, July 9, 1755, the British columns found themselves
scrambling through a narrow defile where a force of just 254 French
troops and 600 Indian warriors lay in wait. Braddock was mortally
wounded in the battle and Washington himself only narrowly escaped
death. All told, over a thousand British and colonial soldiers were
killed on that terrible day, their bodies laid in a common grave.

A mile or so beyond the road, Mason and Dixon found Fort Cumberland commanding a bend of the Potomac. It was a beautiful location, situated on a piece of rising ground where Will's Creek joined
the great river. Mason was surprised, and concerned, that despite Pontiac's recent uprising and the threat of Indian attack this far west, the
fort itself was in a sad state of repair with only ten 6-pound cannon
defending its rotting walls.

On June 24, 1766, Mason sent three men with the zenith sector
back to Captain Shelby's house, while the remaining crew carried on
back toward the east, setting out the offset markers. The 154th milepost was reached on June 28. By July 5, the cutting crew had cleared
an eight-yard-wide corridor and set markers as far as Town Hill.
Mason and Dixon climbed to the top of the lofty summit and surveyed
the swath they had opened through the endless forest. Pleased with
the result, Mason clinically observed, "The Visto shows itself to be the
Arch of a lesser circle of the Sphere, or Parallel of North Latitude."
(The only parallel of latitude that is also a great circle is the equator;
all the rest are small, or lesser, circles.)

Strolling through the scented groves of hickory trees, one huge
leaf caught his attention. He duly measured and recorded its dimensions; seventeen inches long and twelve inches broad. A little later
another prospect opened before them; "This day from the Summit of
Sidelong Hill I saw the Line still formed the arch of a lesser circle very
beautiful, and agreeable to the Laws of a Sphere." It is rare that a surveyor has the satisfaction of seeing the results of his skill drawn visi-
bly across the landscape, unless it is the asphalt of a new and ugly
highway. Darby and Cope, the chain carriers, were also moved by the
result of their labors when, from the top of the North Mountain, they

beheld the gentle, almost imperceptible curve of the vista slicing through the forest trees below. Apart from enjoying the fruits of his labors, Mason was also checking that their work did not contain a gross error and that the line always bent just a little toward the south between him and a distant point.

On Monday, August 4, just as the survey team passed the ninety-sixth milepost on their return journey towards the Susquehanna, a violent summer storm erupted. Lightning flashed and the tumultuous thunder crashed and crackled on all sides. A few minutes later came a "hurricane of wind and Rain." In a land where summer storms are common it was one of the most ferocious the surveyors had witnessed. The inky blackness of the clouds "put on the most Dreadful appearance I ever saw: It seemed to threaten an immediate dissolution to all beneath it." After the torrential downpour and violent concussions, the terrifying storm swept into the east, leaving the forest sodden and strangely silent.

The next day there was another chance to observe a partial eclipse of the Sun. The maximum darkness came at noon, and its precise time would allow them to calculate the longitude (as soon as the information arrived from London and Paris). Shortly before the eclipse started, and again afterward, equal altitudes of the Sun were observed with the Hadley quadrant to find the local apparent time. Despite the flying rain clouds, which frequently interfered with the observations, and missing the precise moment when the eclipse began, Mason and Dixon recorded the event with great accuracy. The image of the Sun was, on this occasion at least, taken "by reflection in Quicksilver [mercury]." Each man took turns using the quadrant; despite the dark filters, staring too long at the brilliant Sun reflected in the mercury might have damaged their eyes.

The end of the eclipse was observed by Mason through the brass reflecting telescope while Dixon estimated the time of the end through the quadrant. Dixon's estimate was 5 seconds later than Mason's; the difference was equivalent to 1 minute 15 seconds of longitude, or just over a mile. Mason carefully recorded the exact location of the observations; 768 yards north of the line and 92 miles 20 chains from the "Post mark'd West." On this particular occasion, the eclipse was nearly total and at its height "very heavy, gloomy darkness took place." It must have been a temptation for the two astronomers to have some

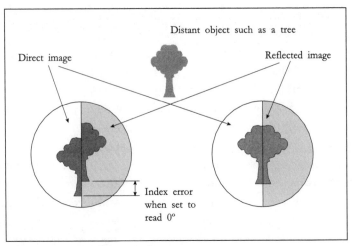

Adjusting the quadrant's index error.

sport with the hired hands by predicting the precise time when the world would be plunged into darkness. For simple folk, an eclipse of the Sun was still an event of mystery and a time of fear. For some it still is.

The next day, just to be certain of their local time, and the rate of their watch, Mason and Dixon reobserved the noon solar altitude with the quadrant. Before making any precise angular measurement, the instrument had first to be checked for index error by making sure the split view through the sight and the mirrors were in coincidence. On the day of the eclipse, Mason noted the error was 1 minute 20 seconds; the next day he found it to be 1 minute 30 seconds, and was annoyed with the instrument's erratic behavior. "I could wish the adjustment . . . were not so subject to change," he wrote, and made a note to complain to John Bird about the annoying problem. From their camp two miles north of the sixty-seventh milepost on August 20, Mason and Dixon were able to observe yet another eclipse, this time of the Moon. Equal altitudes of Vega provided the time on this occasion, happening, as it did, in the dead of night.

From the sixty-first milepost, as they set out the offsets to the true latitude, Mason was again gratified with a view of the vista as it crossed the South Mountain. He was delighted to see that it still "forms a true Parallel of North Latitude." The spectacle never failed to give him

A surveyor admires one of the large boundary marker blocks. (Courtesy Pennsylvania State Archives)

A close-up photo of one of the milestones set in November 1766. (Courtesy Pennsylvania State Archives)

A boundary marker rests near a fence on the Maryland and Pennsylvania border. (Courtesy Pennsylvania State Archives)

A Mason-Dixon "Crown Stone" (so called after the peer's coronet on the Baltimore Arms) on the Maryland and Pennsylvania border. (Courtesy Pennsylvania State Archives)

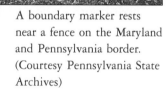

A series of photographs taken in 1906 as part of a U.S. government report filed in 1907 on the resurvey of the Mason-Dixon line.

153

immense satisfaction; he made a similar comment on September 6 from the thirty-first milepost on top of Slate Ridge. The pleasure he drew from these minute observations is clear; it was this attention to detail that made the whole enterprise a success.

The end of the line was in sight and letters were sent by express courier informing the commissioners in Annapolis and Philadelphia that they expected to finish on September 27. The letters also confirmed that the West Line had been measured horizontally and that the hills and mountains had been measured using the 16½-foot levels rather than the Gunter's chain. Posts had been set up throughout the length of the true parallel and at each location where the zenith sector or the transit instrument had been used. By September 25, the offset distances to the boundary latitude were completed and marked with posts all the way to the West Line's intersection with the line running up from the tangent point, "which finished our Instructions." On Tuesday, September 30, the hired hands were discharged for the season and Mason and Dixon departed to their lodgings in Newark. A letter from the commissioners in Philadelphia was waiting for them that together with another that arrived about the same time, contained some eagerly awaited news.

CHAPTER 16

At a Council of the Royal Society

MASON AND DIXON'S proposal to the Royal Society in June 1765 for the measurement of a degree of latitude was approved. Nearly a year before, on October 17, 1765, the Council of the Society had met to consider the proposal and had agreed it "to be a work of great use, and importance." The astronomer royal, Nevil Maskelyne, gave the enterprise his full support and endorsed the skill and excellence of the two surveyors, along with the quality of their instruments and of their American assistants. In supporting the resolution, the society's members expressed their confidence that the measurement would be the most precise ever made. Their confidence was well founded.

The society agreed that Mason and Dixon's fee of £200 for the work was acceptable and furthermore an additional £40 would be made available for the homeward passage, should the proprietors not meet the fare themselves. Nevil Maskelyne gladly agreed to prepare the specification and was instructed by the members "to draw up such further instructions as he thinks necessary." Charles Morton (1716–1799), under-librarian of the British Museum and secretary of the Royal Society, wrote to the proprietors, Lord Baltimore and Thomas Penn, requesting permission for Mason and Dixon to undertake the work in their provinces and to use the proprietors' astronomical instruments.

The two proprietors met on the morning of Thursday, November 7, 1765, to discuss the matter. Relations between the two great landowners were most cordial and, after a pleasant lunch discussing business and the prospect of a final resolution to their costly dispute, they both wrote to Charles Morton confirming their agreement to the Royal Society's proposition. To explain the details of the proposal, it is probable that Maskelyne was present at the lunch meeting, for the next day he penned a very long letter to Mason and Dixon from his office in Greenwich. The astronomer royal's instructions, dated November 8, 1765, were inordinately fussy, and there is the impression that he very much enjoyed writing them. Pedantry was combined with unnecessary labor on matters in which Mason and Dixon would have been more expert than Maskelyne. This interesting letter contains many points of academic interest and throws some useful light onto eighteenth-century geodesy. Maskelyne advised the surveyors that John Bird would be providing ten-foot-long fir measuring rods and a five-foot brass standard, which Maskelyne would dispatch together with the astronomical clock he had used during the 1761 transit of Venus expedition.

Unfortunately, Maskelyne's original instructions, along with the resolutions of the Royal Society, were never to reach Mason and Dixon in the forests of Pennsylvania. The merchantman *Ellis,* which had been carrying the instructions, foundered somewhere between Land's End and Halifax, taking its crew and, wrongly assumed, the Royal Society's instruments to a watery grave. This tragedy was a further reminder of the uncertainties of ocean voyages, uncertainties that would remain, despite improved navigation, until ship design advanced in the latter part of the eighteenth century. In the letters that finally arrived at Newark, Charles Morton added a covering note:

> The enclosed are duplicates of letters sent you from the Royal Society last year: and they are now repeated, because your not writing to us has occasioned a suspicion that the former letters have miscarried. I have nothing to add except what you will perceive, that you are not to expect any instruments than what you already have: and that we shall be glad to hear from you as soon as may be:
>
> I am, Gentlemen.
>
> Your most obedient, and humble servant. C. Morton, S.R.S.

Enclosed with the letters was half an ounce of fine silver wire for their plummet. Another letter, from Lord Baltimore's new secretary,

Hugh Homersley, was also waiting for the two surveyors at their lodgings in Newark. It was a response to Mason's letter of January 6, 1766, and contained the sad news that old Cecilius Calvert had recently died. The letter advised Mason and Dixon that Lord Baltimore "expressed his satisfaction in your Proceedings, and the happy prospect of bringing your great work to a conclusion in the ensuing summer." The letter also confirmed His Lordship's agreement that once the boundaries were completed, and the sooner the better, the surveyors were free to use his instruments for the Royal Society's project. The last letter was from the commissioners for Pennsylvania, informing Mason and Dixon that the next meeting of the commissioners had once more been postponed, to October 28. In the meantime, the two surveyors were free to start the measurement of the degree of latitude. The two men left their lodgings in Newark and headed for the Middle Point stone, south of the Nanticoke. The zenith sector was set up on October 8, 1766, and the preliminary observations began for the first linear measurement in North America of a degree of latitude.

The first stage of the process was to redetermine the precise latitude for the terminal points of the measured baselines. For this, Mason selected ten zenith stars from Dr. Bradley's tables of star positions. To avoid any error in the critical mathematics, Mason and Dixon each laboriously calculated the right ascensions of the selected stars. Every evening just before nightfall, the surveyors prepared themselves for the patient hours of observation ahead lying on the damp ground beneath the zenith sector. For ten long nights, they measured the angular distances as, one by one, the stars sailed past the six-foot telescope of the instrument. As was their wont, the sector was turned through 180 degrees to mean out any error. The next day Mason was annoyed when he noticed that their pendulum clock had stopped for twenty-three seconds for lack of winding.

On the evening of October 11, the transit instrument was set up alongside the zenith sector, and equal altitudes taken of the star Deneb to determine their clock's rate of sidereal time. The time of the star was also logged when it passed by the meridian observed through the zenith sector. The transit instrument was then sighted on the Tangent Line and the time noted when the alpha and beta stars of the Great Bear (Ursa Major) crossed the line; the next night the process was repeated. On the night of Monday, October 13, the transit was once more employed in equal altitude observations, which showed that their clock was gaining at a rate of 61.5 seconds per sidereal day. The clock's error was added to the right ascension for alpha and beta Ursa Major to determine the time when the two stars would cross the meridian. At the precise moment, the transit instrument was locked onto the position and the horizontal axis tightened. A quarter mile to the north, Joel Bailey, following Mason's directions, aligned a candle with the vertical wire of the transit. The two marks established by this method fell exactly at the same spot. The next evening the process was repeated, except that the candle was placed a mile to the north. The process was repeated again on the fifteenth and the sixteenth, when Mason also "turned the axis of the Telescope end for end; that is the Telescope itself was turned upside down: This proved the Ends of the Cylinders to be good." On October 17, the surveyors set up a candle at the quarter-mile mark and, sighting through this, extended the line to the other marks a mile distant. The line fell just a quarter-inch east of the mark established on October 14, quite a phenomenal achievement.

The surveyors now had a cluster of six meridian points, located by the stars alone. All six points fell within three inches and the middle of the cluster was taken as the true north-south meridian. From this point on the meridian, a line was set out at right angles west towards the Tangent Line. Another candle was set on the Tangent Line, 1¼ miles north of the Middle Point, and the transit instrument aligned on its tiny flame. Finally, the point where the two lines intersected was marked with yet another candle. It must have made a strange spectacle; the parties signaling to one another, waving their lanterns, and dark figures moving backward and forward getting on line. One or two of the surveyors on horseback trotted between the parties across the open ground, "level as a floor by nature," delivering the instructions.

The distance from the northern meridian point to the Tangent Line was measured twice with a calibrated chain, and found to be 5 chains 14 feet 0.3 inch. Using the same chain for consistency, the distance from the meridian point to the Middle Point stone was measured as 80 chains, or one mile exactly. In 1760, the American surveyors had established the meridian at supposedly the same spot when setting off on their first line towards New Castle. The marker post still stood, 9 feet 10 inches east of Mason and Dixon's meridian mark. The angle due to this error was about 6.5 minutes of arc, which, over the 80-mile-long

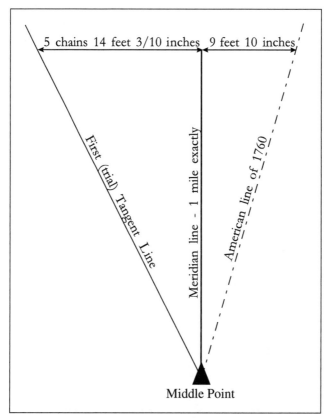

5 chains 14 feet 3/10 inches   9 feet 10 inches

First (trial) Tangent Line

Meridian line - 1 mile exactly

American line of 1760

Middle Point

Establishing the meridian at the Middle Point.

line, would have put the American meridian line 12 chains too far east. Had this been corrected, the error in their first Tangent Line would have been only 21 chains. The reasons for their error may have been due in part to inexperience, but probably the main cause was the quality of their telescope's optics.

The last task before finishing work at the Middle Point was to find its longitude by a form of lunar distances. The transit's telescope was aligned on the meridian candle a mile to the north, then turned to face due south. When the Moon crossed the meridian, the time was recorded as it passed the three vertical wires of the telescope. Similarly, the meridian passage times of alpha and beta Aries and Aldebaron were also observed. After each observation, the telescope was reversed (transited) to check that it still pointed correctly to the distant candle.

Dixon and Mason independently repeated the lunar observations on October 18 and 19. When fully processed back in London, the observations would provide an accurate longitude of the Delaware Middle Point.

Their short interlude working for the Royal Society came to an end on October 20. They packed their instruments and returned to Newark for a short rest and some calculations before setting off to rendezvous with the commissioners. Arriving at Christiana Bridge, Mason and Dixon discovered that the meeting had again been rescheduled. Instead, one of the commissioners from Pennsylvania was on hand with a train of wagons loaded with milestones, carved from the finest English Portland stone. The instructions required that all one hundred stones be placed immediately. For the next three weeks Mason, Dixon, and Joel Bailey supervised the setting out and hole digging for the heavy stones. The Tangent Line was completed, and stones were set into the ground on the West Line as far as the sixty-fifth milepost. The official starting point for the milestones on the West Line was the northeast corner of Maryland and not the "Post mark'd West." Consequently, each of the stones had to be set up seventy-three links east of the original wooden markers to ensure that they lay at exactly one-mile intervals.

The gentlemen commissioners eventually convened at Christiana Bridge on November 17 for a six-day conference and social discourse with their surveyors. For reasons that were later to baffle Thomas Penn, the commissioners agreed with Mason's recommendation that this would be an opportune time to extend the West Line eastward to the banks of the Delaware River before the winter set in. The royal charter for Pennsylvania stipulated that the western extent of the territory should extend exactly five degrees west of the Delaware. To translate this into practical terms, it was necessary to establish the distance from Bryan's field to the river; the commissioners required this task to be Mason and Dixon's next priority.

At the meeting it was also agreed that after the winter break, the West Line should be continued beyond the Allegheny Mountains. However, to do so would require the agreement of the Six Nation Indian Confederation through whose lands, protected by the royal proclamation of 1763, the surveying party must traverse. One suggestion was that an offer should be made to the Indians to purchase the narrow strip of land. It was resolved therefore that if the proclamation's strictures had to be respected, the commissioners would then apply to the war hero General Sir William Johnson, "his Majesty's Agent for Indian Affairs," to negotiate on their behalf. Johnson and his colleague John Stuart were the two agents appointed by the British government to manage the provisions of the proclamation. General Johnson was intimately familiar with Indian affairs, having lived among the tribes. He had even married a Mohawk woman, Mary Brant, who, after Johnson's death, encouraged her people to support the British cause in the Revolutionary War.

That weekend Mason and Dixon found themselves once more in Alexander Bryan's chilly field, setting up their instrument at the "Post mark'd West," but preparing to head east.

CHAPTER 17

Vibration of the Pendulum

ON TUESDAY, November 25, 1766, following the meeting with the commissioners, the chaining party set off from Mill Creek to measure the short distance east to the banks of the Delaware River. They crossed Christiana Creek on the twenty-ninth, measuring its width with the Hadley quadrant. The next day they recrossed the same river before arriving in a freezing, windswept triangle of marshy land between the Brandywine and the Delaware owned by William Pewsey of Philadelphia. On the banks of the main river they erected a tall wooden post "marked E, on the east side . . . in the Parallel of 15 statute Miles South of the Southernmost Point of the City of Philadelphia. This Post is distant from the Post marked West in Mr. Bryan's field 11 miles 20 chains 88 links . . . "

The next morning snow began to fall and the surveyors retreated to nearby Newport to compute their results and thaw out. Before leaving Newport for a Christmas break with the Harland family, Mason sent the trusty Jonathan Cope to remeasure the distance from the Tangent Line to the West Line, as he suspected there had been an error of one whole chain. Mason and Dixon's 1766 work on the West Line had finished for the winter, and would not continue beyond the Alleghenies unless General Johnson had success in his negotiations with the Indians. There was a distinct possibility that the Six Nations might not comply, in which case Mason and Dixon's work for the proprietors would come to a quick and untimely end.

In the meantime, rather than venturing abroad on expedition, Mason decided to dedicate their winter energies to the work of the

Royal Society. Nevil Maskelyne had taken advantage of Mason and Dixon's offer, which was to measure a degree of latitude, by including a request for gravity observations. To this end, Mason had taken receipt of John Shelton's astronomical regulator from the Royal Society. This was the same well-traveled clock used by Maskelyne on Saint Helena and by Dixon at the Cape of Good Hope during the 1761 transit of Venus. It had also been used by Maskelyne at Greenwich, and even accompanied him during the longitude measurements on Barbados. Maskelyne's instructions for setting up the clock were to adjust the pendulum to "the Upper Scratch No 3 . . . which answered to Sidereal time at St Helena . . . " The astronomer royal had calibrated the clock on Saint Helena to keep sidereal time. His purpose in keeping the pendulum the same length was to measure the tiny variations in its rate of swing caused by the different values of gravity. Mason's gravity measurements in Pennsylvania would be added to those from Saint Helena, Cape Town, London, and Barbados. The tiny variations at known latitudes and longitudes would further assist in developing a true shape for Earth.

John Shelton's regulator was set up in the tent in Harland's garden alongside the proprietor's clock, newly fitted with a pendulum fashioned from 40-year-old seasoned walnut. The two precious longcase clocks, wrapped in blankets for protection from the damp and intense cold, were fastened to a huge piece of timber 22 inches broad and 5¼ inches thick, sunk 4 feet into the hard clay ground. Astronomical observations for latitude, longitude, and sidereal time commenced on December 11, when the zenith sector was erected in its tent above the Stargazers Stone in Harland's back garden, "in the same Parallel that it stood in, in the year 1764."

The long chilly nights that followed were spent measuring zenith distances of stars and taking equal altitudes of transiting stars. At the end of a cold night, there was the prospect of Mrs. Harland's hot breakfast as the farmhands assembled. The index mark on the pendulum of the society's clock, which Mason called clock P, was set exactly as Nevil Maskelyne instructed, and the clock was put in motion. On December 16, Mr. Jackson, the Philadelphia clock maker who made the proprietors' timepiece that Mason had nominated as clock Q, hazarded the muddy tracks and deep snow to reach Harland's farm in order to clean and adjust his masterpiece. That same freezing night,

Stargazer's Farm—a view of John Harland's house from the Stargazer's Stone.
(Photograph courtesy Ruth Harlan Lamb)

Mr. Jackson watched Mason observe the "immersion" of a Jovian
moon—that is, the time when one of Jupiter's moons disappeared
behind the giant planet—which would facilitate an accurate determination of the longitude.

Snow flurries swept the barren garden and drifted against the tent;
the winter vegetables became shapeless humps beneath a snowy blan-
ket. Christmas morning dawned cold and cloudy; a little rain fell. The
Harlands and their English guests met at the breakfast table, where
the children sang a Christmas hymn, and Mason's thoughts turned
towards his own dear family, so very far away. The house was decorated
from top to bottom with garlands of holly and green boughs from the
woods. Mason ventured outside at midday to measure the temperature,
which had risen to forty-six degrees Fahrenheit. Inside, the Harland
family, with their friends and guests, celebrated the holy feast with a
plain meal followed by bowls of hot punch, sitting in front of the
blazing log fire. There would be no special presents for the children—
the great Dickensian Christmas was still a hundred years away. Instead, the mellowed adults played with the youngsters and told stories.
Carols were sung and parlor games enjoyed. Each man stood and gave

Astronomical clock (or regulator) by Recordon, 1762. (Photograph courtesy Armagh Observatory, Northern Ireland)

a recitation, or spouted a few lines of nonsense, and Jeremiah Dixon told them a story about a fierce sea battle.

Shortly after Christmas, a strong gust of wind shifted the zenith sector from its position; apprehensive that another accident could seriously damage the proprietors' precious instrument, Mason had it dismantled and stored away. The New Year's Sun rose into a bright blue sky at precisely 7:21 A.M. Outside it was bitterly cold with an air temperature of twenty-two degrees Fahrenheit below freezing. Observing the tedious equal altitudes at night in such temperatures was an enterprise requiring stamina and determination: "the immediate touch of the Brass was like patting one's Fingers against the points of Pins and Needles; the cold was so intense." The weather that New Year alternated between fine, clear days and driving snow or freezing rain; on

January 27 it was so cold that the falling rain froze to the trees, "such that the limbs of the Trees broke in a surprising manner, with the weight of clear Ice upon them." Mason blamed the extreme cold for the fact that when clock P stopped one evening, the pendulum had come to rest ten minutes of arc east of its vertical scale.

Around February 16, Mason made some preliminary longitude calculations, based upon the Paris observatory's predicted apparent times for the eclipses of Jupiter's moons. He calculated that John Harland's backyard was 5 hours 12 minutes 54 seconds (78 degrees 13 minutes 30 seconds) west of the longitude of Paris. Every day, until March 17, 1767, Mason and Dixon meticulously recorded the temperature in the instrument tent and of the air outside. "The vibration of the pendulum," the amount the pendulum swung either side of the vertical, was carefully measured using special scales fitted behind the swinging weights. The difference in time kept by the two clocks, day by day, was determined as usual by equal altitudes observed in winter temperatures that dropped below 10 degrees Fahrenheit.

The Royal Society's clock P was finally dismantled and packed away on February 28. On March 22 Mason and Dixon led their horses from the stable and headed for New Town to keep their next appointment with the commissioners. After waiting a couple of days at an inn in the town, and with no sign of the commissioners, they decided to set out for nearby Annapolis. The next morning they presented themselves at Horatio Sharpe's fine house, only to learn from the governor of Maryland that the proposed meeting had been postponed until April 28, as no word had been received from General Johnson on his negotiations with the Indians. After a few days idling around Annapolis, strolling along the waterfront and admiring the elegant townhouses, the two surveyors returned to the Brandywine.

On April 26 they were back in Philadelphia, meeting some of the Pennsylvania commissioners including Surveyor General John Lukens of Pennsylvania, who was a frequent participant in the commissioner's discussions with Mason and Dixon. The main meeting had been postponed yet again, this time until May 20. General Johnson had still not reached an agreement with the Six Nations that would allow the survey to proceed beyond the mountains and through their territory. The situation was a delicate one; or perhaps the bureaucracy was slow. The Agency for Indian Affairs was a British-imposed institution, staffed by

British officers under Johnson's command, much to the colonists' chagrin. The most likely cause for procrastination and indecision was that the boundary survey would extend some one hundred miles west of the 1763 proclamation's demarcation line. This point cannot have been lost on the Six Nations. All of General Johnson's skill and diplomacy was required to counter its ramifications for white settlement west of the Appalachians.

Meanwhile, John Lukens and Charles Mason enjoyed each other's company and discussed in detail both the work for the proprietors' boundaries and the measurement of a degree of latitude for the Royal Society. Lukens had been involved in the original survey of the Tangent Line and Mason was pleased to have him compare the society's statute yard with that used in the 1760 survey. Laying the two standards side by side, and using a magnifying glass, Lukens compared the lengths, exclaiming to Mason that the society's statute yard was "the thickness of a piece of parchment [approximately $\frac{1}{32}$ inch] shorter than theirs, with which they measured the tangent Line."

After a few days in the pleasant company of the Pennsylvania commissioners, Mason and Dixon returned to languish at John Harland's and continue the various physical observations for the Royal Society. Shortly after, a letter arrived from Philadelphia informing them that General Johnson was still negotiating with the Indians (or not as the case may be), and that the proposed meeting had again been cancelled. On May 24, a parcel arrived from Nevil Maskelyne, mailed from London on February 24; it had taken three months to traverse from Greenwich to the wilds of Pennsylvania. In the package, Maskelyne included a copy of the 1767 *Nautical Almanac,* requested by Mason, and a table for computing the Moon's angular distance from the Sun. The astronomer royal apologized for not including a copy of Mayer's tables of lunar distances, explaining that they were not yet completed. He also expressed his surprise that he had not received any word from the surveyors or any acknowledgment that they had received the Royal Society's instruments, including the precious pendulum clock. However, it appears that Mason must have sent a verbal message to Maskelyne, via some unnamed intermediary, that he would soon be writing. Having reproved the errant Charles Mason, Maskelyne went on to say that the Royal Society had come to learn that its clock had been damaged. The society required it to be sent to England immediately for repairs, as it would be needed for the next transit of Venus in 1769. How the society came by this misinformation is not clear.

The astronomer royal's pleasant letter, in which he signed himself "your sincere friend," included the latest news and gossip from London's scientific community. The lunar distance method for finding the longitude was, apparently, approved of by the public and coming into vogue (no mention of the diligent Harrison or his chronometer). John Bird had been awarded the princely sum of £500 from the Board of Longitude for his methods for dividing measuring circles and "taking apprentice, and instructing workmen in his art." The new achromatic lenses invented by John Dolland (1706–1761) also received praise from the astronomer royal. The new compound lens design, made from glasses of different refractive index, reduced the annoying rainbow effect common in plain lenses. Maskelyne reported enthusiastically that he had recently purchased a new 3.5-foot refracting telescope that magnified 140 times and was fitted with the new lens. The instrument had even proved to be superior to the observatory's 6-foot Newtonian reflector, an instrument that used a silvered parabolic mirror to collect and magnify the faint light of the stars. Maskelyne ended his ebullient letter with a request that Mason write immediately with a progress report on their achievements.

Mason forthwith sent the Royal Society's clock and a covering note with four of his men to Wilmington, where it was loaded on the ferry for the short journey upriver to Philadelphia. There it would be placed on a ship to Britain. On June 2, Mason and Dixon wrote letters to Maskelyne and to Charles Morton, secretary to the Royal Society, bringing them fully up to date. A detailed analysis of the society's clock performance was included, as well as the progress made on the measurement of a degree of latitude.

It was about this time, before the work on the West Line restarted, that Mason and Dixon determined their preliminary value of a degree of latitude for the Royal Society. The astronomical observations at the Delaware Middle Point and the Brandywine were readjusted for the latest values for aberration, nutation, and precession. With the star positions corrected, the zenith distances were adjusted and the latitude differences calculated between the Brandywine, the midpoint, and the starting post in Mr. Bryan's field. The precise angle between the Tangent Line and the meridian was also recalculated and compared to the angle determined by terrestrial measurements, the difference being just five seconds of arc. The whole meridian distance between the Brandywine to the Middle Point was calculated by a combination of plane trigonometry and ground measurements. The result was then transformed, using spherical trigonometry, to a (spherical) distance equivalent to 8,131.93 chains.

By the same processes, the distance between Bryan's meadow and the Middle Point was calculated and the spherical distance found to be 6,955.76 chains. All that remained was to calculate, by proportions, the distance for a degree of latitude. Their preliminary results are summarized in the following:

Brandywine to Middle Point	Latitude observed	Distance measured
Brandywine	39° 56' 19"	
Middle Point	38° 27' 34"	
Difference:	1° 28' 45"	8,131.93 chains
1° of Latitude = 68.73 miles.		

Post mark'd West to Middle Point	Latitude observed	Distance measured
Post mark'd West	39° 43' 23.4"	
Middle Point	38° 27' 34"	
Difference:	1° 15' 49.4"	6,955.76 chains
1° of latitude = 68.81 miles.		

Although Mason and Dixon were aware that Earth was not a perfect sphere, they did not have enough reliable information to compute their solutions on an ellipsoid. The whole purpose of these measurements was to ascertain the ellipsoidal dimensions of Earth. Using the dimensions of Earth derived by Alexander Clarke in 1866, Mason and Dixon's error proves to be less than 0.5 percent. Before Mason and Dixon left Britain, the accomplished Dr. Bevis had calculated that one degree of latitude 15 miles south of Philadelphia, based upon geodetic knowledge as it then stood, should be 69 miles 858 yards. He would be gratified to learn that his calculations were within 620 yards.

At about the same time, Mason and Dixon also determined the value for a degree of longitude along the West Line parallel, which worked out to be 52.86 miles. The Pennsylvania charter stated that its southern border with Maryland should extend 5 degrees of longitude west from the Delaware River. Multiplying 52.86 miles by 5 degrees produced a total distance for the Pennsylvania border of 264 miles 22.8 chains. The point where Mason and Dixon finished in June 1766 was 165 miles 54.88 chains from the "Post mark'd West." To this distance, Mason added the 11 miles 75.76 chains from the post to the banks of the Delaware. The balance, 86 miles 54.56 chains, was the distance remaining to the western limits of the province.

On June 3, word reached Mason and Dixon that General Johnson had finally reached an understanding with the Six Nations and the survey could continue west. A meeting of the commissioners had been called for June 16. Mason sent letters to Lord Baltimore and Thomas Penn in London, informing them of the agreement with the Indians and that his crew were preparing to finish the West Line survey.

The surveyors began to make ready for the final phase of the work. Seven men were dispatched with the zenith sector to Mr. Spear's house on the Youghiogheny River; their instructions were to rendezvous at the place where they had left off in 1766.

Success in General Johnson's negotiations with the Six Nations had hinged on the Indians' trust in the provisions of the 1763 proclamation, which restricted European settlement to the east of the Allegheny divide. The Indians questioned the commissioners' desire to run the survey any farther than the Allegheny divide. For them, the greatest western excursion they could tolerate, and still retain some faith in the word of "the great King over the Waters," was the Monongahela valley.

In his letter to Thomas Penn, Mason clearly thought that Johnson's agreement with the Indian chiefs went only as far as the western extent of Maryland and not to the limits of Pennsylvania. Mason knew that on the West Line, the divide of the rivers was in the region of Savage Mountain. Maryland's royal charter stipulated that the province's southern border was the Potomac River, which rises in the Backbone Mountain region of the Alleghenies and flows east. Its western border was a line due north of the source of the river that crossed the West Line some thirty miles west of Savage Mountain. Mason therefore thought the limit of the survey would lie between these two extremes.

The commissioners of Pennsylvania and Maryland convened on June 16 for a three-day meeting with their surveyors to discuss the final phase of the work. To mark the boundary line, 139 boundary stones, prepared in England for the purpose and shipped by Penn, had arrived in Baltimore (named for George Calvert, First Lord Baltimore) and were ready for collection. In addition, the commissioners required stone cairns raised at the summit of every mountain ridge the line would cross.

On the last day of the meeting, Mason and Dixon received their written brief, probably drafted by the lawyer Benjamin Chew. The commissioners' instructions were to complete the survey to "the End of Five Degrees of longitude from the River Delaware," some eighty miles beyond the proclamation's limits; the consequence of this would manifest itself later.

The commissioner's instructions continued:

> A Number of the Indians have been deputed by the Six Nations (whose Consent hath been obtained to our extending the West Line to the Western Limits of the Province of Pennsylvania) to be present at, and attend you in running the said line. As the public Peace and your own Security may greatly depend on the good Usage and kind Treatment of these Deputies, we commit them to your particular Care, and recommend it to you in the most earnest Manner not only to use them well yourselves but to be careful that they receive no Abuse or ill treatment from the Men you may employ in carrying on the said Work, and to do your utmost to protect them from the Insults of all other persons whatsoever.

The commissioners were echoing General Johnson's concern that given the colonists' hostility towards the Indians, the native guides might receive insults and abuse from the hired hands. Johnson had assured the chiefs of the Six Nations that every effort would be taken to avoid this; it was also British policy. In an addendum, the commissioners added that the liquor rations for the Indians were to be in small and diluted quantities, not more than three times a day. It is also apparent that the commissioners believed the last section of the line might well prove the most hazardous. The dire reference to "the public Peace and your own Security" was not lost on Mason and Dixon. Their brief but bloody encounter with the French navy in the English Channel just six years before, still a vivid memory, mingled in their minds with the Paxton Boys' recent rebellion and the multifarious stories of Indian scalping, torture, and brutal murder.

CHAPTER 18

Not One Step
Further

THE WAGONS ARRIVED at Fort Cumberland on July 7, laden with the precious instruments, tents, and provisions. Not far from the run-down fort, Mason and Dixon were enjoying the cordial hospitality of one Colonel Crisep, on his beautiful estate overlooking the Potomac River. It was less than ten miles from Crisep's home to where work had ceased thirteen months before. Shortly after daybreak the following day, the colonel accompanied his guests on their short cross-country trek. Long before night cloaked the forest trees, camp had been erected, supper cooked, the instruments checked, and the marks of the previous year recovered.

The next morning, the sun rose just before five. The cooks had breakfast prepared, and Mason addressed the men while they ate. He was in somber mood as he read out the strict instructions of the commissioners. Shows of bigotry or disrespect towards the Indian guides, when they arrived, would not be tolerated. The forty men nodded, but many muttered obscenities under their breath, while others checked the keenness of their blades. Following Mason's admonitions, the cutting crews collected their axes and began work, opening up a vista to the east, while the chaining crew set off west, across the proclamation's line of royal prohibition.

The summit of Savage Mountain was crossed on July 14, 168 miles 78 chains from Mill Creek. Below the peak, the laurel swamps and dark pines gave way to tall spruce breaks and sunny glades. The cherry trees and wild flowers "resembled a Garden desolate." A few days later Captain Hugh Crawford with three Onondagas and eleven

Mohawk "deputies" strolled into camp "with instructions to conduct us through their country."

Sixty-five years before Lewis and Clark set out on their epic exploration up the Missouri to discover a passage to the Pacific, Crawford and men like him were already exploring the vast wilderness beyond the American frontier. They were hunters, traders, and trappers, supplying rich furs for the European markets. Crawford had first ventured into the uncharted territories west of the Allegheny Mountains while still a young man, maybe no older than eighteen. Between 1739 and 1755 he wandered the vast territory west and south of Pittsburgh, and down the Mississippi as far south as the Red River. He had explored many of the major rivers that drained into the Ohio, following them up into the rolling hills toward the Great Lakes and south into the steep, narrow valleys of the forested mountains.

He was on good terms with many of the Indian tribes in the region, trading trinkets for furs and animal skins. An intelligent and observant man, Crawford was a natural geographer; in his head he carried a map that was as complete a picture of the Northwest as then existed. The lands he explored were native provinces, where British, French, and Spanish interests were only beginning to emerge. When war broke out with France in 1755, he had been recruited into the army as "a Commander in his Majesty's Service," where his intimate knowledge of the dispositions of the French forts was invaluable. His war service, and his deep appreciation of the ways of the Indians and his familiarity with the land, made him the ideal choice for leading the Mason and Dixon party west. Crawford, then in his late forties, was an impressive figure, clad head to foot in buckskins, a large knife at his hip and his musket always in hand. The Indian guides would have no trouble from the hired hands while Hugh Crawford was around. His easy manner and pleasant demeanor immediately endeared him to the younger Englishmen he had come to lead.

The chief crewmen, Joel Bailey, Will Darby, and Jonathan Cope, together with Mason and Dixon, gathered to listen to Crawford's briefing. There was conflict between some of the tribes to the west. The Seneca were on the warpath against their traditional enemies, the Cherokees. Delaware Indians were also about in large numbers and there was a serious chance of trouble. Mindful of Crawford's words of warning, progress through the forest took on an air of urgency. On

July 25, the party reached the end of their first 10-minute great circle arc, 177 miles 4.45 chains west. Once more, the direction was changed by the offset method as they prepared to head into the rugged Laurel Mountains. Jeremiah Dixon spent his thirty-fourth birthday struggling over the inhospitable terrain and peering behind trees. The top of Little Laurel Hill was crossed on August 1, and five days later they reached the end of the section. Normally, Mason would have set up the zenith sector to observe latitude, but either the ground was unsuitable or he was confident from experience that the great circle offset method was safe enough. Or perhaps Crawford counseled against unnecessary delay. At 189 miles 57 chains they crossed and recrossed General Braddock's fateful military road; a few miles later, they arrived at the banks of the Youghiogheny River. Along the valley seven families still farmed the rich river land, but it was a dangerous frontier country, and many of the pioneer homesteads were abandoned for fear of renewed Indian attacks.

The Youghiogheny River was nearly dry; the water flowing over its hard black stones was scarcely a foot deep. There was no need to measure its width with the Hadley quadrant. Instead they were able to chain straight across via a small islet in the middle of the river. A few miles later, they passed the western boundary of Maryland, unremarked, followed by the end of the third 10-minute arc. On August 16 some of the hands were sent back along the line to retrieve the zenith sector from Mr. Spear's house on the river. The next evening the sector was set up, 199 miles 63.68 chains west from Alexander Bryan's field in distant Mill Creek. Every night from August 17 to 23, Mason and Dixon took turns lying beneath the tall telescope, peering at the misty stars, watched by their curious and silent Indian guides. In modern instruments, the sighting hairs (reticule) in the eyepiece can be softly illuminated so that they are clearly visible against the black night sky. How Mason and Dixon illuminated their wires is not known, but one common trick was to hold a torch near the object lens to throw just sufficient light into the tube to illuminate the reticule. Perhaps Dixon held a candle in such a way, while Mason stared through the instrument. On the other hand, perhaps Joel Bailey held the candle while Dixon booked the readings; we shall never know the simple practicalities, for they were commonplace and not considered worthy of record.

The zenith observations of stars were processed and the latitude calculated. They were 9.9 seconds, or 330 feet, north of the true parallel, a very acceptable error considering the expeditious technique. While they were making the stellar observations, they were visited by a band of thirteen Delaware led by a nephew of Captain Black-Jacobs, an Indian chief killed by General Armstrong during the recent war. The Delaware were not members of the Six Nations "and lived in the region by their [the Confederation's] leave." The nature of the encounter is not recorded, but there must have been a tense moment when the two Indian parties met. Black-Jacob's nephew was huge, "the tallest man I ever saw." The visiting Indians stayed some time, watching the strange antics of the white men as they studied the night sky. What the Indians must have thought of the giant zenith sector can only be speculation, but eventually they melted back into the forests, leaving the survey party wondering and uneasy. John Green, one of the Mohawks, left the party with his nephew "to return to their own Country," and report the encounter to the Six Nations.

The cutting party set to work clearing an eight-yard-wide vista eastward, back toward Savage Mountain. A new direction was set out on the ground starting in the true parallel, and the chaining crew set off again, westward. The land was a bleak, barren limestone wilderness, with sudden deep bottoms and steep cliffs. Chaining was difficult, and they had to resort to using the levels on the steeper inclines. Nevertheless, they were averaging some 8 chains an hour. In all probability there were three chaining crews working leapfrog; a practical and efficient method of progressing, and expeditious under the circumstances. At 211 miles 13.28 chains from the "Post mark'd West," at the foot of the Laurels, they changed direction by the offset method to return to the boundary's true parallel of latitude. The highest summit of the range was reached on September 8, where the party was rewarded with a vast panorama: " . . . from the Summit of the Westernmost Ridge . . . there is the most delightful pleasing View of the Western Plains the Eye can behold. From hence the end of our Line may be seen, and about 10 Miles farther, which reaches a Ridge or Ridges, that divides the Waters running into the Monaungahela from those running into the Ohio." Eight miles north of this beautiful view, the sad remains of General Braddock and his brave soldiers shared their common, desolate grave.

The Cheat River, dammed in modern times to create the long, thin Lake Cheat, was reached on the morning of September 12. The river was some 220 yards wide, but its waters were low and scarcely two feet covered its smooth, sandy bottom. Two of the Mohawk guides thought that the Cheat River marked the limit of their commission. Crawford and the chief of the guides called a council to discuss the matter. The survey team was twenty miles beyond Maryland's western limits, and well past the Allegheny divide. There was still some forty-five miles to go before they reached the full five degrees of longitude west of the Delaware. The limit for the work, agreed to by Johnson with the Six Nations, was, by its very nature, vague, and there was disagreement among the Indian guides over what marked the western extent. A river was a time-honored and logical boundary, and the Mohawk's view was that the Cheat was it. Up to this point, Mason and Dixon had probably restricted mention of their true objective, to run the whole distance to the limits of Pennsylvania, to Hugh Crawford alone.

After lengthy debate, the Indians concluded that the survey could continue beyond the Cheat but whether they would pass the next major river, the Monongahela, some ten miles further, was yet to be seen. The next day was Sunday, and Mason and Dixon decided to rest the crew. The Cheat was well stocked with large, succulent catfish that provided a pleasant diversion for the men and a change of diet for surveyor and Indian alike. The normal practice of supplementing their diet by hunting game with guns had ceased for fear of inadvertently arousing attention. Even the Indian deputies were wary of venturing too far abroad on hunting trips.

At 221 miles west, Mason sent some hands to collect the zenith sector from the last station, then called a halt. The sector was set up on the top of a high bluff, below which the Monongahela River meandered through its wide valley. The tedious round of observations began on the night of September 19. Crawford asked Mason how long the observations would take, and was not encouraged by the answer. The men were getting nervous about their predicament and needed something to occupy their minds. Crawford and Mason decided to have the men build a log cabin, 2 miles downstream, as a temporary store for the zenith sector. In all probability it was in Crawford's mind that the cabin would provide some refuge in case of an Indian attack. The site he chose, carefully selected for the best defense, lay in a narrow triangle of land between the Monongahela and Cheat Rivers.

While the men were occupied cutting timber and building the storehouse, Mason, Dixon, and the other surveyors got on with the astronomical observations. The last readings were taken on September 26 and the following day was spent calculating the result; they were 3.57 minutes, or 5.41 chains, south of the true parallel. That same day a new direction was set out in preparation to move on.

Despite the tree felling, store building, and vista cutting, the enforced ten-day break had still allowed time for the men to reflect and gossip, and to worry. The presence of the strange and silent Indian guides, whom the men neither trusted nor understood, the stalking proximity of hostile Shawnee and Delaware, and the great empty land all about had unnerved them. When it was time go, twenty-six men refused to cross the river and a further fifteen axmen needed coaxing, reassurances, and, perhaps, threats from Hugh Crawford to remain on the payroll. The survey party was down to below half strength, which was a serious concern for Mason, Dixon, and Crawford. Despite the surveyors' strength in firearms and the log cabin refuge, it would be an uneven match if Indians attacked. The men were acutely aware that the scouting Delaware had already assessed their strength and passed on the news.

Pressing forward despite their lingering doubts, the party crossed the almost dried-out Monongahela. Scouting with Crawford on the far side, Mason caught a lizard, "near a foot in Length," and was also surprised by the abundance of surface coal, the mineral that was to bring wealth and prosperity to the region years later. Two miles beyond the river, Crawford and his scouting party reported that another band of Delaware had appeared. Their leader, accompanied by his wife, was Catfish, whose band of warriors included his nephew. Work stopped, and the Indians called a diplomatic council. The Indians, Mason, Crawford, and the surveyors sat in a circle around the campfire while the pipe was passed from hand to hand. The leader of the guides stood to make a speech to Chief Catfish, explaining the purpose of the strange white men with their chains and measures. There was no cause for concern, there was no hostile intent by the British fathers, and the Indians west of the mountains could live in peace just as the great king across the waters had promised. Mason and Crawford presented strings of wampum and some trinkets to Catfish as tokens of peace and goodwill, which for the time being seemed to satisfy the Delaware chief. The Indian visitors departed peacefully with a promise to return.

To be on the safe side, Crawford sent one of the men to Fort Cumberland for fresh hands to replace the twenty-six who had quit and to report the position of the survey party. A few miles later the obliging behavior of the Delaware was explained when a war party of eight Senecas appeared out of the trees. The Seneca were members of the Six Nations Confederation and received a warm welcome from Crawford's Onondagas and Mohawks. The Senecas, armed to the teeth with bows and arrows, tomahawks, and muskets, were headed south for a confrontation with the Cherokees. Their passage through the forest had intimidated the foraging Delaware. The Senecas stayed with the surveyors for a few days; in return, they received gunpowder and war paint from the grateful Mason. On Wednesday, October 7, a fresh contingent of hands arrived from Fort Cumberland and the party was back to full strength—some forty men all told, including axmen and cutters, wagoners, and domestic staff. In addition, there were the twelve remaining Indian guides and the stalwart Hugh Crawford. All were well armed and ready for trouble.

At a distance of 231 miles 20 chains west, the survey team crossed a major Indian warpath running alongside the meandering Dunkard Creek "that takes its name from a small town settled by the Dunchards." The Dunkards were a pacifist religious sect of German origin who had first settled in Pennsylvania in 1719. On the outbreak of war in 1755, hostile Indians had attacked the tiny settlement in the depths of the Pennsylvania wilderness, and razed it to the ground; nearly all its inhabitants had been massacred. A mile and a half beyond the warpath, the chief of the Indian deputies approached Mason and Hugh Crawford to inform them that they had reached the limit of their agreement with General Johnson. The chief stated emphatically that he "would not proceed one step further Westwards." After protracted but fruitless negotiations, the Indians insisted they would not go any further west; it was the end of the line for them.

Mason and Dixon wrote a letter to the commissioners:

10 October 1767, Near the 230th Mile Post.

Sir,

In our last of the 2nd Inst. we informed you of the Desertion amongst our Men at the Monanegehela. Their Places we soon supply'd by Hands from Fort Cumberland and Pitts and should have finished the Line before the End of this Month. But on

NOT ONE STEP FURTHER

the 9th Inst. we crossed a Warrior Path (used by the Six Nations to go against their enemies the Cheroqueas). There we were informed by the Chief of our Indians that he was come to the Extent of his Commission from the Six Nations to go with us on the line; and that he would not proceed one Step further.

Finding they could not be prevailed upon to go further with the line we set up the Sector at the Distance of 233 Miles 13 Chains 68 Links from the Post marked west in Mr Bryans Field and found we were 3 Chains 38 Links to the South of the true Parallel.

We are now opening a Visto in the true Parallel location and have about 25 Miles to cut open. This and placing Piles of Stones on the Ridges &c (to the East'd of the Allegany Mountains) we think we cannot finish in less than Six Weeks.

We shall bring the instruments with us and be at Philadelphia about the End of December if we receive no Orders to the contrary. We have this Day drawn a Bill on Mr Carey for £500 and by the time we have opened the Visto above mentioned of 25 Miles (which will be in 3 Weeks) our Commissary will be in Debt Three Thousand Pounds.

We are Sir, your most obedient humble Servants

Cha Mason

Jere Dixon.

The next evening the zenith sector was set up for the last time, 233 miles 13.68 chains from the "Post mark'd West." While the stellar observations were made, a party of cutters was dispatched to start opening the vista eastward from the Monongahela. Six days later this same party was recalled; the reason is not known, but it may have been as a result of rising tensions in the camp. Another large band of Delaware had showed up, this time led by "Prince Prisqueetom," the eighty-six-year-old brother of the chief of the Delaware Indians, curious to see the white men who had suddenly appeared on his borders. The old man spoke excellent English and seemed peaceful and courteous enough. He told Mason and Dixon that "he had a great mind to go and see the great King over the Waters; and make a perpetual Peace with him; but was afraid he should not be sent back to his own Country." In conversation, Prisqueetom waxed lyrical about the lands to the west around the Ohio and Mississippi Rivers. Mason recorded the old man's descriptions of the rich land and wide meadows, "whose verdant plains never heard the Milk Maid singing blithe and gay."

The zenith distance observations were completed by the evening of October 17, and the latitude for the sector's position was found to be 223 feet too far south. The true point lay just to the east of a ridge of high ground, so Mason first extended the line 3 chains 80 links westward before laying off the 223 feet north. This point was the absolute limit of the great survey, 233 miles 17.48 chains west from Alexander Bryan's farm and 31 miles short of the western boundary of Pennsylvania. Here they raised "a stout post and heaped around it Earth and Stone three yards and a half diameter at the Bottom and five feet High. The figure nearly conical." This was the very spot that became Brown's Hill, near Mount Morris, the site of the Mason-Dixon monument where, on October 11, 1997, the citizens of Greene County commemorated the 230th anniversary of the historic event. No doubt Charles and Jeremiah would have been amused to know that the citizenry celebrated with home-baked Mason-Dixon buckwheat cakes and staged raft races on the creek along which early settlers had feared for their lives.

All that remained of the West Line survey was to cut the eight-yard-wide vista and set up the milestones. On October 20, with a mixture of reluctance and relief, Mason and Dixon turned their backs on the West and set off from whence they had come. They reached the 225th milepost on October 24, where they received a letter from Thomas Penn, dated August 7 in faraway London. Penn was pleased with their progress and that the Six Nations "had consented for the survey to progress to the extent of the province of Maryland." On November 5, the cutting work was finished, and Mason was able to report that there was one complete eight-yard-wide vista running from Dunkard Creek all the way to the Delaware Tangent Line. They were in safe country now, and it was time for Hugh Crawford to leave them. Mason and Dixon bid farewell to their friend and his Indian companions who, together with twenty-seven of the hired hands, headed back to their distant homes. As Mason watched Crawford depart, he reflected on what he had learned about the western marches and the Ohio from his extraordinary American friend and resolved to put it all down in his journal. Combining Crawford's information with his own observations, Mason filled six close-written pages describing the geography and natural resources of the country west of Savage Mountain, along the Ohio as far as the Mississippi and north to the Great Lakes.

Those who remained with Mason and Dixon included the redoubtable Jonathan Cope, Joel Bailey, and twelve laborers, "to Erect Marks in the Line etc." On November 13, it began to snow, and seven days later the weather was so poor that the laborers refused to work. Seven of the men packed their bags and quit, and replacements had to be found from the inhabitants of Will's Creek Valley.

Shortly afterward, the weather improved a little and they were able to move on, but the work was hard and tedious. At each summit, the commissioners' instructions demanded that a large cairn of stones had to be erected. In all, forty-five cairns were needed to mark the highest Appalachian ridges that were crossed by the line. By the end of November, the depleted team were back at Town Hill, where they met up with Richard Farrow, their labor contractor. Farrow and his men had been hauling the thirty tons of stone markers across the mountains and setting them in place; now Jonathan Cope was sent to North Mountain to check that their work was satisfactory. At Coneeocheague, on December 4, a letter was written and sent by express to the commissioners, informing the gentlemen that "Messrs. Mason and Dixon expected to be in Philadelphia on December 15."

Exhausted, the two surveyors finally arrived at the warmth and safety of John Harland's hearth on December 9. A letter awaited them from Benjamin Chew, advising them that the commissioners wished to meet them in Christiana Bridge on the twenty-third. Chew also informed the surveyors that he had written to the Maryland commissioners "expecting them to confirm and put an end to this tedious Business." Chew was becoming impatient, alarmed at the rising costs in the budget, even commenting that the placement of the mile stones "at an Expense which can be borne" was in doubt; indeed, a heap of milestones was abandoned at the bottom of Sideling Hill and rediscovered in 1910.

When Mason and Dixon had written to the proprietors at the start of their epic journey, they had set out their objectives and time estimates, which no doubt formed the basis for Mr. Chew's budget and his complaint:

> . . . to settle the Latitude of the southernmost point of the City of Philadelphia [completed January 4, 1764].

> . . . to find a Point . . . 30 miles west [and] having the same Latitude [John Harland's plantation, completed March 4, 1764].

. . . to measure 15 miles . . . South [Alexander Bryan's field and the Post mark'd West, completed May 18, 1764] . . . and to proceed to run the Parallel of Latitude [not started until March 1765 and completed October 19, 1767].

. . . on the 15 June (1764)... begin the tangent Line [started June 25, 1764, completed November 21, 1764].

Whether Mason and Dixon seriously believed they could complete the basic work and run the West Line "by the end of next Summer" (i.e., 1764) is most unlikely. Nevertheless, from Mr. Chew's weary lament, it seems that all parties had underestimated the difficulties and delays the survey would encounter, and the costs for the project had risen far beyond expectation. All the commissioners were present on December 24 to hear Mason and Dixon's account of their adventures, and to settle the financial accounts with Mr. McClean. On the last day of the three-day meeting, the commissioners informed the two Englishmen that "the Honourable Proprietors of Maryland and Pennsylvania had no further occasion for more lines to be run." The great eighty-year boundary dispute was finally and happily settled, and all in accordance with Lord Hardwicke's dictum. Mason had hoped to receive a formal written discharge from the commissioners, but this was not forthcoming. Instead, they were asked to produce a map of all the lines and determine the value of one degree of longitude on the West Line parallel.

The two tired surveyors returned to John Harland's plantation to start work on the map and calculate a degree of longitude. After a few days rest they returned to Philadelphia and handed over the solution for a degree of longitude to Richard Peters. Mason's covering letter is not only an excellent disclaimer, but also a succinct contemporary statement of mid-eighteenth-century geodesy:

By comparing our mensuration of a Degree of the Meridian with that made under the Arctic Circle [by Pierre Louis Moreau de Maupertuis in Lapland, 1735], supposing the Earth to be a Spheroid of a uniform Density; a Degree of Longitude in the Parallel of the West Line is 53.5549 Miles. But the Earth is not known to be exactly a Spheroid, nor whether it is everywhere of equal Density; and our own experiment [i.e., measuring the degree for the Royal Society] being not yet finished: We do not give in this as accurate.

Mason and Dixon were again back in Philadelphia on January 27, 1768, to deliver the map of the lines, drawn in the neat hand of Jeremiah Dixon, the land surveyor. Taking advantage of the city's facilities, letters were mailed to Messrs. Williams, Kingston, and Carrier; to Nevil Maskelyne, the astronomer royal; and to Dr. Katy, the new secretary of the Royal Society. A letter was sent to John Bird with the latest account of the instruments he had made and a reminder about the faults with the Hadley quadrant. A letter was also dispatched to the two proprietors, Lord Baltimore and Thomas Penn, in London, advising them that the commissioners had no further instructions and that they consequently "were preparing to remeasure the Line for the Royal Society"; that is, to measure the first degree of latitude in North America.

CHAPTER 19

A Degree
of Latitude

MASON AND DIXON'S work on their now famous line is perhaps their most enduring achievement. However, it was their final challenge in North America, the measurement of a degree of latitude, that made geodetic survey history. The theory for the calculation was simple. All they had to do was measure the distance from John Harland's farm, via Alexander Bryan's, to the Middle Point at the south end of the Tangent Line. From knowledge of the observed latitudes and the measured distance, it was a simple matter to calculate, by proportions, the ground equivalent of one degree of latitude. The latitudes had already been observed, during the first half of 1767. The only part missing was the precise ground measurement; it would take nearly four and a half months to complete.

Scientific work began in earnest on February 1, 1768, when Mason visited Joel Bailey's workshop in Chester. Bailey was fabricating two special levels to support the ten-foot-long fir rods tipped with brass made by John Bird and sent by the Royal Society. The rods and measuring levels were meticulously calibrated against each other and against the society's five-foot-long brass standard, under varying degrees of temperature and dampness. Mason's scientific demand for precision was clearly illustrated during the next twenty days of rigorous calibration.

The astronomical instruments, including the zenith sector, were no longer required and were taken to Philadelphia, where Mason and Dixon placed them in the care of Joseph Shippen, secretary of the province, on February 15. The transit instrument and Mr. Jackson's pendulum clock were subsequently moved to Shippen's home, while the reflecting telescope passed into the care of Reverend John Ewing. The zenith sector joined the unused Sisson sector and the Jersey Quadrant in the statehouse. The measuring procedure suggested by Maskelyne, and modified by Mason and Dixon's practical experience, was to stretch a length of cord along the already marked lines. The levels carrying the measuring rods were aligned with the cord to keep them straight. In this manner, by counting cord lengths (done by Mason, Dixon, and Joel Bailey personally) and cross-checking with the number of levels laid (counted independently by the chain carriers), the chance of error was minimized. The final gross check was to compare the new distances with those already measured between the Harland farm and the Middle Point in 1764.

Joel Bailey delivered the twenty-foot-long measuring levels to John Harland's house on February 22. The starting point for the measurement was the Stargazers Stone, where in 1764, the zenith sector had stood in the garden at the latitude of 39 degrees 56 minutes 18.9 seconds north. When the survey party set out next morning, on the first leg towards Alexander Bryan's plantation, it was freezing cold and snow was in the air. Within a hundred yards of Harland's house awaited the first major obstacle: a series of loops in the Brandywine River. Each crossing was measured by the now familiar baseline and horizontal angle method. But it is curious that despite the enormous care Mason took in calibrating the rods and levels, they measured only two of the three angles in each triangle, and then only the once.

During the first week, Mason set the cord's length equal to 13 levels (260 feet). On February 29 (1768 was a leap year), they shortened the cord to 10 levels (200 feet). Every morning and afternoon the four measuring rods, nominated as A, B, C, and D, were compared with the brass standard and the ambient temperature recorded. The variation of each rod against the standard was measured in steps of $\frac{1}{100}$ of an inch, probably with the aid of a microscope. The length of the brass standard had been calibrated to a certain temperature (60 degrees Fahrenheit) and itself would have varied with the changes in temperature. When cold, the brass would shrink and hence measure too long.

The mark that had been placed on April 4, 1764, on the north side of the road from Philadelphia to Nottingham, was reached on March 3; here a gross check on the measurement was possible. Seven days later,

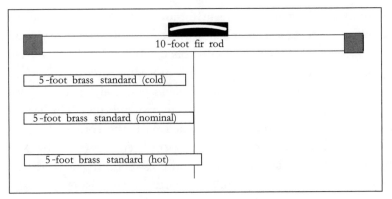

Calibration of rods against the brass standard.

they reached Mr. Bryan's field and tied out at the spot first occupied by the zenith sector in 1764. Having remeasured the distance from Harland's to Bryan's, the surveyors moved three miles due west to where the North Line intersected the West Line. Measuring south from this location, Mason made the cord equal to twelve level lengths, an arrangement he kept for the rest of the work. They reached the fourth milestone on March 18 and there discovered an embarrassing error. They were five levels short of the stone. The chain carriers had dropped a chain length during the original measurement. Other practical problems became manifest; Mason and Dixon were finding it difficult to keep the levels and the precision rods at an equal length. To overcome this problem they decided to abandon the rods and instead use the twenty-foot levels alone. Brass strips were fastened to the wood at precisely marked five-foot intervals calibrated directly against the brass standard.

From the tangent point they followed the Tangent Line southward toward the Middle Point stone, always comparing their new measures against the old. The weather remained cold and wet, and it even began to snow a little. On April 6, they arrived at the Bohemia River, whose width was measured from a short baseline set out on the north bank, observing the subtended angles with the quadrant. During the night, a frost turned the ground iron hard, and the next day it snowed heavily, blanketing the frozen landscape. From somewhere, Mason acquired or borrowed a foot sector, made of ivory by a Mr. Bennet, which he compared with the Royal Society's five-foot standard. This short instrument may have been a scale rule for plotting distances on maps, and Mason was making sure it was accurate. In fact, it had a small error of one part in 400 and was probably discarded.

Friday, April 15, was a miserable day of cold driving rain, which found Mason and Dixon wading through freezing swamp water two feet deep. On this wretched day, unbeknownst to him, the fellows of the American Philosophical Society in Philadelphia met to elect Charles Mason ARS as a corresponding member of the society, an honor justly deserved.* As the month advanced, the daytime temperature began to improve until, by the end of the month, it reached seventy degrees Fahrenheit. It also began to rain very heavily, and the swamps and low ground were quickly drenched. The measuring party kept doggedly to its path, even measuring through a four-foot-deep millpond that, Mason wryly noted, he "did not attend." Another error of one chain was discovered at the forty-third milestone, making the distance between it and the forty-second milestone too long. A thunderstorm broke on May 4 and brought the work to a temporary halt, adding its unwelcome inundation to the already high swamp waters. Nevertheless, the rate of progress was good; they were achieving some 1.4 miles a day.

The next day, in distant London, the Royal Society was in session interviewing the newly commissioned Lieutenant James Cook. He was to command a ship jointly sponsored by the society and the Admiralty to conduct, among other scientific endeavors, observations of the 1769 transit of Venus. The transit board in attendance that spring day included Nevil Maskelyne and the Royal Navy's longitude champion, Captain John Campbell, who had sponsored Cook's appointment. The astronomer royal recommended his observatory assistant, Charles Green, to accompany Cook, and he, too, was present before the august body. Cook and Green were offered 120 guineas each for victualing, and Green was granted a fee of 200 guineas for his services, plus an additional 100 guineas should the voyage's duration exceed two years. The society also arranged for the procurement of the scientific instruments for the transit, comprising two 2-foot Short reflectors, a Hadley quadrant

---

*Dixon was nominated with Mason but, for some unknown reason, was not elected until April 1, 1768.

constructed by Jesse Ramsden, a Shelton astronomical clock, and a
dipping needle for magnetic observations. Mason and Dixon, blissfully
unaware as they waded through the swamps of Delaware, would also
be recruited by the society. Meantime, they had arrived at the twenty-
third milestone on the Tangent Line, where they discovered an empty
hole. An aggrieved homesteader had contemptuously expressed his
opinion of proprietorship and absentee landlords by digging the stone
up and tossing it away.

In the riparian regions west of Dover, the rain continued to lash
the surveyors, filling swamps and ponds to overflowing. The wooden
levels were taking a battering but their precision was holding up,
despite the severe soakings. When the measuring party found the
depth of water in Marshy-Hope obliged them to wade through it up
to their necks, Mason "did not attend" once more and found alternative employment. But he did complain that the Royal Society's brass
standard had received a thorough soaking. On May 29, they reached
John Twiford's friendly house on the Nanticoke, where they were able
to dry out and renew their old acquaintances over Sunday lunch. The
measurement across the river was postponed until the chaining party
had completed its work as far as the Middle Point marker stone.

Mason and Dixon returned to the Nanticoke on Monday, June 6,
to measure its width; this was the last measurement needed to complete the work. They set out a 480-foot baseline on the north bank
and measured the angles formed by this baseline with a Hadley quadrant. This was not the same instrument used on the West Line, which
had been faulty, and where it came from is not recorded. It had an
ivory engraved scale "divided as Mr Bird's but the maker's name was
not upon it." By triangulation, the river's width was determined to be
633.4 feet. A final few days were once again spent in the company of
John Twiford and his family at a place Mason loved and to which he
hoped one day to return:

> Situated on the most Rural and delightful Banks of River
> Nanticoke. Here is the most pleasing Contemplative View I've
> ever seen in America; the River makes a turn from the South-
> ward to the Eastward nearly at Right Angles and not one
> House to be seen for 4 Miles: But Nature's genuine produce of
> Pine and Cedar on both sides its rural Bank's, for which Ships

resort from all parts to supply distant Climes destitute of so great a blessing.

Taking leave of their friend, the survey team departed first for Dover, then went on to Mount Pleasant and finally Newark, where the remaining hands were paid off. They spent a day with the Harlands before proceeding to a meeting with the commissioners of Philadelphia to report that all the fieldwork was completed. Benjamin Chew informed them that a full meeting of the commission was necessary before the Englishmen could be discharged.

For this last meeting, two hundred copies of Dixon's plan of the lines were required. The matter of the maps was discussed with Reverend Ewing, who had the original plans. He recommended a local engraver, Henry Dawkins, to make the printing plates of the two map sheets needed to cover the entire survey area. Mason and Dixon returned briefly to the Brandywine for one last time, to say farewell to their good friends, then returned to their lodgings in Philadelphia. Ten days were spent recalibrating the rods and levels against the brass standard and a brass yard that came with the zenith sector. They discovered, by many trials, that the two differed by 0.015 inch, which equated to some 15.84 inches per mile. Which standard was correct is not known; however, the length of the brass yard was carefully scribed onto the Royal Society's 5-foot standard that would accompany them back to England.

On July 18, Mason had to explain to a disappointed Benjamin Chew that Dawkins, the engraver, had completed only half the work and refused to proceed any further. Why Dawkins declined is not recorded, but the work was removed from his workshop and given to another local engraver, James Smither. When completed, the two engraved plates were passed to Robert Kennedy, a local printer, to run off the desired number of copies. On August 16, Mason and Dixon collected all two hundred of Kennedy's beautifully printed copies of Smither's "Map of the Provincial lines under ye Hand and Seals of the Comms of Maryland & Pennsylvania" and delivered them to the commissioners.

Several of the maps became legal documents for the provincial government's archives and for the two proprietors' records. On these copies, which the commissioners "DO certify that this Map is a true and exact plan and Survey," were appended the signatures and seals of all the commissioners. An explanation key on the eastern map succinctly described the work achieved, all in accordance with Lord Hardwicke's ruling of 1750:

A The beginning of the line run in the year 1751 from Cape Henlopen on Fenwicks Island to Chesapeak Bay

B The exact middle of that line and beginning of the tangent line

BC The tangent Line

CD A Line drawn due north from C the tangent point till it Intersect

DE The parallel of Latitude or west Line distant 15 Miles South of the most Southern part of the City of Philadelphia

F The point where the Meridian CD cuts the Circle drawn at 12 Miles distant from the Town of Newcastle.

On Wednesday, August 17, Reverend Peters visited Mason and Dixon to inform them that the commissioners were preparing to have a final meeting at Chestertown on the following Thursday. The meeting and festivities lasted three days, during which the accounts were settled, and "the whole work of our part relating to the Business we had been engaged in for the Honorable Proprietors of Maryland and Pennsylvania, was entirely finished."

Some critics, especially those of a legal mind, have challenged the commissioners' "true and exact" statement, arguing that from later twentieth-century surveys the Mason-Dixon line has shown variability from a true parallel. From a modern perspective, they are right; but from the historical and factual, they are in error. Lord Hardwicke's ruling was that the dividing line between Pennsylvania and Maryland was to be a line of constant latitude lying fifteen miles south of Philadelphia. At that time, latitude could only mean what we today refer to as astronomical latitude. Any other sort of latitude was unheard of: latitude was just latitude. Thus, substituting Hardwicke's understanding of the definition for one of a number of modern-day latitudes would be incorrect and a little obtuse. In 1849, a survey of part of the boundary lines was made by Colonel J. D. Graham of the U.S. Corps of Topographical Engineers. Commenting on the quality of Mason and Dixon's tangent line, Graham wrote with satisfaction that it "did not show two inches of deviation to the right or left of the centre of the post at the end of the due north line."

After two weeks relaxing in the City of Brotherly Love and enjoying Philadelphia society, its cultivated pursuits, late-night scientific discourse, and drinking with their American Philosophical Society colleagues, the two English surveyors said farewell and departed for New York. A further couple of days were spent sight-seeing, eating, drinking, and enjoying the nightlife of the bustling island metropolis. At 11:30 A.M., at the top of the spring tide on the warm morning of September 11, 1768, after four years and ten months in America, the two friends boarded the Halifax packet, homeward bound for Falmouth, Cornwall: "Thus ends my restless progress in America, C. Mason."

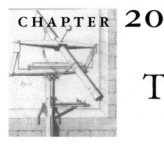

CHAPTER 20

The Last Transit

AFTER A TURBULENT crossing of the Atlantic, the two intrepid companions landed at Falmouth around the middle of October. The Royal Society's instruments were off-loaded together with the baggage and souvenirs of the trip as though Mason and Dixon were English gentlemen just returning from a sojourn in the colonies. From Falmouth, they traveled up the precarious road to London by stagecoach, and checked into the Prince of Wales Arms at the corner of Leicester Fields. This fashionable corner of London, dominated on the north side by the earl of Leicester's elegant mansion, then lay at the edge of town and overlooked the green of Saint James's. Leicester Fields was home to the artist Sir Joshua Reynolds, the first president of the Royal Academy, an eminent body that had just received royal approval. The painter William Hogarth had been a resident until his recent death. The king's surgeon, John Hunter, also lived there. Leicester Fields was also a convenient spot from which to visit John Bird, who worked a stone's throw away in the Strand.

Mason and Dixon sent letters to the two proprietors, advising them of their safe return, as well as to Nevil Maskelyne and John Bird. Mason's first priority was to see his family. Leaving Dixon to his own devices in London, Mason took the stage west to Cheltenham, in Gloucestershire. We can only imagine the emotions that passed when, for the first time in over five years, the children were reunited with the tall stranger who was their father. Mason could afford to stay only a short time with his family, as there was still much to do in London, but the city was not far away. After a week he rejoined Dixon at the Prince of Wales to complete their business with the proprietors.

On November 15, a letter arrived at the inn from Thomas Penn, sent from Hope House, his home in distant Windsor. Mason and Dixon learned that Mr. Penn would be in London on Thursday for a meeting at three o'clock. There was much to discuss over the excellent luncheon at the House of Lords. The commissary accounts had been settled in America, but there was also their fee to arrange. Mason took along his journal records to show and discuss with Penn, explaining how he and Dixon had undertaken the arduous project. The fate of this journal was unknown until 1861, when it mysteriously turned up in the cellar of Government House, Halifax, Nova Scotia.

Apart from renewing friendships and enjoying family life again, Mason and Dixon had to write up the results of all their work for the Royal Society and calculate the final value of the degree of latitude. The *Philosophical Transactions of 1768,* the society's journal, contained these results under the title "Observations for Determining the Length of a Degree of Latitude, in the Provinces of Maryland and Pennsylvania in North America." Nevil Maskelyne provided an introduction and Mason announced the answer as being 68.7291 miles. In the following year, they also published in *Transactions* the results of their work in John Harland's backyard: "Astronomical Observations Made at the Forks of the River Brandiwine in Pennsylvania, for Determining the Going of a Clock Sent Tither by the Royal Society, in order to find the Difference of Gravity between the Royal Observatory at Greenwich and at the Place where the Clock was set up in Pennsylvania."

While Dixon was enjoying London and Mason readjusted himself to family life, the Royal Society and the astronomer royal were well advanced with their plans for the forthcoming transit of Venus. The year 1769 would be another momentous one for astronomy and the last opportunity for a century to observe the event. The 1761 transit had not been without some problems, and the observations had not proved conclusive. The fact that Mason and Dixon never reached Sumatra had been one of the disappointments. Nevertheless, the coordination of the international effort had been impressive and owed much to the efforts of Mason's acquaintance Jérôme Lalande, as did the 1769 event. In the *Nautical Almanac* for 1769, Nevil Maskelyne included his detailed "Instructions Relative to the Observation of the Ensuing Transit of Venus." He would observe the phenomenon himself on June 4 from Greenwich, using the two-foot Short reflector. Even before Mason and Dixon had left America for England, Cook's converted 370-ton collier, HMS *Endeavour,* had already sailed for the Pacific. It had left Spithead on August 25 with Nevil Maskelyne's assistant Charles Green aboard, bound for Tahiti and with just nine months to complete the long voyage. The Pacific adventure was just one aspect of the Royal Society's joint undertaking with the Admiralty. When the time came for the transit, Cook's expertise as a proficient astronomical observer would be crucial. Sadly, Charles Green never again set eyes on England; scurvy, dysentery, and overwork exacted their final toll, and *Endeavour's* crew buried him at sea on January 29, 1771.

In Philadelphia, the American Philosophical Society was making preparations for a grand entrance onto the stage of international science. For the society, it was an opportunity to add an accurate longitude value to Mason and Dixon's latitude for their city. The society formed a Transit Committee, which selected three different observing sites for the transit, just in case the weather interfered. The sites chosen were David Rittenhouse's plantations at Norriton, twenty miles northwest of the city; Lewes in Sussex County, near Cape Henlopen; and Statehouse Square in Philadelphia. David Rittenhouse, provost of the University of Pennsylvania and a distinguished mathematician, astronomer, and surveyor, was one of the experts who supervised Mason and Dixon's boundary survey. At his suggestion, the American Philosophical Society built an observatory at a cost of £60, in the courtyard of Philadelphia's Statehouse. A reflecting telescope, fitted with a Dolland micrometer, was purchased at enormous expense from the London instrument maker Edward Nairne. Thomas Penn graciously granted the society use of his wonderful zenith sector as well as the transit and equal altitude instrument, all of which were installed within the new observatory building. Penn also acted as an intermediary between the American Philosophical Society and the Royal Society and the astronomer royal in London, to coordinate efforts and share information.

In early 1769, Mason and Dixon were again retained by the Royal Society on a six-month contract, to conduct transit of Venus observations. Jeremiah Dixon was sent to Norway; his companion on this occasion was the astronomical observer William Bayly (1737–1810). Bayly, the son of a Wiltshire artisan, had come to the notice of Maskelyne because of his mathematical prowess. The astronomer royal employed him as an assistant at the Royal Observatory and would engage him as the astronomer on Cook's voyage of 1772 and, later, on the fateful expedition of 1776–1780. Dixon and Bayly sailed for Norway aboard the *Emerald,* arriving on May 7 at Hammerfest on Kvaløya, at seventy-seven degrees north latitude. Among their instruments was an astronomical pendulum clock, made by John Shelton (perhaps the well-traveled instrument with which Dixon was so familiar), that had just been calibrated in the Greenwich Observatory. During a visit to the observatory on April 17, Daniel Bernoulli (1700–1782), the outstanding Swiss mathematician, had noticed the clock in the mural room ticking majestically alongside one of John Harrison's busy little chronometers.

With Dixon and his instruments safely ashore, a local fishing boat took Bayly along the treacherous coast to Meagerly Island, sixty miles northeast from Hammerfest, to make separate transit observations at the North Cape of Norway, should the Norwegian weather interfere. In addition to viewing the transit of Venus from the most northerly of all the observing sites, Dixon and Bayly had also been instructed to map the treacherous coastline and islands around Norway's northern cape.

Charles Mason, with his assistants, was sent to Cavan, Ireland, at the end of May. Among his instruments was an eighteen-inch-radius quadrant made by his friend John Bird. This beautiful instrument was made for the Royal Society in 1767 and is now on display in London's Science Museum. From Cavan, Mason observed the transit of Venus and the accompanying partial solar eclipse of June 4. On that great day, the Sun rose just after four in the morning; to its left the tiny black dot that was Venus was beginning to appear and to the right of the Sun lay the invisible disk of the approaching Moon. At about seven o'clock that evening, the long-awaited transit, the last for a hundred years, began; silhouetted against the brilliant disk lay the tiny black circle of Venus. Mason's stay in Cavan lasted until September, during which time he observed some immersions of the satellites of Jupiter, the time when the tiny moons disappeared behind the great gas giant, in addition to the transit and the eclipse. He also observed the appearance of the famous comet that was said to have heralded the birth of Napoléon Bonaparte. Had he known it, Bonaparte's nemesis, the baby Arthur Wellesley (later the Duke of Wellington), lay in his mother's arms in nearby Dublin.

For Dixon, in the Land of the Midnight Sun, the sight was even more spectacular. The Sun was in the sky all the time, neither rising nor setting. At the high latitudes, the partial eclipse was more profound than in Ireland, and nearly the whole of the Sun's disk was covered. Even the tiny disk of Venus was briefly obscured by the passage of the Moon.

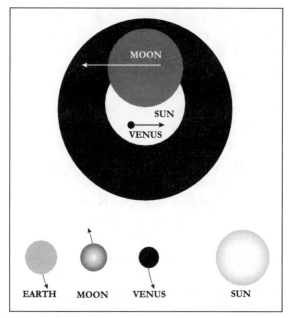

The transit of Venus. Above: view of the transit and
eclipse as it appeared through the telescope. Below:
schematic of the clestial mechanics.

In far away Pennsylvania, the American Philosophical Society's
campaign was a resounding success. David Rittenhouse confirmed his
earlier observations that Venus possessed an atmosphere. Unfortunately,
due to disagreement within the Transit Committee, there were no arrangements for joint publication of the American results. William
Smith, Rittenhouse, John Lukens, and John Sellers, who observed at
Norriton, sent their report to Thomas Penn, who passed it to Nevil
Maskelyne for publication in the Royal Society's *Philosophical Transactions.* The Cape Henlopen astronomers, including Owen Biddle and
the ever practical Joel Bailey, Mason and Dixon's right-hand man, sent
their report to Benjamin Franklin, who had it published in the same
issue of *Philosophical Transactions.* The observers at the Statehouse observatory, among whom was Reverend John Ewing, missed the deadline
and their report was not published until 1771. However, history had
been made. American astronomical science had come of age, and
exactly two hundred years later a U.S. astronaut walked on the moon.

CHAPTER 21

Legacy

WHEN NEVIL MASKELYNE, the "seaman's astronomer," succeeded to the esteemed position of astronomer royal on February 26, 1765, his first priority was to publish the *Nautical Almanac,* so useful to mariners. He personally supervised its content of nautical tables, lunar distances, and other information until his death. Maskelyne's administration was also marked by many improvements in the methods and equipment used by the Royal Observatory, the place he loved and where he died on February 9, 1811. He was a mild and genial man, of "estimable character," but a man of his class. He was awkward when dealing with the "lower orders" or the less mentally endowed, even to the point of pomposity. The astronomer Sir William Herschel remarked, after their first meeting in 1782, "That is a devil of a fellow!"; it was a great compliment.

Despite being deeply convinced that the lunar distance method was the most reliable and accessible way for the majority of mariners to find longitude, Maskelyne accepted the task of evaluating John Harrison's timepieces. Harrison's chronometers were for their day the most precise mechanical instruments ever devised, but Maskelyne, and many of his fellow scientists, seriously doubted that their precision could be reproduced in sufficient numbers, or at an affordable cost, to meet the demand. Poor reproductions would expose unwitting mariners to even greater perils if they trusted the accuracy of an inferior chronometer. Undoubtedly, Maskelyne believed himself the most qualified person to test Harrison's timepieces, knowing full well that he would be charged with conflict of interest. The testing and trials of

the chronometers exposed him to unfair and repeated attacks, especially from Harrison's supporter, the watchmaker Thomas Mudge,
against whom Maskelyne defended himself with great dignity. Nevertheless, the astronomer royal should have taken a greater interest in and
made a greater effort to understand the new technology. In later years
he came to both respect and admire many of the quality clock-and-
chronometer makers, but he never really understood the new machines.

Supporters of Harrison's invention, however, were more than sufficient, and vocal enough, to ensure the chronometer would succeed.
Many watchmakers began to copy and improve on his astounding H4.
Nevertheless, had Maskelyne and the Board of Longitude endorsed the
chronometer as early as 1765, the instrument would still have taken
years to be mass-produced. In the meantime, Maskelyne's Nautical
Almanac offered an affordable alternative. By the time chronometers
were becoming more available, in the late 1790s, the *Almanac,* a set of
tables, and a decent sextant could be purchased for less than 12
guineas, compared with over 60 guineas for a chronometer.

The first print run of the *Nautical Almanac* was ten thousand copies,
and it was snapped up by merchant marine and Royal Navy navigators. In the spirit of scientific cooperation, Maskelyne always ensured
his tables were available to his colleagues in France, and even to those
in the new United States of America. During the early years of the
Napoleonic conflicts, copies still got through the lines. Longitude, it
seems, transcended war. Longitude by lunar distances survived until
the end of the nineteenth century and tables continued to be published
into the twentieth; how many thousands of lives and precious cargoes
owed their well-being to nautical tables is beyond estimation.

After the transit of Venus campaign in Ireland, Charles Mason
moved to Tetbury to be close to his friend Robert Williams. He was a
frequent visitor to the house, and within a few months was engaged
to Williams's daughter, Mary. They were married in Saint Kenelm's
Church, Sapperton, in 1770, and set up home in nearby Bisley.

Sometime after Mason's remarriage, Jeremiah Dixon returned to his
native Cockfield, in County Durham, where he lived the comfortable
life of a "gentleman." He occasionally practiced as a land surveyor and
worked on the estates of Auckland Castle and Lanchester Common,
preparing maps of the estates and laying out the new field boundaries
of the Parliamentary Enclosures. In a directory of practicing land sur-

veyors, compiled from contemporary references, it is conspicuous that no Jeremiah Dixon is listed. This seems strange, given his skill and experience, and perhaps further research will one day throw light on this talented but enigmatic man. In 1773, for his outstanding contributions to science, he was elected a Fellow of the Royal Society. Jeremiah Dixon never married, although he became quite a wealthy man. He died on January 22, 1779, at the age of forty-five, and was buried in the Friends graveyard at Staindrop. In his will, he bequeathed much of his estate in trust to a Margaret Bland and her two daughters.

In 1772, the forty-year-old Nevil Maskelyne proposed to the Royal Society a method to measure the attractive forces of a mountain mass. It was known that variations in the Earth's mass affected the direction of the local vertical, as Mason had cautioned the American commissioners. A better understanding of this strange phenomenon would improve mapmaking and the knowledge of Earth's true shape. In 1773, the Royal Society sent Charles Mason on a reconnaissance of the Scottish Highlands to identify a suitable mountain for Maskelyne's experiment. Ideally, the chosen mountain would be symmetrical and afford easy access. After a summer tour exploring the hills and glens, Mason selected the Perthshire peak of Schiehallien as the best option. From June to October 1774, zenith distances of stars were observed on the west and east sides of the hill. By comparing the small differences from each location, the deviation of the vertical (plumb line) caused by the mass of Schiehallien was measured. The result of the deflections was just 11.56 seconds of arc. In 1775, for his "curious and laborious observations on the attraction of mountains," Maskelyne was awarded the society's greatest accolade, the Copley Medal. Mason received little or no recognition for his work.

Charles Mason continued to work for the observatory under Maskelyne's direction. Sponsored by the Board of Longitude and using the late James Bradley's observations, he compiled a catalog of 387 stars that was included in the *Nautical Almanac* for 1773. He also made further corrections to Mayer's lunar tables for the Board of Longitude comparing the results with his own comparisons from 1,220 of Dr. Bradley's "places of the moon." These latter were published in the *Almanac* for 1774 and continued to be included many years later. His last major publication was in 1778 as "Lunar Tables in Longitude and Latitude According to the Newtonian Laws of Gravity."

The early years of the 1770s saw Britain's relationship with its American colonies deteriorate at an alarming rate. Benjamin Franklin, his work done, knew he was needed back home. On March 20, 1775, he quietly slipped away from London and arrived in Philadelphia on May 5. The next day he was elected to the second Continental Congress, meeting in Philadelphia's Carpenter's Hall. On July 4, 1776, Congress secretly passed the Declaration of Independence, and a few days later it was read aloud to colonial Americans from the stage of the observatory in the Statehouse yard, where the transit of Venus had been observed.

In August 1776, Sir William Howe, supreme commander of the British land forces in America, captured New York. Howe's elder brother Richard, Admiral the Lord Howe of Langar, arrived in the colonies with a large squadron of warships. A man whose sympathies were with the colonial Americans, Admiral Howe tried for conciliation and had discussions with Franklin, John Adams, and Edward Rutledge, but neither side could come to terms. For good or ill, the die was cast.

The degeneration into war came as no surprise to Mason, and his heart must have sunk when he heard the news of the British occupation of Philadelphia late the following year. The Continental Congress fled to York to carry on the vital business of government. In Philadelphia, many of the city's valuables were hidden or buried. The famous Liberty Bell was taken down and, under the floorboards beneath the bell's supports, John Bird's transit and equatorial instrument was hidden away to lie forgotten for 135 years.

Mason's correspondence with his old friends across the ocean became impossible and he was concerned for their well-being. Benjamin Chew had been an early casualty among the British Loyalists when he refused to relinquish his crown appointment as chief justice and found himself under house arrest for a year in New Jersey. David Rittenhouse, an ardent revolutionary, became the Treasurer of Pennsylvania. In 1792, George Washington appointed him as the first director of the U.S. Mint. Reverend John Ewing, commissioner from Pennsylvania, outspoken Presbyterian, and a particular friend of Mason's, was also an American revolutionary. With the signing of the Declaration of Independence, Ewing declared he "would offer no prayers to George III."

The entry of France, Spain, and the Netherlands on the American side turned the war into an international conflict. With General Charles

Cornwallis's surrender of the British army in October 1781, the war in America ended, although it continued on the high seas. By 1780 Britain was in desperate straits; American privateers harassed shipping around its coasts and European enemies controlled the waters of the English Channel. Popular British support for the American war had never been great, and with the prospect of a wider defeat, the government was forced to come to terms with its position. On November 30, 1782, Britain and America signed a provisional peace accord in Paris that recognized the legitimate independence of the former colonies. When the news arrived in Philadelphia, "a great flag was hoisted on a lofty mast on Market Street Hill, and the people fastened their eyes on it by the hour, transferring to the emblem the veneration they felt for the achievers of the peace." There was a great fireworks display for the vast crowds that gathered to celebrate the victory. "The houses at night were illuminated generally, save those of the Friends, which, of course, afforded fine sport for the rabble in breaking in the dark panes." The following year the first American flag seen in Britain was flown from the mast of the *William Penn* when it arrived in the Thames. There was such an outcry in London that the crew had to keep a watch in case they were boarded. Hailed by John Adams as "one of the most important events that ever happened on this globe," the final peace treaty between Britain and the United States of America was signed in Paris on September 3, 1783.

With the war over and normalcy returning, Charles Mason reconsidered his old ambition of returning to North America with his family. He had received a paltry £1,317 from the Board of Longitude for his diligent work on the nautical tables, which, according to a friend, the French astronomer Jérôme Lalande, fell well short of his expectations. He had grown embittered toward the scientific community he had served so well and resentful toward Maskelyne and the Board of Longitude, which was dominated by learned men of rank and consequence. Neither was he honored by the Royal Society with a fellowship, unlike his friend Dixon.

Middle-aged, disillusioned, and in failing health, Mason nevertheless had enough money from the proprietors' survey and the Board of Longitude to return to Philadelphia, where he would be assured of a warm welcome from friendly, democratic, and enlightened men. Leaving England for the last time, Mason and his large family boarded the Falmouth packet in July 1786. On September 27 he wrote to the elderly Benjamin Franklin, with whom he was well acquainted from their days in London, advising of his return to Philadelphia. With him at "the Sign of the George," an inn on Second Street, were his wife, Mary, his seven sons, and a daughter, "all in a very helpless Condition." Despite ill health, Mason resumed many of his old acquaintances and friendships in the city, but by early October he was bedridden and dying. He passed many of his papers and astronomical works to the keeping of his friend John Ewing, who had become the provost of the University of Pennsylvania. His last request to his old friend was for the lunar tables to be further improved and published in the United States. On October 25, 1786, to the great distress of his friends and family, Charles Mason quietly passed away. He was laid to rest a few days later in the Christ Church burying ground, a plot of American soil 3,452 miles 53 chains southwest of the grave of his old friend Dixon. Born an Englishman, Mason died a citizen of the United States, in a land he loved.

The remaining thirty miles of the Mason-Dixon line were completed in 1785, all the way to the full five degrees of longitude west of the Delaware, in accordance with the original royal grant and Mason's calculations. The work was undertaken by John Lukens, Reverend John Ewing, David Rittenhouse, Thomas Hutchins, and the astronomer Andrew Ellicott, who seventeen years later instructed a young Meriwether Lewis in navigation by lunar distances.

Regrettably, John Ewing did nothing with Mason's astronomical works or his lunar tables, and passed the papers back to the widow. Mary Mason returned to England to pursue her late husband's claim for compensation from the Board of Longitude for his almanac work, with indifferent success. At a meeting of the board on December 1, 1792, her claim was denied and she was given a take-it-or-leave-it offer of a meager £100 for her husband's papers; she received a further £100 the following year. Mason's eldest sons, William Charles Mason and Doctor Isaac Mason (who remained in Philadelphia), also tried to get recognition for their father's work and won a paltry £3 18s.

Mason and Dixon's great legacy to science and surveying still endures, and it deserves the highest recognition.

Their instruments remained in use for many years. Bird's six-foot zenith sector was used in 1769 on the New Jersey and New York boundary survey and again in 1785 for the Pennsylvania and New

Tranquillity where once there was violence: a young girl
stands beside a Mason-Dixon line "Crown Stone" on the
West Line dividing Maryland from Pennsylvania, June
12, 1951. (Courtesy Maryland Historical Society)

York line. The sector was on display for a while in Lancaster, the temporary capital of Pennsylvania following the War of Independence,
from where it was moved to the courthouse in Harrisburg, in 1812. In
1878, it was transferred to the State Library in Harrisburg, but tragically a fire destroyed the building in 1897, consuming with it all trace
of John Bird's magnificent instrument. In 1912, during the restoration
of the bell tower of the Philadelphia Statehouse, Bird's transit and
equal altitude instrument was rediscovered lying beneath the floorboards. Eric Doolittle, the astronomer of the Flower Observatory, who
first examined the instrument, even found traces of the original spider-
web of the eyepiece reticule. The transit is now on permanent display
in Philadelphia's Independence National Historical Park.

Mason and Dixon's great boundary survey was the first and, for many years, the most ambitious geodetic survey ever conducted, and it set a precedent. Thomas Jefferson's Northwest Ordinance of 1785 provided for the surveying of the vast territory lying west of Pennsylvania and north of the Ohio River to the Great Lakes. The U.S. government wholeheartedly adopted Mason and Dixon's principles, methods, and demands for accuracy. Survey teams became more and more common in the United States in the last years of the eighteenth century and on into the nineteenth century. The professionalism and precision set by Charles Mason and Jeremiah Dixon were followed and improved upon by subsequent U.S. surveyors. The legacy of those two great English surveyors became the inheritance of the U.S. Geological Survey and the National Geodetic Survey, the country's mapping organizations.

Mason and Dixon's contribution to measuring the shape of Earth was also an outstanding achievement. Never had such an accurate linear distance been measured, and it would be many years before the feat was equaled. The Delaware baseline remained the only meridian arc in the West until well into the nineteenth century. Mason and Dixon's precise distance measurements were in the old imperial feet, links, chains, and miles. The only decimal unit was the link, being $\frac{1}{100}$ of a chain. The phenomenal development in the physical sciences in the seventeenth and eighteenth centuries highlighted the difficulties of a chaotic variety of nonrelating measurements. There was talk of a natural physical unit of measurement, first proposed by Gabriel Mouton, a French clergyman, in 1670. Mouton thought a natural unit of length could be based on the decimal division of a degree of longitude.

In 1791 the revolutionary government of France requested the Académie Royale de Sciences to devise a set of new and "natural" physical units. The Académie declared, before any formal measurements were made, that the new unit of length, the *meter,* would be equal to $\frac{1}{10,000,000}$ part of the north quadrant of the meridian arc passing through Paris. The survey of the arc, or at least the French portion, began in 1792 and extended from Spain to Dunkerque under the direction of astronomer and hydrographer Pierre-François-André Mechain (1744–1804) and Jean Delambre (1749–1822). At the completion of the project in 1799, the French arc was combined with the earlier work of Pierre Bouguer to give a value for Earth's semi-major axis of 6,376,428 meters and a flattening of $\frac{1}{311.5}$. The British followed suit in 1802 when mathematician and astronomer William Mudge measured the first major arc for the British Ordnance Survey, the nation's new mapping organization. The measurements started from Dunnose, in the south of England, and extended as far as Clifton in the northeast. The principles Mudge adopted were the same as used by Mason and Dixon; he also used a zenith sector, very similar to John Bird's instrument, to measure the latitudes.

The next leap forward in the science of geodesy came in 1830 when Maskelyne's successor, Astronomer Royal George Airy, published his famous figure of Earth.* Known universally as Airy's Spheroid, it was immediately adopted by the British Ordnance Survey and remains to this day the official spheroid for the British Isles. In calculating the parameters for his spheroid, Airy used the two French meridian arcs, an improved version of Mudge's British arc, the spectacular Indian arcs measured by the celebrated Surveyor General Sir George Everest, Carl Friedrich Gauss's German arc, and Fredrich von Struves's great Russian arc.

But for the Western Hemisphere, Airy's first and only choice was the American arc, as measured by Charles Mason and Jeremiah Dixon.

---

*See Appendix, "Figures for the Earth."

Appendix

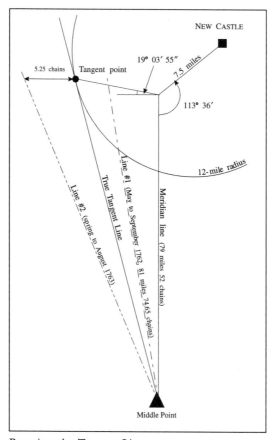

5.25 chains   Tangent point

NEW CASTLE

19° 03′ 55″

7.5 miles

113° 36′

12-mile radius

Line #1 (May to September 1762, 81 miles 74.65 chains)

True Tangent Line

Line #2 (spring to August 1763)

Meridian line (79 miles 52 chains)

Middle Point

Running the Tangent Line.

207

The Tangent Line

SPRING–DECEMBER 1761: the surveyors first ran a line in the meridian, due north, from the Middle Point toward the New Castle circle. Once across the boundary circle, they placed a mark 79 miles 52 chains north of the Middle Point. They next ran a radial line from the courthouse to the mark, a distance of 7 miles 40 chains, and measured the angle of intersection, 113 degrees 36 minutes. From the two measured sides and the included angle, it was calculated that an angle of 19 degrees 03 minutes 55 seconds north from the radial line would place them close to the tangent point. It was also calculated that the Tangent Line should be at an angle of 3 degrees 32 minutes 05 seconds west of the meridian line.

MAY–SEPTEMBER 1762: line number 1 was run toward the tangent point to a marker 81 miles 74.65 chains from the Middle Point. The angle at the tangent was measured with "Lord Baltimore's large theodolite" and found to be 26 minutes too great; they were too far east of the tangent. After more calculations, line number 2 was begun, 16 minutes 40 seconds west of the previous line.

SPRING–AUGUST 1763: measuring along line number 2, the surveyors reach the tangent point but miss the 12-mile post by 5 chains 25 links too far west. Further calculations were made, but there was no more fieldwork.

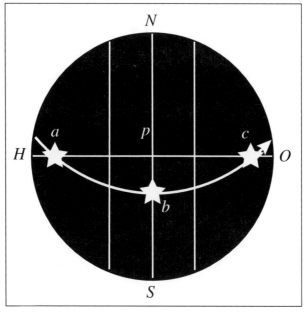

Setting the zenith sector in the meridian by equal
altitudes.

Setting the Zenith Sector

Mason describes his method for aligning the zenith sector in the
meridian—that is, aligned due north-south—as follows:

> Brought the Instrument into the Meridian by making several
> stars pass along the horizontal wire in the middle of the Tele-
> scope. The method pursued in doing this is as follows: Let *HO*
> be the horizontal, and *NS* be the vertical wire, Then we bring
> a Northern star (one as far north of the zenith as the limit of
> the Arch) to the Horizontal wire at *a,* and it will describe the
> arch of a circle *abc,* (the Telescope inverting). If *ap* be appar-
> ently equal to *pc,* it is truly in the Meridian, if not equal, we
> proceed by trial until they are equal; which may be done with
> four or five stars to great exactitude as we find by comparing
> the time of the stars passing the wire *NS,* with the time they
> transit the Meridian as found by Equal Altitudes.

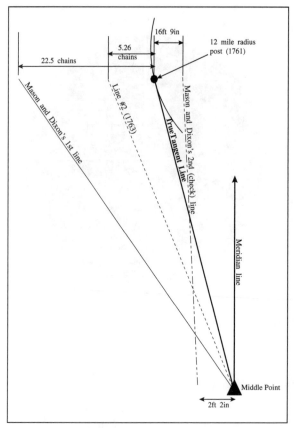

Lines to establish the tangent.

Running the Tangent Line

Mason and Dixon calculated, by proportions, a table of offset measurements needed to move the original mileposts of the 1763 line number 2 into the true tangent. To check the earlier assumption for the method used, Mason's original calculations have been reworked in a computer spreadsheet. Whereas Mason used seven-figure log tables, which probably took him a day, the spreadsheet method took just twenty minutes.

Milepost	A From Mason and Dixon's line to survey line #2	B Mason and Dixon's offset from 12-mile post, proportioned back to the Middle Point	C Line #2 offset from 12-mile post, proportioned back to the Middle Point	D Mason and Dixon's offset + surveyors' offset from 12-mile post (A + C)	E Offsets from survey line #2 to true tangent line (B − D)
	Chains. Links	Chains. Links	Chains. Links	Chains. Links	Chains. Links
81	17.25	22.50	5.26		
80	16.25	21.96	5.14	21.39	0.57
70	12.14	19.22	4.50	16.64	2.58
60	9.80	16.47	3.85	13.66	2.82
50	8.17	13.73	3.21	11.38	2.34
40	6.46	10.98	2.57	9.03	1.95
30	4.40	8.24	1.93	6.33	1.91
20	2.13	5.49	1.29	3.42	2.08
10	0.58	2.75	0.64	1.22	1.52
0	0.00	0.00	0.00	0.00	0.00

The error at the 12-mile-radius post was 16 feet 9 inches east of the post. Another table of offsets was drawn up; this time the terminal mismatches were proportioned over the whole length of 80 miles (column F below) and compared with the measured variance (column G). The difference (column H) was the check error, the values of which entirely satisfied Mr. Mason.

Milepost	F Mason and Dixon's second line, proportioned between the Middle Point and tangent	G Measured offsets from Mason and Dixon's second line to true tangent	H Difference
	Feet	Feet	Feet
80	−16.33	16.58	0.25
70	−14.02	12.92	−1.10
60	−11.71	10.50	−1.21

Milepost	F	G	H
	Mason and Dixon's second line, proportioned between the Middle Point and tangent	Measured offsets from Mason and Dixon's second line to true tangent	Difference
	Feet	Feet	Feet
50	−9.40	10.92	1.52
40	−7.08	8.41	1.33
30	−4.77	8.25	3.48
20	−2.46	4.67	2.21
10	−0.15	0.00	−0.15
0	2.17	−2.17	0.00

Setting Out the West Line

Mason calculated that the greatest offset at the midway point of the arc (E to B) would be 17.14 feet. The observations and the calculations required expert knowledge of spherical trigonometry as well as accomplished astronomical observing skills. In their lodgings at Newark, Mason meticulously wrote out the complicated procedure in his journal.

> March 1, 1765. Began to prepare for running the Western Line: the method of proceeding as follows.
>
> Let P be the Pole, $ABCD$ the Parallel to be drawn.
>
> AC the arch of a Great Circle. At pleasure suppose = 10 minutes [of arc] which we shall set out with on the first station, and in order to find the direction AC, there is given in the Right Angled Spherical Triangle EPA
>
> AP = Complement of Latitude = $50° \ 16' \ 42.''6$ [i.e., 90 degrees minus the Latitude]
>
> AE = One half AC = $5'$
>
> Hence Angle PAE = $89° \ 55' \ 51''$ [by calculation: azimuth = 90 degrees − Sec(Tan 0 degrees 05 minutes 00 seconds)/(Tan 50 degrees 16 minutes 42.6 seconds)] the angle from the North

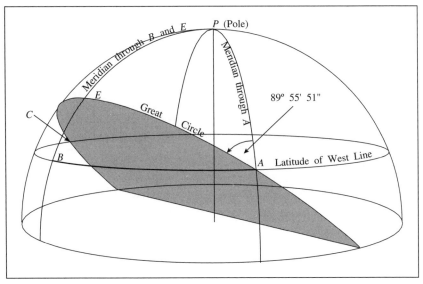

A 10-minute arc of the great circle. The great circle is the arc passing through *A, E,* and *C.* The distance *B* to *E* equals 1,714 feet.

Westward: and to lay off this angle with the transit Instrument by the Stars; Let *P* be the Pole *Z* the zenith and *S* the place of the star. Then in the oblique angled Spherical Triangle *SPZ,* there is given

SP = the star's distance from the Pole

ZP = the Compliment of the Latitude.

Angle *SZP* = 89° 55′ 51″ = the star's azimuth from the North when it will be on the direction *AEC* above. To find the angle *SPZ* or angle at the Pole when the star is on the said azimuth.

The angle *SPZ* being added to the star's Right Ascension: if to the Westward of the Meridian or subtracted if the Star is to the Eastward; give the Right Ascension of the Mid-Heaven, when the star is upon the azimuth Required. In this manner the Right Ascension of the Mid-Heaven for different stars is as follows. ——— Next to find by the clock when the star will be on the said azimuth, two equal altitudes of the same star before the time are observed, whence the time is gained. At this instant of time [i.e. the sidereal time] the Middle Wire is

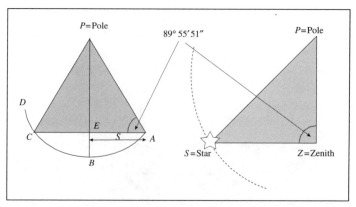

Setting out the West Line. Left: the arc *ABCD* is the true latitude; *AEC* is a great circle. Right: the astronomical triangle *SPZ*. The direction *Z* to *S* is the same as *A* to *C*.

brought to bisect the star, and in that position (The axis of the Telescope, etc., being Horizontal) the vertical axis is made fast: Then the Telescope is brought parallel to the Horizon, and a Mark set by the help of a candle (at the distance of ½ or ¾ of a mile) so that the middle wire bisects it.

In this manner we proceed with 3 or 4 different stars and find that at the distance of ½ a mile the extremes of the distances of the marks made by the different stars will not in general exceed 5 or 6 inches.

The line *AC* being run with the transit Instrument, at *C* we set up the Sector to prove or correct the work, by observing the zenith Distances of the same stars that were observed at the point *A*.

Using spherical trigonometry (in which, unlike plane trigonometry, the sum of the angles exceeds 180 degrees), Mason calculated that by sighting along a line 89 degrees 55 minutes 51 seconds west of true north, they would be looking along the line of a great circle. To find this direction from the night sky they first chose a star that would cross the line at a low elevation. By adding the 89 degree 55 minute 51 second angle to the star's right ascension, they determined the time when the star would be in the required direction. They then observed meridian equal altitudes with the transit instrument to find the sidereal time and to determine the error of their watch; local sidereal time equals the right ascension of a star when it is on the meridian.

Adjusting the 10-Minute (11-mile) Segment of the West Line

In the figure the line actually run was *W* to *S* rather than the exact great circle direction *W* to *B*. The 43 yards error over a distance of some 11 miles represented an inaccuracy of only 0.2 percent. The meridian colatitudes *PW* and *PD* are equal, so by calculating each hypotenuse *Pa, Pb,* and so on, and deducting these from the colatitude, the offsets from the great circle to the true latitude were deduced. By arithmetic proportion, the offsets from the line (*W* to *S*) were calculated and the two sets of offsets added together. This complex and tedious procedure would be repeated time and again as they moved ever westward.

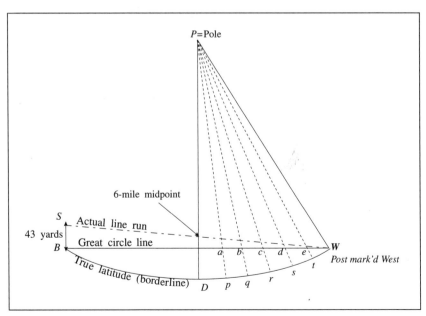

Adjusting the 10-minute (11-mile) segment of the West Line.

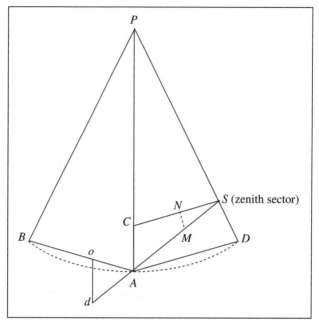

Running the sections from the Susquehanna.

Running the Sections from the Susquehanna

In the complicated figure, PD = PA = PB = colatitude of the West Line; that is, 90 degrees minus the latitude. PS = the colatitude of the zenith sector where it stood on May 19, and the direction SC, found by stellar observations, is the line from the sector parallel to the great circle DA. First, Mason and Dixon set out the radius SN = 1.187 miles long and from N set out 60.5 links at a right angle to the line SNC. Using their seven-figure logarithms, they then calculated the angle NSM, which worked out to be 0 degrees 21 minutes 55 seconds precisely. They had previously calculated the angle PSC; hence, they were able to calculate the angle PSA by adding NSM. By a laborious process of spherical trigonometry, the angle dAo was calculated to find the direction A to B. Once more they resorted to linear measurement; they made Ad = 24.71 links, and set out do = 21.7 links at right angles to Ad. In actuality, the line DAB is very nearly a straight line, and the angle at d would have been as near a right angle as would make little difference.

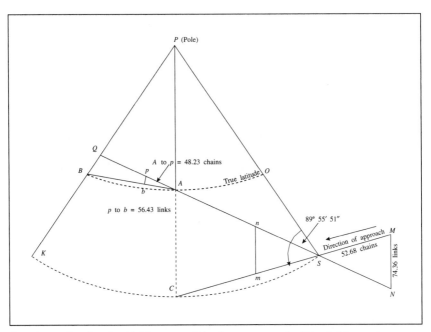

Starting point for the 1766 season. S is the sector at the North Mountain. A marks the spot for the first change of direction.

Starting Point for the 1766 Season

In his journal, Mason explains the geometry for setting out the direction of the great circle arc. "Here P, the Pole: OAB the true Parallel. S, the Sector at the North Mountain SCK the Parallel at the said Mountain, MSC the direction we came in. MN the said direction changed which we went off in. MN the Quantity changed = 74.36 Links to the Eastward of S."

Mason computed that an angle of 0 degrees 14 minutes 14 seconds south of their last direction would put them back on course for the true parallel at point B, 10 minutes or 11.37 miles to the west. To turn the small angle into the dimensions of a right-angled triangle, they first measured a distance of 48.23 chains from A to p, then calculated that Sin 0 degrees 14 minutes 14 seconds multiplied by 48.23 chains equaled 56.43 links; actually it should have been 56.64 links. This offset was set out from p to b, due south; any small error in guessing the direction of due south would have had a negligible effect.

The transit instrument was set up at *a* and sited on *b* for the chaining direction.

Figures for the Earth, 1743 to 1984

Date	Spheroid name	Semi-major axis (m)	Flattening 1/f	Notes
1743	Académie Royale de Sciences	6,397,300	216.8	Meridian arcs, Peru/Lapland
1798	Académie Royale de Sciences	6,376,428	311.5	Meridian arc, France (defining meter)
1830	G. B. Airy	6,377,542	299.3	Compilation, meridian arcs, worldwide (including Mason and Dixon's American arc)
1830	G. Everest	6,377,276	300.8	Meridian arcs, India and France
1841	F. W. Bessel	6,377,397	299.2	Meridian arcs (in *toises*)
1858	A. R. Clarke	6,378,293	294.3	Meridian arcs
1860	F. G. W. von Struve	6,378,298	294.7	Meridian arc, Russia
1866	A. R. Clarke	6,378,206	294.5	Compilation, meridian arcs, worldwide
1880	A. R. Clarke	6,378,301	293.5	Compilation, meridian arcs, worldwide
1906	F. R. Helmert	6,378,200	298.3	Meridian arcs and gravity observations
1910	J. F. Hayford	6,378,388	297.0	
1948	Krassovsky	6,378,245	298.3	
1960	J. Fischer	6,378,155	298.3	Satellite
1984	US DoD/WGS84	6,378,137	298.3	Satellite, gravity, etc.

(Geodesy, Bomford, 3rd edition)

Bibliography

Archives

American Philosophical Society, Philadelphia
Astronomical Society of South Africa, Cape Town
Institution of Surveyors, Australia
Maryland State Archives, Baltimore
Museum of the History of Science, Oxford
National Maritime Museum and Old Royal Observatory, London
Pennsylvania State Archives, Harrisburg
Religious Society of Friends in Britain, London
Royal Institution of Chartered Surveyors, London
Science Museum, London

Books and Articles

Bedini, Silvio A. *The Transit in the Tower: English Astronomical Instruments in Colonial America.* Annals of Science, vol. 54. Washington, D.C.: n.p., 1997.

Bell, Whitfield J., Jr. *Patriot-Improvers: Biographical Sketches of Members of the American Philosophical Society. Vol. 1: 1743–1768.* Memoirs of the American Philosophical Society, vol. 226. Philadelphia: American Philosophical Society, 1997.

Biddle, Col. C. A. *The Textbook of Field Astronomy.* London: Her Majesty's Stationery Office, 1958.

Bomford, G. *Geodesy.* 3rd ed. Oxford: Oxford University Press, 1980.

Briggs, A. L. *Social History of England.* London: Weidenfeld and Nicolson, 1995.

Brinkley, Alan, Frank Freidel, Richard N. Current, and T. Harry Williams. *American History: A Survey.* 8th ed. New York: McGraw-Hill, 1998.

Brown, Curtis M., Walter G. Robillard, and Donald A. Wilson. *Evidence and Procedure for Boundary Location.* New York: John Wiley and Sons, 1981.

Buckner, R. B. *Surveying Measurements and Their Analysis.* Rancho Cordova, Calif.: Landmark Enterprises, 1983.

Burkard, Lt. Col. Richard K. *Geodesy for the Layman,* 4th ed. Washington, D.C.: Defense Mapping Agency, 1998.

Close, Col. Sir Charles. *Early Years of the Ordnance Survey.* London: Institution of Royal Engineers, 1926.

Coolidge, Susan. *A Short History of the City of Philadelphia, from Its Foundation to the Present Time.* Philadelphia: Arden Press, 1880.

Cope, Thomas D. *Collecting Source Material about Charles Mason and Jeremiah Dixon.* Proceedings of the American Philosophical Society, vol. 92/2. Philadelphia: American Philosophical Society, 1948.

Danson, E. F. S. *First Point of Aries.* London: Civil Engineering Surveyor, 1995.

———. *Plane and Geodetic Co-ordinates.* London: Civil Engineering Surveyor, 1991.

Garraty, John A. *A History of the United States.* 7th ed. New York: HarperCollins, 1991.

Greene County Observer-Reporter, Pennsylvania, October 1998.

Harvard University, the Collection of Historical Scientific Instruments. *Quest for Longitude: Proceedings of the Longitude Symposium.* Cambridge, Mass.: Harvard University Press, November 1993.

Headlee, Alvah John Washington. *The Accompt of the Hands Settling the Lines between Maryland and Pennsylvania: Mason Dixon Survey.* Philadelphia: Historical Society of Pennsylvania, 1976.

Hogben, L. *Mathematics for the Million: How to Master the Magic of Numbers.* London: Pan Books, 1967.

Horn, Pamela. *Life and Labour in Rural England, 1760–1850.* London: MacMillan Education, 1987.

Hoskins, W. G. *Making of the English Landscape.* London: Hodder and Stoughton, 1970.

Howse, Derek. *Nevil Maskelyne: The Seaman's Astronomer.* Cambridge, U.K.: Cambridge University Press, 1989.

Jackson, Helen. *A Century of Dishonor: A Sketch of the United States Government's Dealings with Some of the Indian Tribes.* 1881. Reprint, Norman: University of Oklahoma Press, 1995.

Jenson, Merrill, ed. *English Historical Documents.* Vol. 9: *American Colonial Documents to 1776.* London: Eyre and Spottiswoode, 1955.

Keyes, Nelson Beecher. *The American Frontier.* New York: Hanover House, 1954.

Law, John. *Indian Snapshots.* Calcutta: Thacker Spink, 1912.

Mason, A. Hughlett. *Journal of Charles Mason and Jeremiah Dixon.* Memoirs of the American Philosophical Society, vol. 76. Philadelphia: American Philosophical Society, 1969.

Middleton and Chadwick. *A Treatise on Surveying.* Vol. 2. 6th ed. London: E. & F. N. Spon, 1955.

Milne-Tyte, Robert. *Bloody Jeffreys: The Hanging Judge.* London: Andre Deutsch, 1990.

Minow, Helmut. *Historische Vermessungsinstrumente.* Wiesbaden: Verlag Chmielorz GmbH, 1990.

Morison, Samuel Eliot, Henry Steele Commager, and William E. Leuchtenburg. *The Growth of the American Republic,* vol. 7, 5th ed. New York: Oxford University Press, 1980.

Richeson, A. W. *English Land Measuring to 1800.* Cambridge, Mass.: MIT Press and Society for the History of Technology, 1966.

Robbins, A. R. *Military Engineering,* vol. 13 pt. 9. London: Ministry of Defence, 1976.

Scholes, Percy A. *The Oxford Companion to Music.* 6th ed. Oxford: Oxford University Press, 1945.

Sobel, Dava. *Longitude: The True Story of a Lone Genius Who Solved the Greatest Scientific Problem of His Time.* N.p.: Fourth Estate, 1996.

Star Almanac for Land Surveyors. London: Her Majesty's Stationery Office, 1991.

Trevelyan, G. M. *English Social History.* London: Longmans, 1944.

Index